Syndromes of Corruption

Corruption is a threat to democracy and economic development in many societies. It arises in the ways people pursue, use, and exchange wealth and power, and in the strength or weakness of the state, political, and social institutions that sustain and restrain those processes. Differences in these factors, Michael Johnston argues, give rise to four major syndromes of corruption: Influence Markets, Elite Cartels, Oligarchs and Clans, and Official Moguls. Johnston uses statistical measures to identify societies in each group, and case studies to show that the expected syndromes do arise. Countries studied include the United States, Japan, and Germany (Influence Markets); Italy, Korea, and Botswana (Elite Cartels); Russia, the Philippines, and Mexico (Oligarchs and Clans); and China, Kenya, and Indonesia (Official Moguls). A concluding chapter explores reform, emphasizing the ways familiar measures should be applied – or withheld, lest they do harm – with an emphasis upon the value of "deep democratization."

MICHAEL JOHNSTON is Charles A. Dana Professor of Political Science and Division Director for the Social Sciences, Colgate University.

D1127677

Syndromes of Corruption:

Wealth, Power, and Democracy

Michael Johnston

Charles A. Dana Professor of Political Science
Colgate University
13 Oak Drive
Hamilton, NY 13346
USA
Tel: +1-315-228-7756
Fax: +1-315-228-7883
mjohnston@mail.colgate.edu

CAMBRIDGE
UNIVERSITY PRESS

CAMBRIDGE UNIVERSITY PRESS
Cambridge, New York, Melbourne, Madrid, Cape Town, Singapore, São Paulo

CAMBRIDGE UNIVERSITY PRESS
The Edinburgh Building, Cambridge CB2 2RU, UK

Published in the United States of America by Cambridge University Press,
New York

www.cambridge.org
Information on this title: www.cambridge.org/9780521618595

First published 2005

Printed in the United Kingdom at the University Press, Cambridge

A catalogue record for this book is available from the British Library

ISBN-13 978-0-521-85334-7 hardback
ISBN-10 0-521-85334-6 hardback
ISBN-13 978-0-521-61859-5 paperback
ISBN-10 0-521-61859-2 paperback

For Betsy,
always.

Contents

Figures

Tables

Preface

"I have seen the future, and it is very much like the present, only
longer ..."
                                    Dan Quisenberry,
                critic, social commentator, and right-handed reliever

There was a time not long ago when few policymakers or scholars cared
much about corruption. Whatever the reasons for that long dry spell – the
scarcity of systematic evidence, a wish to avoid the appearance of naïveté,
vested institutional interests, or just an honest reluctance to venture into a
domain full of colorful stories and characters but seemingly devoid of
theoretical interest – by the end of the 1980s corruption was climbing
back onto the agenda. During the years that followed it became a certified
"hot topic" drawing the attention of governments, international aid and
lending agencies, business, and a growing number of scholars in many
disciplines. By now we have learned a great deal about corruption,
its links to development, and the complexities of reform, and possess
a body of knowledge, data, and experience impossible to envision a
generation ago.

For all that has been accomplished, however, we seem to have reached
a plateau. As I suggest in the early chapters of this book, the dominant
view of corruption is a partial one, treating bribery – usually involving
international aid and trade, and often at high levels – as a synonym for
corruption in general. Much empirical work focuses on statistical analysis
of single-dimensional corruption indices, or case studies that are richly
detailed but not integrated into a comparative framework. Those two
research traditions remain largely separate, rather than complementing
each other. The effects of corruption are often reduced to economic data,
facilitating statistical work but too often equating human wellbeing with
trends in GDP, and saying even less about justice. Much of the debate has
been driven by groups advocating the bundle of changes commonly called
globalization – outlooks and policies that I see as more positive than not,
but that have a way of framing corruption issues in terms of obstructions
to free markets, and reform as primarily a task of continued economic

liberalization. Finally, while much is said about understanding diverse settings, reform recommendations tend to vary rather little.

This book is hardly a direct assault on those interests and outlooks: we have learned far too much during the past fifteen years to say that the major debates and findings are fundamentally wrong in any sense. Rather, it offers the thoughts of a friendly critic who does not want the future of corruption research, at least, to be "very much like the present, only longer." While I am critical of some of the arguments, findings, and policies of liberalization advocates, and of several US government agencies, I have been involved in their debates and work as a scholar and consultant, and have always been given a fair hearing. I have methodological reservations about Transparency International's famous Corruption Perceptions Index, and express them at many points in this book. But (full disclosure here) I also have been associated with the US chapter of TI for a decade, share the organization's overall goals, and have great respect for what TI – and its index – have done to put corruption issues on page one and keep them there.

Instead, I argue for a more differentiated and comparative view of corruption, and of the reforms we must pursue. The goal is to start with deeper trends and difficulties in development and trace their implications for the contrasting sorts of systemic corruption problems various societies experience. Those development issues, and corruption itself, are found in affluent market democracies as well as in societies undergoing more rapid change. Indeed, some of the corruption problems of those poorer and less democratic countries originate in more developed parts of the world. I propose the existence of four major corruption syndromes, consider case studies of each, and engage in some speculation – useful, I hope – about the different sorts of reform required for each. That discussion emphasizes the ways we should (and should not) deploy familiar reform measures, rather than searching for silver bullets. As I note at the beginning of the final chapter, it is highly unlikely that all who care about corruption will be persuaded by the chapters to come. Instead, the goal is to spur renewed debate over just how corruption differs in various settings, what the underlying causes of those contrasts might be, and what needs to be done by way of more appropriate remedies.

Whatever the merits and failings of this book, it could not have been written without a great deal of support and advice. My wife, Betsy, and our sons Michael and Patrick, have put up with more talk about corruption and reform than anyone should have to endure in one lifetime. Colgate University, and before that the University of Pittsburgh, have encouraged me to teach and do research in this field for (egads . . .) thirty years now. Colgate's Research Council has provided funding for research assistants; the Office of Dean of the Faculty, and the Division of Social Science, have supported travel to numerous conferences. Friends and colleagues at Colgate and elsewhere, including Jessica Allina-Pisano, Miriam A. Golden, Yufan Hao, Sahr J. Kpundeh, Sharon Lean, Bert Levine, Stephen Morris, Nikolay Naydenov, Madalene O'Donnell, Anne Pitcher, Susan Rose-Ackerman, and Bertram Spector have been kind enough to read and comment on sections of various drafts. Professor Antonio Azuela of the Autonomous National University of Mexico and Javier González of the Ministry of Public Functions provided excellent guidance on the topic of presidential reforms in Mexico. Ian Helfant of Colgate's Russian department and his student Amanda Egan provided quick and polished translations on several occasions, and Rena Safaraliyeva of Transparency International – Azerbaijan was an invaluable intermediary in the process of obtaining permission to use the cover image of this book. Cindy Terrier and Linda Rauscher at Colgate have always provided unfailing administrative and clerical support, and my student research assistants over the years, including Richard Kim, Frances Masih, Jerri Pittsley, Tiffany Thompson, and Cecilia Wagner contributed in a variety of ways.

During the 2002–3 academic year I had the good fortune to be a Member of the School of Social Sciences, and a National Endowment for the Humanities Fellow, at the Institute for Advanced Study in Princeton, New Jersey. The Institute provided superb support, a real community of scholars working on corruption and other issues and, best of all, a year's unencumbered time. All have proven essential to the development of this book. Michael Walzer organized a stimulating thematic seminar at the Institute with a focus on corruption issues. I benefited immensely from his comments, and from those of Clifford Geertz, Eric Maskin, Philip Bond, Brenda Chalfin, Neil Englehart, John Gerring, Jennifer Hasty, Rasma Karklins, Madeline Kochen, Wolf Lepenies, Sankar Muthu, Roberto Serrano, and Ralph Thaxton. Linda Garat, the Members' Secretary, was indispensable. My thanks to all at the Institute, and to NEH, for a great year. I also thank Professors William Heffernan and John Kleinig, at John Jay College, City University of New York, for the opportunity to present an early version of my corruption typology at an excellent conference they organized in September, 2002. Anne Lauer and her colleagues in Washington gave me excellent feedback about cases in the course of a series of presentations in recent years. Members of a seminar at Harvard University's Weatherhead Center for International Affairs, directed by Professor Susan Pharr, provided challenging questions and suggestions in response to my presentation on Asian cases in October, 2004. The advice of John Haslam of Cambridge

University Press, and of his anonymous reviewers, has been useful in many ways. All of these people helped make this a better book, and of course none bears any responsibility for its shortcomings.

In the mid-1970s I began teaching my upper-level lecture course on political corruption. It began as a discussion of the United States with a few comparative examples added, and has evolved into an examination of international corruption and development issues in which the US is but one of many examples. Over the years I have also had the opportunity to visit a variety of countries to study and take part in their reform efforts, to lecture, and to participate in conferences. The students, scholars, citizens, and officials I've met along the way have never failed to provide questions, challenges, and new ideas. That is one part of the future I hope will be very much like the present.

EARLVILLE, NEW YORK

January 5, 2005

1   Wealth, power, and corruption

Three questions

Two decades of liberalization of politics and markets, and of increasingly rapid movement of people, capital, and information across regions and around the globe, have reshaped societies in all parts of the world – in many ways for the better. But these developments have been accompanied by renewed worries about corruption. New opportunities to pursue wealth and power abound, but so do new ways to use and exchange them illicitly, and to move the proceeds across borders almost instantaneously. Corruption benefits the few at the expense of the many; it delays and distorts economic development, preempts basic rights and due process, and diverts resources from basic services, international aid, and whole economies. Particularly where state institutions are weak it is often linked to violence. In part because of corruption, for millions "democracy" means increased insecurity and "free markets" are where the rich seem to get richer at the expense of everyone else.

These problems raise fundamental questions about the ways people pursue and exchange wealth and power, and about the ways societies and their economies are governed. For a generation now we have delegated major questions of justice, accountability, and reform to markets, or have tried to reduce politics and government to market-like processes. Social and state institutional frameworks essential both to sustaining democracy and markets, and to checking their excesses, have been deemphasized or defined as problems to be solved by further liberalization. Meanwhile, developing societies are expected to attain levels of transparency and probity that advanced societies took many decades to reach, and to do so while competing in world markets and undergoing political transformation. Compounding the problem has been a "one size fits all" view of corruption as consisting essentially of bribery, varying only in degree across societies, and of reform as the process of making developing societies more like the West.

1

But while affluent market democracies resemble each other in many ways, poverty and dictatorships come in many varieties – and so does corruption. Responding to these diverse problems is both an analytical and a political challenge: we need to understand the contrasting corruption problems of different societies, and to emphasize the value of government, politics, and substantive "deep democratization," if the benefits of global political and economic change are to be more justly shared.

Contrasting syndromes

This is a book about corruption and development, with a focus upon the ways wealth and power are used and exchanged in diverse settings. I address three questions: What are the links among political and economic liberalization, the strength or weakness of state, political, and social institutions, and the kinds of corruption societies experience? What syndromes of corruption result from various combinations of those influences and how do they differ? What kinds of reform are – and are not – appropriate for contrasting corruption problems?

Like most other analysts I maintain that corruption is undemocratic and broadly harmful to economic growth. This book, however, differs from most others in four important ways. First, I argue that it makes little sense simply to array societies on a single scale ranging from high to low corruption. Instead, I identify four distinctive corruption syndromes that reflect and perpetuate deeper problems of democratic and economic participation and institutions. Second, I include the corruption problems of advanced as well as of developing societies in the analysis. Affluent market democracies have corruption problems of their own that – along with the conceptions of reform they have fostered – do much to shape the difficulties and opportunities facing developing societies.

Third, I take issue with many current prescriptions for reform by arguing that it is not enough simply to identify aspects of an ideal market-democracy model that developing societies seem to lack. Instead, we must examine the forces and interests that actually are at work there and that drive the abuses those societies experience. Doing so will produce reform strategies that differ from one society to the next, but that also draw support from lasting interests in society. Finally, a major theme of the book is the value of institutions, politics, and the state. Since the 1980s corruption has frequently been seen as an effect, and cause, of incomplete economic liberalization, and public institutions and politics treated mostly as obstructions to that process. Public-sector reforms have thus emphasized narrow goals of "good governance" while liberalization of economies and politics has proceeded without essential institutional foundations. I argue, by contrast, that reform is a matter not only of improved public management but of justice. It requires "deep democratization": not just elections but vigorous contention over real issues among people and groups capable of defending themselves politically, and of reaching political settlements sustained by their own lasting interests. Such contention, and the social "ownership" of institutions it fosters, helped create democracy in societies where it is now strong (Rustow, 1970). Without that sort of social foundation even our best reform ideas are unlikely to take root.

I will develop these arguments in eight chapters. Chapter 1 takes up the nature of syndromes of corruption. Chapter 2 examines the "new consensus," driven by economic liberalization, that has emerged regarding corruption and its links to democratization and development. In chapter 3 I propose four syndromes reflecting commonly found combinations of political and economic *participation* and *institutions*. *Influence Market* corruption involves efforts on the part of private interests to rent access and influence within well-institutionalized policy processes, often through political figures acting as middlemen. It is the sort of corruption most characteristic of advanced market democracies, but while it has shaped basic conceptions of reform it differs in important ways from that found in many other places. *Elite Cartel* corruption occurs among, and helps sustain, networks of political, economic, military, bureaucratic, or ethnic and communal elites, depending upon the society in question. It helps them defend their hegemony in a climate of increasing political competition and only moderately strong institutions. *Oligarch and Clan* corruption takes place in a risky, and sometimes violent, setting of rapidly expanding economic and political opportunities and weak institutions. It is dominated by figures who may be government officials or business entrepreneurs, but whose power is personal and attracts extensive followings. *Official Moguls* are government officials, or their protégés, who plunder an economy with impunity. Institutions and political competition are weakest of all in this category, and economic opportunities are often scarce and bitterly contested. A statistical analysis in chapter 3 uses measures of participation and institutions to assign about one hundred countries to these four categories.

Chapters 4 through 7 put the proposed syndromes to the test through a series of case studies. Influence Markets are explored in the USA, Japan, and Germany (chapter 4) while Elite Cartels in Italy, Korea, and Botswana are the focus of chapter 5. I consider the Oligarchs and Clans of Russia, Mexico, and the Philippines in chapter 6, and the Official Moguls of China, Kenya, and Indonesia in chapter 7. The corruption problems found within any one group will not be identical; indeed, some countries are examined because they stretch the boundaries of their categories. No more can short case studies take up all major cases or aspects of corruption in any one country. Still, the four ideal-type syndromes are clearly visible in the case studies, and contrasts among them generally correspond to those proposed in chapter 3. Finally, chapter 8 links the notion of corruption syndromes to broader questions and suggests ways in which anti-corruption strategies must be tailored to the contrasting realities of diverse societies. The results are not offered as any kind of "toolkit" for dealing with corruption; they do, however, help us understand how corruption problems vary in complex settings, and how both analysis and reform must take deeper development problems into account.

Linking two analytical traditions

Despite the boom in interest in corruption over the past fifteen years, surprisingly little of the resulting research has been broadly and systematically comparative. Much recent work has been cross-sectional, often applying statistical measures and models to large numbers of countries to account for their scores on various single-dimension corruption indices. A second tradition of longer standing describes cases or societies in rich detail with extensive attention to history, culture, and social context. Both strategies are essential: the former can identify broad contrasts and trends, and can estimate the strength of the relationships among a number of variables. The latter often tells fascinating stories about corrupt processes and reminds us that they are embedded in complex human interactions. But both approaches have their limits: cross-sectional work and corruption indices impose a common model upon all cases and are not particularly sensitive to qualitative variations. In effect those models assume that corruption is essentially the same in Denmark, the United States, Botswana, and China, varying only in extent. Descriptive case studies, on the other hand, usually do not lead to systematic comparisons transcending particular times and places; indeed, some scholars doing this sort of work resist the basic idea of comparisons. Cross-sectional work tends to overemphasize commonalities while case studies can overstate contrasts and uniqueness.

I seek a middle level of comparison – one that does not supersede those traditions but links them. The development processes behind the syndromes will be operationalized using statistical indicators, but what they suggest about corruption in specific societies will be tested against descriptive cases. Those case studies, in turn, will be compared to each other within the framework of the syndromes argument. This strategy can tell us whether expected patterns of corruption are found in practice, how they reflect deeper patterns of participation and institutions, and how they affect political and economic development. Those findings not only point to major reform opportunities but also help explain why some past efforts to control corruption have failed, or have even done more harm than good.

Rediscovered territory

After a generation during which it drew very little interest from scholars and policymakers, the issue of corruption shot back up the international policy agenda in the early 1990s. Possible reasons for this include, *inter alia*, the end of the cold war, which both reduced the geopolitical import-ance of many corrupt regimes and intensified pressures upon aid and lending budgets; growing global competition among firms, capital man-agers, and countries seeking investment, which made it difficult to justify corruption as an "overhead expense"; the difficulties attending most democratic and market transitions; and longer-term ideological shifts in the ways the public and private sectors are viewed (Elliott, 1997a; Glynn, Kobrin, and Naím, 1997).

There has also been a sense that corruption itself is growing rapidly. As suspect regimes lost their ideological cover and other countries moved toward democracy and open markets, many scandals came to light – some new and others of longer standing. "Corruption" is both a provocative term and an attractive *ex post* explanation for a host of development and policy problems (Sindzingre, 2005); not surprisingly those seeking action on the problem have portrayed it in dramatic terms. International cor-porations, and aid and lending institutions, have begun to look at corruption within target nations, and within their own programs and operations, more forthrightly. Both economic growth and failed expecta-tions among those left out have created newly assertive social groups in many countries; particularly where dissent is risky, corruption issues are one way to take regimes to task without directly challenging their claims to rule (Johnston and Hao, 1995). Corruption has also become the focus of sus-tained international advocacy: Transparency International, founded in 1993, quickly expanded its reach and continues to work hard on many levels. New kinds of evidence and detection techniques also contribute to a sense that corruption is on the rise.

In fact no one knows whether corruption is actually growing (Williams and Beare, 1999). It is a secretive process in most cases, with all who know of illicit dealings having an interest in concealing them. Rose-Ackerman (1999: 4) points out that "extensive corruption" is a complicated notion: does it mean activity that is frequent, or open and overt, or takes place at high levels, or involves large stakes? Notions of what is or is not corrupt, and of what levels are acceptable, may change rapidly. Much of the concern has, however, reflected a keener appreciation that the costs of corruption, once widely disputed, are real and can no longer be rationalized. For these reasons and more, by the early 1990s major government, international aid, business, and civil-society organizations were committed to reform.

But while this renewed interest is welcome – indeed, overdue – the vision that has emerged over the past decade is a partial one at best. Too often corruption is reduced to a synonym for bribery or rent-seeking, and viewed primarily as a problem in economic development. But the starting points from which societies embark on development and reform can vary considerably. So can the pace of change and the range of forces backing or opposing it. Given those sorts of differences it would be surprising if corruption varied among the world's countries only in amount; yet few theories and reforms systematically address such basic contrasts. A first step toward identifying major syndromes of corruption and their implications is to understand major underlying variations in the ways people pursue and exchange wealth and power.

The roots of the syndromes: participation, institutions, and corruption

That the revival of interest in corruption took place during an era of global liberalization and integration is no coincidence: the connections among those developments and heightened concern over the ways people use and abuse emerging opportunities are numerous. But the new emphasis on corruption has been limited in a variety of ways by the interests and worldviews of the organizations and interests spearheading debate and policy change. Indeed, I will argue in chapter 2 that a "new consensus" emerged during the 1990s – one that treats corruption mostly as bribery, and as both effect and cause of incomplete, uneven, or ineffective economic liberalization, with the state judged primarily in terms of the extent to which it aids or impedes market processes. The ideas underlying that consensus are not illusory, but development problems come in many forms reflecting a variety of deeper difficulties. Political liberalization – democratization – is not just a mirror image of the proliferation of markets. Neither process can succeed on its own: both require a solid institutional footing – precisely what is lacking, in various ways, in many developing countries. The pace and balance of the two kinds of liberalization can vary markedly as well. How are such differences linked to contrasting kinds of corruption, and indeed what sorts of variations are most important? The most fruitful comparisons, I will argue, emphasize not just perceived amounts of corruption, or various techniques such as bribery versus extortion versus patronage, or cultural variations (though the latter will be critical to our discussion of reforms). Instead, the most important contrasts are found at deeper levels – in patterns of *participation* and the strength of *institutions* in, and linking, the political and the economic arenas.

Balanced and sustained democratic and market development depend upon – and indeed, as a developmental ideal are defined by – open, competitive, but structured *participation* in politics and the economy, and legitimate, effective *institutions* that protect and restrain activities in those arenas while maintaining boundaries and paths of access between them. Vigorous economic competition, by itself, does not necessarily produce broad-based growth; sound policies and institutions that facilitate and protect property rights, investment, entry into markets, and a moderate redistribution of wealth are also a part of the mix. Similarly, political competition alone – even if expressed through elections – is not enough: elections must be legitimate and decisive as well as competitive, and access, rights, and liberties *between* election campaigns are just as important. Open, competitive participation is essential if people are to express their preferences freely and have them weighed fairly by decision-makers – for Dahl (1971: ch. 1), critical aspects of democracy – and if they are to be able to reward effective government and oust the incompetent or abusive. People who have real political and economic alternatives will be less vulnerable to exploitation and dependency; competition weakens the ability of any one economic interest or political faction to dominate its own arena. But participation must also be structured and orderly: total *laissez-faire* in the economy is likely to enrich the few and impoverish the many, while a political free-for-all among twenty or thirty parties will not yield democratic mandates. Insecurity can induce politicians, unsure of their hold on power, to enrich themselves as quickly as they can, and entrepreneurs to buy official protection while insisting on maximum short-term returns (Scott, 1972; Keefer, 1996).

Terming such a balance *a* development ideal, rather than *the* ideal, is deliberate: while powerful arguments can be mounted for a way of life guided by free political and economic choices within open, competitive processes, such a vision of society is by no means free of difficulties or shared by all. At the same time it is a view that enjoys broad-based support at many levels, and one that is the stated justification and goal of many of the policies now reshaping the global system. For most societies the practical question is not whether to join in the pursuit of that ideal but how to make the best of the changes being implemented in its name. Another point is equally important: while this ideal may seem just another way to mandate the affluent market democracies of the West as models for societies everywhere, it is not. As we shall see, those advanced societies, too, fall short of this ideal in significant ways – problems reflected in the kinds of corruption *they* experience. Nor, finally, is this an argument for neoliberalism by another name: while a free and open economy is a part of the picture outlined above, state, political, and social institutions strong enough to preserve the openness and fairness of economic competition, and to restrain its excesses, are equally important. So, too, is a free, competitive, and accountable political system. As I will argue in later chapters, reform – really, the pursuit of this ideal – requires careful attention to the wellbeing of ordinary citizens, and a long-term "deep democratization" enabling and encouraging those citizens to mobilize in defense of their own interests.

A complex balance

Maintaining vigorous yet balanced participation and institutions is a complicated business, even in relatively advanced societies (Weingast, 1993; Schneider, 1998). This is so in part because liberal political and economic processes are *asymmetrical* in significant ways. Democratic politics rests not only on open competition, but also on normative assumptions of equality and fair play encapsulated by the notion of "one person, one vote." Self-interest generally drives the process, but contention among such interests must stay within certain boundaries. Ideally, democratic processes will not only express diverse private interests but also *aggregate* them[1] into broadly accepted public policies. Markets, by contrast, incorporate few presumptions of equality, either in process or outcome; such rights and accountability as exist are grounded primarily in ownership, not citizenship. Gains are presumed to be private and separable, rather than public and aggregated. Indeed, many "public" aspects of the process – externalities – are excluded from market calculations, or are taken seriously only because of government policy. Economic competition, while open to new participants, is continuous and much less structured than politics, with a wider range of uncertainty in outcomes. Losers are routinely driven out of markets, and winners enjoy advantages, in ways that lack legitimate political parallels. Political regimes hold power over a limited territory and population, while markets are increasingly integrated into global processes that can overwhelm local actors and policies.

---

[1] I thank Dr. Salvador Valdes-Prieto, Centro de Estudios Publicos in Santiago, Chile, for his comments on this point.

If such asymmetries did not exist connections between wealth and power would be much less complicated issues, and corruption would not be a problem. More or less anything, including official power and resources, could be bought and sold, and public office or other political resources could be used like any other in the pursuit of private gain. Neither political interventions in the economy, nor economic influence in the political realm, would threaten fundamental values and processes. But these contrasts do exist, and thus institutions are needed both to sustain competitive participation and to restrain its excesses. Courts, for example, enforce both public laws and private contracts; standards of fair play, such as honest elections and basic rules of business transparency, require legislation and enforcement mechanisms. Clear and accepted boundaries and distinctions are needed between state and society; public and private roles and resources; personal and collective interests; and market, bureaucratic, and patrimonial modes of allocation (Johnston and Hao, 1995). Without such boundaries major economic interests may dominate politics or powerful politicians can plunder the economy.

Institutionalized paths and rules of access between the political and economic arenas are just as important as boundaries, however. They are essential for maintaining accountability of state to society, and for feedback that can send critical signals to policymakers. Still, officials need enough autonomy to carry out their work in an uncompromised, authoritative fashion, while groups in society and the economy cannot simply be the tools of top politicians and bureaucrats. Maintaining that balance is complicated enough in mature democracies; in transitional societies creating accepted boundaries and paths of access can be a fundamental challenge. Where they do not exist, or are insufficient – as in contemporary China, where new political interests unleashed by market reform have few if any legitimate outlets, and bureaucrats carve out domains for themselves in the economy (Hao and Johnston, 2002) – they will be created corruptly.

Balanced and integrated participation and institutions as outlined above embody a developmental ideal – one that will also figure into our discussions of reform. No society attains that ideal in every respect, nor is movement toward it necessarily permanent. Problems can appear in many forms: participation can be weak, restricted, or manipulated in differing ways; institutions can be too rigid, too weak, too remote, too accessible, or poorly coordinated. In some places institutions will be stronger than participation, while in others the opposite may be true (a classic account appears in Huntington, 1968). In subsequent chapters I will explore the ways such difficulties can foster characteristic kinds of corruption. But for now the point is this: high-corruption societies do not just diverge from the ideal but *differ from each other*. We should also remember that serious corruption problems do not mean that participation and institutions are absent in a society; rather, they may take on many forms (O'Donnell, 2001). Civil society and political parties might be weak, for example, but extended patron–client networks can dominate politics and segments of the economy. Legitimate markets might be moribund while illicit ones thrive. Courts and the police may be ineffective while private armies hold extensive power and territory. Wealth and power will still be sought and exchanged, and institutions will emerge, even if informally and in ways that serve only a few. Thus we need to understand not only how developing societies differ from the ideal – and certainly not just how they differ from affluent market democracies – but rather focus upon the forms of participation and institutions that actually are at work there.

Problems with participation and institutions not only contribute to corruption but shape it in a variety of ways. In some countries most corruption involves private wealth interests' quest for influence within state bureaucracies or legislative bodies, while in others powerful government or military officials seize portions of the economy with impunity. Electoral corruption in some countries may consist of vote-stealing and intimidation of citizens, while in others it revolves around the theft of public resources to reward followers and to buy support. Sometimes corrupt incentives are used by elites to keep elections from being genuinely competitive in the first place. Some varieties can draw elites together into more or less organized networks, while other kinds are linked to deep divisions and contention among them. In some societies corruption is closely linked to violence, but elsewhere serves as an alternative to it (Huntington, 1968), enabling excluded groups to buy their way into economic or political processes. Bribery may be the predominant form of corruption in some countries – particularly those that have done most to shape the recent revival of interest in the problem – but in others extortion, nepotism, extended patronage abuses, fraud in elections, taxation or customs, political–business collusion, or outright official theft may be the biggest challenges. I suggest in chapters to come that particular syndromes of corruption are linked, via participation and institutions, to deeper problems in development, and that understanding those origins and contrasts is critical to devising appropriate and effective reforms.

What is corruption?

Corruption is a deeply normative concern and can be a matter of considerable dispute. Indeed, in many of the countries discussed here contention over *who gets to decide* its meaning is a central fact of political life.

Definitions are a matter of long-running debate (see Nye, 1967; Heidenheimer, 1970; Scott, 1972; Thompson, 1993; Thompson, 1995; Johnston, 1996; Philp, 1997; Philp, 2002), and I can scarcely settle the issue here. While I begin this discussion with a basic definition of corruption itself my main focus will be upon *systemic corruption problems*, a somewhat different idea aimed at exploring contrasts rather than resolving them in advance.

What makes an activity corrupt?

Corruption involves the abuse of a trust, generally one involving public power, for private benefit which often, but by no means always, comes in the form of money. Implicit in that notion is the idea that while wealth and power have accepted sources and uses, limits also apply. But in rapidly changing societies it is not always clear what those limits are, and the term "corruption" may be applied broadly (Hao and Johnston, 2002). Even in more settled societies its meaning is open to dispute, manipulation, and change. Distinctions between "public" and "private" can be difficult to draw (Jowitt, 1983; Wedel, 2001), particularly in the midst of economic liberalization and privatization. Policy changes may redefine public roles as private, or delegate power and resources to organizations that straddle state/society boundaries, in the process changing rules and accountability. Benefits and costs may be intangible, long-term, broadly dispersed, or difficult to distinguish from the routine operation of the political system (Thompson, 1993). Particularly where the problem is severe, corrupt demands and expectations can be so ingrained into a system that they go unspoken.

And by what standards do we identify "abuse"? One school of thought advocates definitions based on laws and other formal rules because of their relative precision, stability, and broad application (Nye, 1967; Scott, 1972). Critics reply that laws may have little legitimacy (or may even be written by officials to protect themselves), that definitions of corruption must address the question of its social *significance* – not just its nominal meaning – and that cultural standards or public opinion thus offer more realistic definitions (Peters and Welch, 1978; Gibbons, 1989). Relying upon cultural standards alone, however, may so relativize the concept, or impose so many distinctions and subcategories upon it, that its core meaning and useful comparisons are obscured. Still others contend that any definition based upon the classification of specific actions ignores broader issues of morality and justice, and neglects important political values such as leadership, citizenship, representation, deliberation, and accountability (Dobel, 1978; Euben, 1978; Moodie, 1980; Philp, 1987; Thompson, 1993).

I define corruption as *the abuse of public roles or resources for private benefit*, but emphasize that "abuse," "public," "private," and even "benefit" are matters of contention in many societies and of varying degrees of ambiguity in most. If our goal were to categorize specific actions as corrupt those complications would be a serious difficulty; indeed they are reasons for the inconclusive nature of the definitions debate. But at a systemic level, particularly where the problem is severe, such contention or ambiguity can be useful indicators of difficulties or change at the level of participation and institutions. Disputed boundaries between the "public" and the "private," for example, can signal critical institutional weaknesses. Where officials flout formal rules with impunity, that may indicate that countervailing forces in politics or the economy are weak or excluded. Such systemic issues can be critical to understanding how contrasting syndromes of corruption might arise and why the contrasts among them matter.

My primary focus is thus not upon corruption as an attribute of specific actions, but rather upon *systemic corruption problems*: uses of and connections between wealth and power that significantly weaken open, competitive participation and/or economic and political institutions, or delay or prevent their development. Systemic corruption problems disrupt the developmental ideal sketched out in the preceding section *in a variety of ways* symptomatic of underlying participation and institutional problems. Looked at this way corruption is both a symptom of development difficulties – and thus a useful diagnostic tool for understanding what those problems are – and a reinforcing cause.

This approach differs from the task of defining a corrupt act in important ways. Some systemic corruption problems might involve uses of wealth and power that are legal but still impair institutions and preempt the participation of others. Indeed, I will argue in chapter 4 that such is the case in the United States and many other market democracies. Further, it is meant to accommodate developments central to some of our syndromes and cases. The boundaries and functions of the "public" domain are changing (as they always have done), and the nation-state's dominance is under stress from both above and below – so much so that in some countries its claims to rule are not convincing. Even where institutions are strong, more activities and key decisions are taking place in essentially private arenas through markets, or market-like processes, subject to less restrictive rules and mechanisms of accountability. Specific activities might be defined or redefined as corrupt or acceptable in the course of such changes, but key connections between wealth and power, and the strength and balance of participation and institutions, might remain the same – or, be changing in ways that the classification of specific actions cannot capture. Indeed, I will suggest in my concluding chapter that continuing economic liberalization and changes in the role of the state may eventually drain much of the meaning out of behavior-classifying definitions of corruption.

At the same time this approach, with its emphasis upon institutions, does not disregard politics and public institutions. Given the recent controversies over power and accountability within private organizations as diverse as Enron, the Roman Catholic Church, the US Olympic Committee, United Way charities, and intercollegiate sports programs – to name just a few examples from the United States, where public–private boundaries are relatively clear – that may seem unduly restrictive. But governments remain important sources of decisions, benefits, and punishments nearly everywhere. If they were not, few would bother to corrupt them. Where they fail to perform those functions authoritatively and justly, that is a serious problem. Corporate fraud can closely resemble corruption in behavioral terms, and may be linked with it in numerous ways. In the business sector wealth and power may be essentially the same thing. Private-sector abuses of trust may signal deterioration of a society's social and normative fabric. But my primary concern is with relationships among political and economic participation and institutions, as noted above, not with categorizing specific actions, and we gain nothing by stretching our notions of corruption to include all forms of high-profile wrongdoing. We already have many concepts, such as fraud, theft, and failure to perform fiduciary duties, that are readily applicable to the private sector. My emphasis, therefore, will be primarily upon systemic corruption problems, with weak states or public–private boundaries being important aspects of some of the syndromes of corruption we will consider.

Conclusion

International development policies and the aspirations of people and societies around the world have been powerfully affected, over the past generation, by the ideals and difficulties that will be the focus of this book. A healthy synergy between emerging markets and democratization was widely hoped for as the 1990s began, but has more or less been left to chance: liberalized politics and economies were expected to support each other, even if nobody knew quite how that would come to pass. Participation, in forms both helpful and harmful, proliferated while state institutions were being deemphasized, rolled back, or even defined as causes of corruption and barriers to development. Thus, for many citizens "democracy" has meant increased poverty and insecurity in personal life, and ineffective leadership and policy in the public realm.

A parallel argument can be made about markets: some transitional economies have experienced spectacular, if uneven, success (China and, more recently, India), or have at least sustained generally positive trends (Poland, Hungary, Chile, Botswana). But others have endured periods of chaos (Russia, post-1997 Indonesia), a drift backward toward illiberal practices (Belarus), or outright failure (Argentina and several African economies). In Brazil the election of President Lula da Silva in November, 2002, was widely judged a popular backlash against economic liberalization and its perceived social consequences. The Asian economic meltdown of the late 1990s, with its serious damage to emerging economies that had long been the envy of many other societies, raised further questions about corruption, markets, and the role of the state.

Advanced countries have their periods of political and economic difficulty, and they too experience corruption which, I will argue, is more serious than most corruption indices seem to suggest. There are poor democracies, such as India, and wealthy undemocratic societies such as Kuwait and Singapore. There are third-wave success stories too, such as Spain, Poland, and Chile. So the connections we will explore in this book are complicated, and the four syndromes of corruption I will propose are but a first step toward disentangling them and designing appropriate policy responses. Still, the optimism of the late 1980s and 1990s has given way to a more sober appreciation of the challenges of liberalization and development – and as optimism has cooled, the focus on corruption has intensified. The United States government, through its Millennium Challenge Accounts initiative, has made corruption and good government a priority issue affecting the way major development aid resources will be distributed and withheld. International anti-corruption agreements sponsored by the United Nations, the Organization for Economic Cooperation and Development, and the Organization of American States reflect similar commitments on an even broader scale. As we contemplate such initiatives, and as we reassess the effects of a generation of liberalization and deemphasis of the state, a clear understanding of the nature and origins of corruption has never been a higher priority.

Too often in the policy debate, however, corruption has been seen as a generic problem. Its deeper origins, the ways it is embedded in political and economic processes, and its role as a symptom of diverse and problematical relationships between wealth and power, public and private interests, and state and society, are acknowledged but only poorly understood in depth. The institutions and norms of affluent market democracies are posited as the obvious goal of reform; as a result, reform recommendations vary little from one society to another. How rapidly changing societies *get to* a better place is reduced to recommendations for technical changes in "governance" and calls for "political will," while the very different places from which they embark on that journey seem to matter little.

How did we arrive at that view of corruption and reform? Whose interests and worldviews does it reflect, and what is missing from it? What are its implications? And how well does it actually account for the patterns of corruption and development we see in real societies? Those questions are the focus of chapter 2.

2 The international setting: power, consensus, and policy

New life for an old issue

Corruption is back on the international agenda after a generation's absence because important economic and political interests put it there. Policymakers have changed the ways we pursue international development and reform, while international businesses and the governments that increasingly have a stake in their success have extended their reach both in the world economy and in policy debates. Scholars and advocacy groups have produced important new theories and data that have moved us beyond old conundrums regarding corruption. Many of these activities reflect business- and trade-oriented worldviews, organizational interests, and analytical outlooks advocating liberalized markets and politics, in that order.

With respect to corruption this worldview and the power behind it have at least three major implications. First, and most visible, is the general trend toward liberalization and privatization of economic activity, along with the withdrawal of the state into more limited and technical kinds of functions, that has marked global development for a generation. Those changes affect the ways people pursue, use, and exchange both wealth and power and, as we shall see, shape corruption syndromes in critical ways. Second, businesses based in affluent countries play major roles in the corruption that occurs in developing societies, often with the blessings of their home governments: until recently some affluent societies allowed their international businesses to deduct foreign bribe payments from their tax bills. Third, a new consensus has emerged over corruption's origins, consequences, and remedies. Many who share in the consensus are driven by a genuine desire to improve the lives of people in developing societies, and have done much to pursue that goal. Still, despite the power of its backers and scope of its claims the consensus remains a partial vision – one that imposes a common diagnosis and reform strategy upon diverse cases. Consensus approaches work well at a high level of generality but tell us much less about the societies where the problem is worst.

All three of these developments are important concerns in this book. The broad trend toward economic liberalization, and the questions it raises about the role and soundness of state, political, and social institutions, will play a direct role in the process by which I define corruption syndromes and locate countries within them (chapter 3). The role of some international businesses in the corruption problems of specific countries will become evident in several of the case studies to come (chapters 4–7). This chapter deals primarily with the third connection: the ways policy and analytical aspects of the consensus worldview have converged at a global level to influence both corruption and the ways we understand it. Corruption has come to be seen as both cause and effect of uneven or incomplete economic liberalization, and of an intrusive, ineffective state. Rank-ordering countries from high to low corruption effectively defines the problem as the same everywhere, and its scope and effects are judged primarily in economic terms. Reform is seen as moving societies toward a neoliberal ideal of market economics, and market-like political processes, facilitated by a lean, technically competent state that is little more than a kind of referee in the economic arena. Anti-corruption agendas thus tend to vary rather little from one country to the next.

The problem is not that these ideas are utterly wrong: there are, as we shall see, good reasons to believe that corruption delays, distorts, and diverts economic and democratic development, and new data and scholarship have taught us a great deal. Rather, the difficulty is that the dominant worldview is incomplete: it diverts our attention from complex and contrasting underlying causes, and from qualitative differences in various societies' experiences with corruption. At the level of reform much is said about fitting anti-corruption strategies to differing societies, but the most frequent approach is still to assemble "toolkits" of ideas that may have worked somewhere, while providing little guidance on what to do, and what *not* to do, in particular settings. This book cannot demolish the consensus worldview – indeed, in some respects it builds upon it. Rather, my goal is to change the ways we think about corruption, to increase our awareness of how and why it varies among and within societies, and to offer a more realistic view about the challenges of reform.

Consensus and its limitations

Calling any state of opinion a "consensus" is inherently risky; indeed, ideas continue to evolve over issues such as the role of state institutions in development and reform. Still, it is striking how quickly past debates over corruption – so often hung up on definitions, divided over the question of effects, and mired in a paralyzing relativism – have given way to extensive agreement. The *definitions* issue has not so much been resolved as bypassed – wisely, for the most part – in order to focus upon processes that would qualify as corrupt by any definition. Still, bribery – particularly at high levels in the course of international aid, trade, and investment – has become a *de facto* synonym for corruption. Within that relatively narrow focus there is little debate anymore as to broad *effects*: strong theory and evidence suggest that corruption delays and distorts economic growth, rewards inefficiency, and short-circuits open competition (Kaufmann, Kraay, and Zoido-Lobatón, 1999; Rose-Ackerman, 1999: chs. 2–5; Hall and Yago, 2000; Mauro, 2002). Findings relating to democratic development are less plentiful (Doig and Theobald, 2000; Moreno, 2002), in part because within the consensus politics and the state have often been seen as impediments to economic liberalization. Still, evidence suggests moderate-to-low levels of corruption in most democracies (for a dissenting view see Lipset and Lenz, 2000). Far more serious problems occur where state institutions (Knack and Keefer, 1995; Rose-Ackerman, 1999), civil society (Ruzindana, 1997; Johnston, 2005a) and civil liberties (Isham, Kaufmann, and Pritchett, 1995) are weak, where political competition is impaired (Johnston, 2002; Della Porta, 2004), and where officials operate with impunity. *Relativism* – a sense that each society's corruption issues are shaped in unique ways by historical and cultural variations, and that comparisons among diverse societies are therefore suspect – reflected laudable motives but discouraged all but the vaguest generalizations. That position has been overrun by numerical rankings of countries on worldwide league tables of corruption, and to propositions and findings extending across large numbers of societies (see, for example, Friedman, Johnson, Kaufmann, and Zoido-Lobatón, 2000; Sandholtz and Koetzle, 2000; Triesman, 2000; Kaufmann, 2004). Reticence about discussing corruption in developing countries and in agencies and programs seeking to aid them has given way to a recognition that it can no longer be written off as a matter of differing customs or values.

Partial visions

Whether or not it fully qualifies as a "consensus" this outlook has moved us beyond some old, stale debates. We know much more than we did a generation ago, and there are far more resources with which to study the problem. But in other respects there may be *too much* consensus. The revival of interest has been driven primarily by business, and by international aid and lending institutions – groups that tend to view corruption as cause and consequence of incomplete or uneven economic liberalization. The state and politics are, often as not, seen as parts of the problem, rather than as essential elements of development and reform (Weingast, 1993; Schneider, 1998). Governing is reduced to public management functions while complex questions of democracy and justice are to be addressed through technically sound "good governance" rather than politics. There is little attempt to differentiate among corruption problems, either between or within societies; instead, much research seeks to explain variations in whole countries' scores on one-dimensional corruption indices. There are thus few variations in suggested reforms, and little guidance as to which remedies should be applied first, later, or not at all.

Some of these limitations could be seen in anti-corruption strategy statements issued in the late 1990s by major international organizations. The United States Agency for International Development, in its 1998 *USAID Handbook for Fighting Corruption*, presented good case studies of Hong Kong, Mexico, and Tanzania (USAID, 1998: 21–39), and offered a useful overview of anti-corruption measures (*ibid.*: 8–15). But while the document acknowledged the need for flexible responses and discussed social as well as institutional causes, there was little systematic comparison of cases. The World Bank strategy document "Helping Countries Combat Corruption" offered a range of good-governance measures and advocated continued economic liberalization, but treated anti-corruption reform in very general terms and did not differentiate among types of cases (World Bank, 1997: chs. 2–6). The UNDP discussion paper "Corruption and Good Governance" proposed attacking the "micro" logic of bribery (UNDP, 1997: 52–59) but did not extend the analysis to other varieties of corruption; proposed reforms again dealt mostly with improved law enforcement and public management (*ibid.*: ch. 3). The Organization for Economic Cooperation and Development (OECD), in *Corruption and Integrity Improvement Initiatives in Developing Countries* (1998), discussed some conceptual issues but did not distinguish systematically among types of cases. Emphasis was on political will at top levels, law enforcement, institutional reform and technical skills, mobilizing civil society, and economic liberalization (OECD, 1998). The Year 2000 *Sourcebook* of Transparency International (TI) acknowledged four types of bribery (Transparency International, 2000: 16–17), but beyond a mention of extortion did not explore other sorts of corruption. Indeed, at one point it asserts that "corruption in China … is really no different from that in Europe" (*ibid.*: 15–16).

A similar outlook is reflected in TI's best-known publication – the Corruption Perceptions Index (CPI).[1] The CPI is an annual "poll of polls" in which results from varying numbers of surveys are averaged into scores for well over 100 countries, rating the extent to which they are seen as corrupt. Several of those component surveys specifically ask respondents to judge the extent of bribery, or of demands for bribes, in a country. Others sample international or domestic business people; some ask recipients the extent to which corruption harms the business environment, again framing the corruption issue in terms of bribery, business, and markets. CPI scores, like all other single-score country-level indicators, reduce potential qualitative differences to matters of degree, while obscuring contrasts within societies (Khan and Sundaram, 2000: 9–10; Johnston, 2001a).

What is wrong with this picture? Certainly not that these reports or the CPI draw upon bad ideas; nor is it that every case or country requires a unique policy or theory (although understanding the significance of what they have in common would seem to require more attention to contrasting cases). In some cases the organizations sponsoring these documents are restricted as to the in-country issues they may address. On the plus side, USAID has amassed significant anti-corruption capacity, and the OECD Anti-Bribery Treaty is a landmark achievement. The CPI, like TI and its many national chapters, has helped make corruption a priority issue in places where those in power would rather it be ignored. TI carefully documents the sources and methodology of the CPI[2] (Lambsdorff, 1999), is candid about the index's limitations, and in any event is not responsible for the ways the data are used by others. CPI results do fit in expected ways with other development measures, giving them significant construct validity, and there is little reason to think that the overall rankings are radically wrong. Indeed, I will make limited use of the CPI later on in this book.

The problems, instead, are those of worldview and analysis. As the overall emphasis on international business might lead us to expect, "corruption" is too often treated as a synonym for "bribery" – in effect, as a particular kind of *quid pro quo* set apart by its illegitimate nature but otherwise open to analysis as just another process of exchange. Bribery, particularly when viewed broadly enough to include extortion (where an official demands payment), probably is the most common form of corruption; it is certainly the easiest kind to model. But nepotism, official theft and fraud, and conflict-of-interest problems, for example, do not fit

[1] Available at http://www.transparency.org/cpi/.
[2] See http://www.transparency.org/cpi/index.html#cpi.

the bribery model well. In some corrupt exchanges, such as patronage and nepotism, considerable time may elapse between receiving the *quid* and repaying the *quo*, and the exchange may be conditioned by many factors other than immediate gain (Johnston, 1979). In practice *quid* and *quo* may be difficult to link and compare. In other cases, such as "constituent service" by legislators, illicit activities may be all but impossible to distinguish from legitimate ones, and corruption may lie not in an exchange but in cumulative effects upon the quality of political processes (Thompson, 1995; Moroff, 2002). Still other varieties – corruption-violence linkages, electoral fraud, embezzlement, or using official resources for under-the-table business – are not exchanges at all. *Political* corruption is generally underemphasized compared to bureaucratic varieties.

Other problems are evident at the level of corruption control. The political risks of confronting corruption and the collective-action problems inherent in mobilizing citizens to fight it (Johnston and Kpundeh, 2002) are too often reduced to calls for "political will." Most consensus reforms amount to recommendations that developing societies emulate laws and institutions found in advanced societies; countermeasures are generally seen as ends in themselves, with little attention paid to how they originated and won support in societies where they are now in place. Stronger fiscal and managerial controls, greater transparency and accountability, monitoring by an independent judiciary and free news media, greater competition in politics and the economy, and a stronger civil society – to name some frequent recommendations – do help check corruption in many societies. But they did not emerge from nowhere; often, in fact, they were the *results* of democratization and political contention, and were devised by groups seeking to protect themselves rather than as plans for "good governance" in society at large. To be effective they require continued support from significant interests in society and legitimacy with respect to basic social values. Where anti-corruption forces are new such social support may be weak, or may need time to gather strength. Reforms, even when technically sound, can do more harm than good if they lack key resources and social backing: as we shall see, the premature implementation of competitive elections during the 1990s arguably made corruption more rapacious in Kenya and Indonesia.

The analytical and policy trends outlined here extend across a range of institutions and interests, and for each statement I have made there are of course exceptions. Moreover, there are signs of change: by the late 1990s the value of institutions for sustaining and restraining liberalized economic and political processes was once again widely acknowledged, after fifteen years during which economic liberalization stood nearly alone at center stage. Enhancing state capacity is now a top priority for institutions such as the World Bank (see, for example, Levy and Kpundeh, 2004). Agencies such as USAID are taking a more nuanced view of corruption as a problem embedded in social contexts, and are working on ways to distinguish among differing varieties. Still, interests and institutions primarily concerned with economic development will continue to set the anti-corruption agenda for some time to come. To make that agenda more responsive to the diversity and complexity of corruption we need to understand underlying causes of corruption and how they vary among the world's societies. Those contrasts are of more than theoretical interest: in rapidly changing societies they make for qualitatively different development and corruption problems, not just differences in amounts.

Change from within

Years ago Denison Rustow (1970: 341–350; see also Anderson, 1999) pointed out that the factors that *sustain* democracy where it is strong – literacy, affluence, multiparty politics, a middle class – are not necessarily the same as those that brought it into being *to begin with*. He argued that democracy grew out of "prolonged and inconclusive political struggle ... [T]he protagonists must represent well-entrenched forces ... and the issues must have profound meaning to them" (Rustow, 1970: 352). In those struggles, "Democracy was not the original or primary aim; it was sought as a means to some other end or it came as a fortuitous byproduct of the struggle" (*ibid.*: 353). Much the same is true of reform. Checks and balances, accountable leaders, liberal markets, competitive elections, and administrative transparency do much to control corruption in countries where it is the exception rather than the rule, and where they enjoy broad-based legitimacy. It does not follow, however, that the *absence* of such factors is what explains corruption where it is extensive, nor that putting them in place will control the problem. Historically, many societies reduced corruption in the course of contending over other, more basic issues of power and justice (Roberts, 1966; Johnston, 1993). Checks against various abuses were not so much schemes for good governance as political settlements – rules that contending interests could live with and could enforce by political means, allowing them to pursue their own interests while protecting themselves against predation by others. The institutions and norms of low-corruption countries not only shape political and economic participation; in a long-term sense they are also the products of such participation. They ratify and enforce underlying settlements regarding the uses, and limits, of wealth and power. They were created and continue to work not just because they are "good ideas," but because they engage and protect lasting interests in society.

Thus, an understanding of corruption where it is common requires not just an inventory of what seems to be missing by comparison to low-corruption countries, but an analysis of what *is* influencing their political and economic development. What sorts of political and economic opportunities exist, who puts them to use, and what are the trends in those two arenas? What institutions shape, restrain, and sustain economic and political participation, and how effective are they? Such influences do not easily reduce to any single dimension; countries including affluent market democracies diverge from the ideal laid out in chapter 1 in many different ways. As a result, we should expect to encounter many kinds of corruption problems reflecting differing origins, affecting societies in distinctive ways, and requiring appropriate, carefully tailored counter-measures. Recognizing and understanding those contrasts, however, have proven to be difficult within the limits of the consensus worldview.

Why worry about corruption?

If development does reflect complex and interrelated influences, why single out corruption for such concern? Looked at one way it is just another form of influence, decisionmaking, and exchange, and "development," broadly speaking, entails broadening and deepening such processes. Moreover, while corruption is formally illegitimate it does not follow that approved procedures and institutions are necessarily moral or effective. Official policy may be inherently unjust; a Ministry of Development that pursues fundamentally flawed policy will fail at its mission even if corruption is eliminated. Calling new policies and procedures "reforms" does not make them beneficial; often the language of reform masks agendas that benefit very few. A poor but non-corrupt country would still face all of the problems associated with being poor.

Indeed, during the first round of debate over the developmental effects of corruption, roughly between the late 1950s and the mid-1970s, one side held that corruption might have considerable political and economic benefits (Leff, 1964; Bayley, 1966; for opposing views, Andreski, 1968; Myrdal, 2002). Corruption, the argument ran, was a way for elites to build their political backing in society and to win cooperation in both parliaments and bureaucracies, a way for entrepreneurs and investors to break through bureaucratic bottlenecks, an informal price system in tightly regulated economies, and a cushion against the worst social dislocations of development. A somewhat different argument (Leys, 1965) suggested that corruption be judged against actual alternatives available at a given time, rather than in comparison with ideal processes; some of those alternatives might be more harmful than corruption. Still another view is that established and acceptable ways of doing things come to be labeled corrupt by outsiders who do not understand the informal functions such behavior might play in society. Such actions or exchanges might confer or reaffirm status, build social alliances, or reduce conflict among people and groups, for example. To judge such activities solely by their systemic political or economic effects may be to ignore other, less tangible, benefits at a personal or community level. Reforms that do not address those social functions in alternative ways may well be doomed to fail.

These views have many drawbacks, however. Too often they rest upon hypothetical examples and treat corrupt dealings in isolation, rather than exploring their broader and longer-term implications (Rose-Ackerman, 2002). Some who have argued for informal social functions of corrupt activities tend to look much harder for beneficial implications than for harmful ones; too often it is assumed that if a particular way of exchange, or of seeking and using power and status, has existed within a society for some time it must be superior to ideas originating elsewhere. As we shall see below, recent research makes it difficult to maintain that there is something inherently good about corruption. Still, the contrasting views that have been debated over the years are useful reminders that corruption cannot really be understood without reference to the political, economic, institutional, and social setting within which it occurs.

The costs of corruption

Over the past fifteen years new evidence and refined theories have shown that on the whole corruption delays and distorts political and economic development. Unlike functionalist arguments these findings focus on real processes and systemic, measurable consequences, rather than upon specific or hypothetical deals in isolation (Rose-Ackerman, 2002). Corrupt transactions, via the signals they send and incentives they confer, can ripple through an entire economy or political system. Bribes that win public contracts for an incompetent bidder, for example, reward inefficiency and may discourage efficient firms from entering a country's economy. "Speed money" paid to bureaucrats does not break down administrative bottlenecks (Wei, 1999); instead, it tells other officials that they too can make money by dragging their feet.

Some of the damage done by extensive corruption is clear and direct: when political figures and their business cronies divert aid and investment to offshore bank accounts, poor nations become poorer. Where political and bureaucratic discretion is put up for rent due process, civil liberties, and basic rights are endangered, and official policies become a sham. In both instances benefits and advantages are likely to flow to the few and the well-connected while costs are extracted from society at large – ultimately, from the poor and powerless most of all. Other effects are intangible, collective, and long-term in nature: where corrupt connections guide decisionmaking, democratic values and participation become irrelevant and opportunities are denied to many who need them most. At times petty benefits flow to poor people or ordinary citizens: Palermo's local politicians sometimes gave voters one shoe before an election, and its mate afterwards if the ballot had been cast as expected (Chubb, 1981). But those short-term incentives come at a long-term cost: they are given not for their own sake but to maintain control, and accepting them means forgoing political choices. Such costs are no less real for being difficult to measure.

From corrupt deals to systemic effects

How do the costs of specific corrupt deals become so harmful to development? Consider, in light of the ideal sketched out in chapter 1, the well-known formulation proposed by Klitgaard (1988: 75):

> **Corruption equals *Monopoly* plus *Discretion*, minus *Accountability*.**

Klitgaard uses this formulation to identify and analyze situations conducive to bureaucratic corruption. Officials can use the prospect of lucrative contracts to extract corrupt payments, for example, if they can exploit a monopoly – power to award contracts not available elsewhere – and discretion – the ability to choose among bidders. A lack of accountability means that there is little to prevent exploitation and no recourse for the losers. Bidders who pay the bribes likewise short-circuit competitive bidding, reward the corrupt use of discretion, and subvert transparent, accountable procedures. Klitgaard's equation is not intended to explain why particular individuals do or do not become corrupt, or how a specific client will respond to corrupt demands or opportunities. It does a better job of explaining bureaucratic corruption, and bribery, than other varieties. It is, however, a very useful model of situations most likely to foster corruption (see also Rose-Ackerman, 1978; Della Porta and Vannucci, 1999; Della Porta and Rose-Ackerman, 2002).

For our purposes Klitgaard also shows how corruption and its underlying dynamics subvert structured, competitive participation and sound institutions. *Monopolies* by definition disrupt competition and, when combined with *discretion*, encourage rigged processes rewarding connections rather than open, honest decisionmaking. Political machines, for example, are electoral monopolies giving bosses the discretion to reward their backers and punish their enemies, with little fear of being called to account for their actions. *Discretion* in the absence of *accountability* is antithetical to strong and effective political and market institutions: boundaries between politics and the economy, or between public and private interests, are weakened or subverted. So are rules of fair play, making access to decisionmakers a marketable commodity. Connections and boundaries between wealth and power will be controlled by corrupt officials and their cronies, not by laws or accountable agencies. Markets as well as politics and policy can become distorted: in South Korea, for example, politically favored industrial combines (*chaebols*) received preferential interest rates and access to credit while those refusing to send cash to the Blue House (Korea's presidential residence) were left to fend for themselves in much more expensive capital markets, and suffered official harassment (Moran, 1999; Kang, 2002a). Serious corruption thus reflects and perpetuates weaknesses in participation and institutions, the prospect of corrupt benefits creates incentives to undermine both, and the result is that further corruption is facilitated while opposition to it becomes difficult – or even dangerous.

Economic consequences

The economic costs of corruption can be seen in both individual transactions and their extended consequences (Rose-Ackerman, 1999: ch. 2; Rahman, Kisunko, and Kapoor, 2000; Moreno, 2002). By substituting illegitimate payments and preferments for free exchange and a fluid system of market-clearing prices, corruption introduces and rewards inefficiency in dealings between the state and private interests (Elliott, 1997b; Seyf, 2001; Rose-Ackerman, 2002) and preempts competition among firms. In the short term, corrupt influence may seem cheap and expeditious, compared to routing complex and expensive bids through legitimate channels. But bribes and extortion payments are an expensive way to obtain results for which one already qualifies, or that could be the rewards of efficiency. Resources are diverted into corrupt payments while the costs of negotiating with agencies, providing data, filling out forms, allowing inspections, and awaiting outcomes are actually compounded as officials contrive new requirements and delays. Corruption tends to be more extensive, and aggregate growth and investment lower, in countries with extensive bureaucratic delays, and there is no evidence that corruption "cuts through red tape" (Mauro, 1998; Mauro, 2002; see also La Porta, Lopez-de-Silanes, Shleifer, and Vishny, 1999; Gupta, Davoodi, and Alonso-Terme, 2002; Tanzi and Davoodi, 2002a; Tanzi and Davoodi, 2002b; Lambsdorff, 2003a; Lambsdorff, 2003b). Surveys of businesses and bureaucrats show that where corruption is extensive bureaucratic requirements and delays tend to be significantly *greater*, not less (Kaufmann and Kaliberda, 1996; Wei, 1999; Hellman, Jones, and Kaufmann, 2000; Reinikka and Svensson, 2002; Hellman and Kaufmann, 2004). Moreover, corruption is a risky and unreliable form of influence: officials powerful enough to create monopolies and resist accountability are also powerful enough to renege on their side of a deal. Corrupt deals place the payers outside the protection of the law and create a trail of incriminating evidence that can be used to impose further pressure.

Between corruption and reduced growth there are several causal connections. Primary among them are effects on investment (World Bank, 1997; Mauro, 1998; Seyf, 2001). Wei (1997; Wei, 2000; see also Mauro, 1998; Fisman and Svensson, 2000) has shown that corruption amounts to a heavy "tax" on foreign direct investment, and estimates that an increase in corruption from the low levels of Singapore to the much higher levels of Mexico is equivalent to a 21 percent levy on investment. Investment seems to be damaged most where corruption is high *and the predictability of its rewards is low* (World Bank, 1997; Campos, Lien, and Pradhan, 1999), likely reflecting the negative effects of poorly functioning institutions (Knack and Keefer, 1995). The quality and implementation of environmental policy also suffers in corrupt regimes (Esty and Porter, 2002), as do health and education efforts (Gupta, Davoodi, and Tiongson, 2001). Mauro (1998) finds that public spending in high-corruption countries tends to be diverted from education toward activities like major construction projects where sizeable bribes are readily available (see also Rauch, 1995; Ruzindana, 1997). Significant corruption is associated with low-quality regulation, services and infrastructure (Rose-Ackerman, 2002), and with ineffective tax collection and administration (Mauro, 1998). International aid is less likely to be used effectively in high-corruption countries (IMF, 1995; Isham, Kaufmann, and Pritchett, 1995; Kilby, 1995). Corruption diverts talent – official as well as entrepreneurial – resources, and effort away from productive activities into rent-seeking (Murphy, Shleifer, and Vishny, 1993; Mauro, 1998; Gaviria, 2002). It encourages inefficient contracting for unneeded services: Daniel O'Connell's legendary political machine in Albany, New York, employed sixty-eight janitors to maintain the six-story City Hall, nearly as many as worked in the Empire State Building (Kennedy, 1983: 341).

Consistent with our discussion of participation and institutions, data also point to significantly higher levels of corruption in economies with low levels of competition, poor anti-trust policies and enforcement, and markets dominated by a few large firms (Ades and Di Tella, 1994). Elliott (1997b), Ades and Di Tella (1999), and Blake and Martin (2002) find a negative relationship between corruption and the overall openness of an economy. Some of the most serious harm is done to small businesses that might otherwise be protected by strong institutions and rules of fair play: many are forced into the informal sector (Kaufmann and Kaliberda, 1996; Rose-Ackerman and Stone, 1996) and their potential for offering marginal groups a stake in the economy is lost. For those reasons so-called "petty corruption" should be seen as a serious concern (Elliott, 1997b), not just as an echo of illicit dealings at higher levels.

Extensive corruption tends to be associated with widespread, persistent poverty, though here causality runs in both directions (UNDP, 1997). Some countries remain poor because they are corrupt, but they may also have extensive corruption because they are poor. Where legitimate alternatives are scarce the incentives to make and demand payments can be all the more intense. Meanwhile, corrupt deals are unlikely to contribute to growth: beyond a certain point where payments make up for low salaries (a complex issue: see Besley and McLaren, 1993), illicit returns are likely to be spent on luxury goods or to flow out of corrupt countries toward economies offering better returns and safe numbered bank accounts.

Affluence is not, by itself, evidence that a country does not have significant corruption problems (Kang, 2002a) – nor is democracy. Moreover, GDP trends by themselves are a decidedly incomplete measure of a society's wellbeing, and focusing only on domestic economic consequences would give many affluent countries a "pass" on corruption issues that they may not have earned. Indeed, chapters 4 and 5 will discuss several established democracies in which politicians trade in bureaucratic or legislative access made all the more valuable by the strength of the institutions involved. In less-institutionalized democracies, we shall see that corruption helps a range of elites build networks and secure their positions. They *may* then pursue growth-oriented policies relatively effectively, but that is by no means guaranteed. I will suggest that spurring economic growth in that way can have significant costs later on.

Implications for political development

Open, competitive political processes – including but not limited to elections – are also undermined by corruption (Doig and Theobald, 2000; Moreno, 2002; but see also Lipset and Lenz, 2000). Two of the three political opportunities seen by Dahl (1971) as essential to the development of a polyarchy – the opportunities to signify preferences, and to have those preferences weighed equally by decisionmakers – are incompatible with the monopoly influence and lack of accountability that feature in Klitgaard's equation. A political monopoly held by an extended patronage network, or created through electoral fraud, may make it pointless or risky to express opposition views, while illicit use of discretion in policymaking means that the preferences of non-favored groups and citizens will carry little weight. Similarly, genuine freedom to vote, form independent organizations, and compete for popular support – all parts of Dahl's (1971: ch. 1) list of basic democratic guarantees – can be circumvented by corrupt officials and their private clients. Where civil liberties are secure, and some political or economic alternatives remain, victims of corruption may confront the problem directly. But where corrupt networks dominate politics, citizens will more likely respond in what Alam (1995) calls *evasive* ways – dropping out of politics or the mainstream economy, forgoing economic benefits, or moving away – or in *illicit* ways, fighting back with corrupt influence of their own. Such responses may protect individuals in the short run, but do little to enhance democracy and nothing to reduce corruption; in the long run they play directly into the hands of corrupt interests. The belief that corruption is pervasive appears to encourage tax evasion by citizens (Torgler, 2003; Uslaner, 2003), which in turn weakens government's capacity to respond to political mandates and pay adequate salaries. Intangible political costs can be serious too: a perception of corruption can undermine both the legitimacy of regimes and leaders and levels of interpersonal trust (Seligson, 2002; Anderson and Tverdova, 2003).

Because corruption, as a form of influence, requires scarce resources *haves* (money, access, expertise) it typically benefits the "haves" at the expense of have-nots. Patronage networks may bring large numbers of people into the political process, but they do so on the terms and in the interests of the leadership – controlling rather than mobilizing client groups and their interests. The biggest potential asset of the poor, or of ordinary citizens – the strength of numbers – can be divided and conquered by giving and withholding tangible rewards on the basis of politicized discretion (Wilson, 1960; Webman, 1973; Johnston, 1979). Where playing the role of political opposition means little more than cutting oneself out of the spoils, structured political competition may implode into one-party clientelism or a disorganized scramble over petty stakes. Either way corruption is a poor substitute for politics. When political change threatens elites' security hyper-corruption may result as those unsure of their hold on power take as much as they can, as quickly as they can take it (Scott, 1972: ch. 5).

Established democracies benefit from strong civil societies, working consensus on standards of fair play and the limits of political and economic influence, independent judiciaries and opposition groups, and from the voters' ability to throw out the government without toppling the constitutional regime. Social sanctions – both the force of public disapproval (Weber, 1958; Elster, 1989) and the various ethics codes and penalties that can be enforced by professional and business associations – can also be meaningful restraints. Perhaps the most important asset in such societies is the very legitimacy that government and the law accumulate over time through effective performance. But here too corruption can do political damage – effects that are worrisome both in themselves and because of their implications for the intangible anti-corruption strengths just noted (Lauth, 2000).

Consider, for example, the vitality of political competition. Doig (1984) argues that the most serious cases of corruption tend to arise where political competition is weak (see also Blake and Martin, 2002; for contrary US evidence, Schlesinger and Meier, 2002). Entrenched elites can buy off or intimidate opposition parties and voters or construct backroom coalitions so broad that even when a given faction loses votes it can retain a share of power. In such settings there may be few political options and organizational vehicles available to would-be reformers. In federal systems, opponents can at least appeal to higher levels of government for support: in many American cities during the nineteenth and early twentieth centuries, anti-machine groups persuaded state governments to intervene in local corruption. But decentralization comes at a price (Fjelsted, 2002; Gerring and Thacker, 2004), for it also leads to a vast proliferation of access points through which private interests can seek influence or exercise veto power by means both legitimate and illicit, and may create political stalemates that encourage bribery to speed matters along.

Where building political monopolies and extracting corrupt benefits dominate elite agendas parties may dig in within their own bailiwicks in both state and society, avoiding competition while cultivating the financial backing of favored interests. Where they share power in a jurisdiction they may carve up public budgets and payrolls among themselves (e.g. the *Proporz* practices of Germany's local party organizations outlined in chapter 4). Such politics may build only limited public trust and commitment; citizens may see the process as a rich man's game, and their own choices at election time as unconnected to the wellbeing of their families and communities. The "corruption" in such cases – particularly in established democracies – may come more in terms of damage to democratic values and processes than actual lawbreaking (Thompson, 1995);

indeed, entrenched officials can write election legislation that does little to restrain their own campaigns and their contributors' activities.

Contrasting corruption problems

Recent scholarship thus makes a strong case that corruption harms economic and democratic political development. But two further points emerge from the preceding discussion. First, corruption is *both* a cause and an effect of such difficulties – in many ways, a *symptom* of deep-rooted problems in the emergence of, and balance between, participation and institutions. Second, these interconnections are complex and variable: there are many possible permutations of, and strengths and weaknesses in, participation and institutions. Corruption is thus unlikely to be the same problem everywhere, and scores along one-dimensional indices may tell us little about different sorts of societies.

Corruption as people live it

People and societies experience corruption in diverse ways. Patronage machines (Mexico's PRI), informal enterprises and self-dealing in a gray area between the public and private sectors (China), extensive payments by candidates to voters (Japan), politicized credit and development policies (Korea), a sense of scandal surrounding private interests' contributions to parties and candidates (the United States and many other democracies), official theft of public land for use as rewards for prominent political backers (Kenya), and extortion practiced by police upon small businesses and farmers (many poor countries) draw upon contrasting kinds of power and resources, capitalize upon diverse institutional problems and social vulnerabilities, create different sorts of winners and losers, and embody differing distributions of, and relationships between, wealth and power.

Contrasts abound at other levels too. Democratization in much of Central Europe, and in the Philippines, has not markedly reduced corruption. Democracy in India continues to survive despite significant corruption and desperate poverty; Italy and Japan are established democracies with relatively strong economies and a long tradition of extensive corruption, marked in the past by major scandals. In some places corruption and violence are closely linked, while in others the former may be a substitute for the latter (Huntington, 1968). For thirty years high levels of corruption coexisted with (and in some ways may have aided) rapid economic growth in East and Southeast Asia, while in Africa it helped keep people and countries poor. In the US and many other democracies

M S

private interests try to buy influence within government; in many more places powerful government officials reach out and plunder the economy. Some of these examples fit the consensus worldview better than others. All suggest that corruption problems may vary in important ways.

The scope and implications of corruption will vary from case to case, and may take on several forms within any given society or part of it. Officials' leverage varies with the type, and number of competing sources, of benefits they can offer (Johnston, 1986a); upon the number of officials offering comparable goods, the relationships among them, and queuing arrangements (Rose-Ackerman, 1978; Shleifer and Vishny, 1993); upon the extent and quality of political oversight of the bureaucracy (Rose-Ackerman, 1978); and upon the ability of the press, civil society, and political competitors to demand accountability. Corruption can change qualitatively too, not just rising and falling in severity but taking on new participants, stakes, and practices as one regime gives way to another or as major new commodities, opportunities, and even reforms emerge. Many nations launching democratic and market transitions experienced a surge of corruption and scandal – which are not synonymous – as established elite relationships gave way to a more fragmented scramble for spoils, new economic and political opportunities began to open up, and the weaknesses of formerly monopolistic state and political institutions became apparent.

Broader patterns

Such contrasts begin to become apparent when we examine connections between corruption and development more closely. The United Nations Development Program's 2003 Human Development Index (HDI)[3] – based on 2001 data, the most recent HDI data available – and TI's 2003 Corruption Perceptions Index[4] offer at least an initial look. The HDI is a composite score, on a zero-to-1.0 scale, of many factors affecting human wellbeing, including not only GDP per capita but also life expectancy, literacy, and access to education. It thus reflects not only affluence but also the effectiveness of public institutions and policies. The TI index, as noted, ranks countries in terms of how corrupt they are *perceived* to be. A score of ten on the CPI stands for clean government and zero indicates

---

[3] Report and data available at http://www.undp.org/hdr2003/.

[4] Data and documentation for current and past years available at http://www.transparency.org/cpi/index.html#cpi; I use the 2003 TI index here because it includes many more countries than indices of years past. It draws upon a number of surveys gathered between 2001 and 2003, and for countries included in both the 2001 and 2003 indices scores correlate at $+.99$ ($p = .000$).

extensive corruption; to make the following discussion more intuitive, I have subtracted scores from ten so that a *larger* value indicates perceptions of *more* corruption.

For the 128 countries appearing on both indices, the simple linear correlation between HDI and the "inverted" TI index is -.71 (p = .000): extensive corruption does indeed appear strongly linked with lower levels of development. But a scatter plot suggests that matters are more complicated (figure 2.1).

A number of cases in the upper left – Scandinavian countries, New Zealand, Australia, the UK, and Canada among them – enjoy high levels of development, democratic politics (Singapore (SIN) and Hong Kong (HK) are notable exceptions on the latter point), and are perceived as relatively free of corruption. As we move toward the lower right we find countries regarded as more corrupt, and facing increasingly serious development problems. The quadratic regression line suggests that as corruption increases its costs mount up at an increasing rate.

But the connection is not simple or consistent. Quite apart from problems with the indices themselves, links to development appear strongest where corruption is perceived to be least important: as CPI scores rise the data points are less and less tightly clustered around the regression line. A large number of societies, arrayed across the top of the plot, enjoy high levels of development despite widely varying amounts of apparent corruption. Moreover, affluent Italy (ITA), for example, has a slightly worse CPI score than much-poorer Botswana (BOT), and ranks only slightly above Namibia (NAM). Chile (CHL) and Argentina (ARG) are similar in terms of Human Development, but have very different TI scores. Indeed, if we leave out the affluent (and reputedly low-corruption) market democracies in the top left and focus on those where corruption is perceived to be most important, the relationship resists any simple description. There, it seems, we have many different possible corruption-and-development stories to tell.

Equally intriguing is the blank space in the lower left: there are apparently few if any low-corruption/low-development societies. It is tempting to infer that countries in the lower right will move up the development scale once they bring corruption under control. More likely is that advanced societies have minimized it in the course of building institutions, guaranteeing rights and opportunities, and making other basic changes that have also aided development (Rodrik, 2003) and that help people pursue and defend their own interests. Development, in turn, likely creates political and economic alternatives that leave people less vulnerable to corrupt exploitation. And it is also worth remembering that HDI scores reflect GDP statistics to a significant extent; in fact, if we

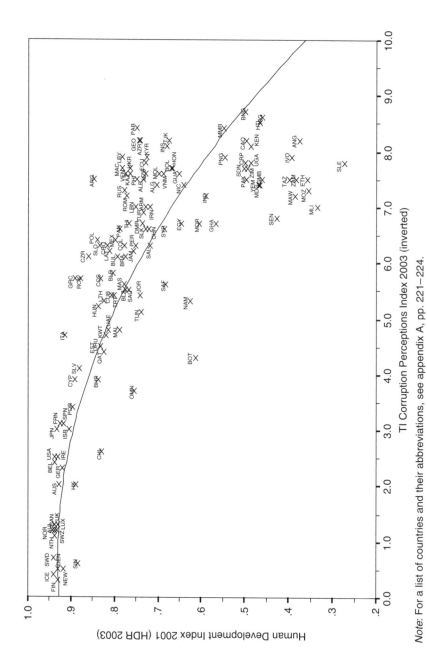

Note: For a list of countries and their abbreviations, see appendix A, pp. 221–224.

Fig. 2.1: Human development and corruption perception indices, 2003

compare TI scores to non-GDP parts of the development index the relationships are far weaker than those seen above. That, ultimately, may reflect the trade-and-business issues raised by GDP figures and informing the TI index. Understanding those processes, as well as untangling the complex distribution of high-corruption cases, would seem to require close examination of patterns of participation and institutions within a framework that can make sense of a variety of contrasts and variations.

Conclusion

Is the consensus view wrong, then? In many ways, no: there is little reason to doubt that corruption harms development, feeds on (and reinforces) institutional weakness and unfair political and economic advantages, and creates further political and economic problems. But that view is *incomplete*: while it is a powerful account at a high level of generality (as in the statistical relationships between corruption perceptions and development data) it does not tell us much about the underlying causes and contrasting corruption problems found in diverse societies. The affluent market democracies that serve as models for liberalization and reform resemble each other in many ways; by contrast, there are many kinds of authoritarian regimes, many roots of poverty, and many types of institutional weakness. This poses the intriguing hypothesis that corruption is not just a single problem but rather one that is embedded in diverse contexts – and that where it is most serious its origins and implications may vary the most.

In the remaining chapters of this book I offer the argument that we can identify and compare major syndromes of corruption originating in underlying patterns of political and economic participation – in the ways people pursue, use, and exchange wealth and power – and in the strength or weakness of the institutions that sustain and restrain those diverse social activities. This approach offers not only a better understanding of the contrasting ways the problem develops and functions in real settings; it can also suggest countermeasures appropriate in differing settings, and ways to avoid doing unintended damage through unwise reforms. Such arguments require detailed comparisons of evidence on participation and institutions, and that is the agenda in chapter 3.

3   Participation, institutions, and syndromes of corruption

Opportunities, constraints, and corruption

Understanding corruption in real social settings, and identifying the variations among cases that are most important, requires careful study of the contrasting political and economic opportunities available in various societies, of the people and groups who seek and use (or who are closed out of) them, and of the institutions and norms that influence their choices. But what are the most important contrasts? Varying techniques (bribery, patronage) or the locations within the state seem natural beginnings, but the prevalence of a particular technique or venue of corruption would seem to be a response to the opportunities and constraints present in a given situation. Categorizing corruption by the scale of benefits involved would require much more information than we typically have and still might not tell us very much: does a case of a given monetary value have the same significance where corruption is the rule compared to places where it is the exception – or in a country where state officials have the upper hand versus another where they are at the mercy of economic interests? Corruption may well follow some regional patterns – African/Asian contrasts are a prime example – but that is all the more reason to search for deeper influences.

In this chapter I propose four corruption syndromes called "Influence Markets," "Elite Cartels," "Oligarchs and Clans," and "Official Moguls." These syndromes, and the names suggesting their distinctive aspects, reflect frequently encountered combinations of stronger or weaker participation and institutions. I then employ widely used country-level indicators of participation and institutions to sort ninety-eight countries into corresponding groupings. Those data by themselves cannot tell us whether corruption varies in the expected ways: that is the task of the case studies presented in chapters 4 through 7. But they do provide a basis for selecting cases for study that is less likely to build in expected results beforehand.

Corruption as an embedded problem: sources of variation

Over the past generation most societies have experienced liberalization of politics, economies, or both – at times on a dramatic scale. Early in the 1990s it was hoped that the shift to markets would fuel growth, and thereby democratization, while lean, accountable governments would best encourage markets. Most early enthusiasm focused on liberalization, with institution-building taking a distinctly secondary role. At times the state was seen as a necessary evil at best. But reality has turned out to be much more difficult. Liberalization has usually not been moderately paced and balanced: often, rapid political transitions and soaring social expectations have given way to much slower and more difficult processes of economic change, or moves toward markets have been stymied by state institutions that are ineffective, repressive, or both.

In fact sound institutions are not impediments to free political and economic participation, but rather help to protect it. In well-institutionalized systems the state, political organizations, and civil society both moderate political demands and aid in their expression, enhancing government's capacity to respond through sound policy; economic processes take place within a framework of sound property rights, enforceable contracts, and open, verifiable transactions. A state that cannot guarantee property rights and basic liberties, collect taxes, enforce contracts, and provide legitimate channels for the expression of interests will be ineffective and unresponsive, and will invite private efforts to perform those functions, often by way of corruption or violence. Where political organizations and civil society are weak or non-existent officials may wield power with impunity and conflicts in society are less likely to remain moderate. There will not necessarily be *no* growth in economic or political participation, but much of it may take place outside the official institutional framework, obey few rules or boundaries, and serve only a powerful few. A 1997 pyramid scheme in Albania, for example, resulted in the loss of nearly a third of the nation's savings and a violent upheaval (Percival, 1997; Jarvis, 2000). On the political side, personal factions or even private armies can supplant parties and interest groups (O'Donnell, 2001), and *mafiyas* can become the means of contract enforcement (Varese, 2001). Particularly in a setting of weak institutions, unbalanced growth in political and economic opportunities allows dominant groups in one sphere to exploit the other.

Searching for patterns

The issue raised by these relationships is not just more versus less corruption. Rather, I argue that the state and trends of participation and institutions influence the _kinds_ of corruption we encounter – participants, relationships among them, benefits at stake, and implications for development. To search for syndromes of corruption is, in effect, to ask *what are the underlying developmental processes, and problems, of which a society's corruption is symptomatic?* Huntington (1968), for example, suggested years ago that where economic opportunities are more plentiful than political ones, ambitious people use wealth to seek power. Where political opportunities abound and economic ones are scarce, by contrast, power pursues wealth. Where institutions are weak, other contrasts may emerge: a weak state may be vulnerable to illicit private pressures, unable to restrain the conduct of officials, or both. Civil society may not exist, or not be strong enough to sustain social trust and channel demands through accepted norms and networks. Some states protect property rights effectively and intervene in the economy in judicious ways; in others, ownership and contracts mean little while state intervention enriches officials and their favored clients. Weak institutions not only allow citizens and officials to seek illicit gains, at times with impunity; they also create incentives for more corruption as people seek protection in an uncertain environment.

Underlying variations in participation and institutions will not determine every detail of a country's corruption problems: personalities, events, crackdowns and reforms, and popular responses can all play roles. International influences, both long-term (e.g. pressures for political and economic liberalization) and more immediate (the activities of multinational businesses and international aid and lending bodies) are also critical, as will become apparent in several case studies. Further, some kinds of corruption, such as payoffs and shakedowns involving police and customs officials, are found more or less everywhere. I seek a middle level of comparison – to identify, account for, and explore the significance of contrasting corruption issues that are manifestations of four major syndromes. The goal is to know what is at stake in a country's corruption, how people and groups pursue, use, and exchange wealth and power, and how those processes are abetted or constrained by institutions and competing or opposing interests. Relative *amounts* of corruption, to the extent that they are even knowable, will be a secondary concern at most.

Four categories

Participation and institutions can combine in a variety of ways, and for every generalization there will be exceptions. The evidence available also varies widely among societies. The challenge is to identify country categories broad enough to preserve important commonalities, to avoid creating categories too numerous or similar to be useful, and yet to bring out contrasts among the sorts of conditions expected to shape various societies' corruption problems. In this section I will propose four categories reflecting commonly encountered combinations of participation and institutions, and will discuss the sorts of corruption problems they seem likely to have. In the next part of this chapter the four groupings are tested using country-level statistical indicators and a cluster analysis; the question at that point is whether the expected groupings are observable. The actual sorts of corruption found in societies in each group will be the focus of case studies in chapters 4–7. These categories do not exhaust all possible combinations of participation and institutions – far from it. They are only useful simplifications, offered as ideal types (for a discussion of that Weberian idea see Coser, 1977: 223–224) intended to highlight patterns and connections for closer study.

Participation and institutions too come in many forms, but as suggested in chapter 2 my main focus is on the ways wealth and power are sought, used, and exchanged on a national scale, and on the state, political, and social structures that both sustain and restrain those activities. With respect to open, competitive, and orderly participation, then, we want to differentiate among societies in terms of range and openness of political and economic opportunities they offer. Strong institutions, in the sense I will discuss them here, are able to protect economic, political, and property rights, guarantee fair play, justice, and honest procedures, and protect society from abuses by the powerful. It is entirely possible for weak institutions of those sorts to coexist with a coercive state and/or durable individual interactions and community organizations (many African societies, for example, have ineffective states and a vibrant social and communal life). Conversely, strong political and economic institutions are not guarantees that all is well at other levels: the United States, for example, scores well on institutional indicators yet, if Putnam (2000) is correct, has a civil society in decline. Many other factors figure into the full picture of participation and institutional portrait in any society, and one purpose of the case-study chapters will be to bring out those complexities; for now, however, I seek relatively clear-cut definitions of ideal types.

Types of political and economic systems, and levels of institutional strength, tend (with exceptions) to fall into identifiable patterns. Let us consider four possibilities to be tested in the next section against country-level data. Established democracies, for example, tend to have mature market economies in which liberalization is largely a *fait accompli*; where open and competitive politics and markets have been in place for a long time economic and political institutions are likely to be strong. Several Western European countries, Canada, Japan, and the United States are a

Table 3.1: *Projected syndromes of corruption*

| Syndrome | Participation | | Institutions | |
	Political opportunities	Economic opportunities	State/society capacity	Economic institutions
Influence Markets	**Mature democracies** Liberalized; steady competition and participation	**Mature markets** Liberalized, open; steady competition; affluent	**Extensive**	**Strong**
Elite Cartels	**Consolidating/reforming democracies** Liberalized; growing competition and participation	**Reforming markets** Largely liberalized and open; growing competition; moderately affluent	**Moderate**	**Medium**
Oligarchs and Clans	**Transitional regimes** Recent major liberalization; significant but poorly structured competition	**New markets** Recent major liberalization; extensive inequality and poverty	**Weak**	**Weak**
Official Moguls	**Undemocratic** Little liberalization or openness	**New markets** Recent major liberalization; extensive inequality and poverty	**Weak**	**Weak**

few examples. But there are also consolidating or reforming democratic/
market societies in which political competition is still emerging or undergoing significant change; often their economies are becoming more open
and competitive too. Institutional frameworks in such societies seem likely
to be moderately strong, but weaker than those in the first group. The most
consolidated post-communist democracies of Central Europe, Chile,
Botswana, and South Korea might be examples of the second group.

Countries in a third group are undergoing major transitions in politics
and their economies. Many kinds of change are happening at once;
political and economic opportunities are both rapidly expanding, and
relationships between them will be difficult to predict. Weak institutions
are both a result of rapid, broad-based change – even when institutions
are well-designed and supported, which will often not be the case, considerable time will be needed to acquire legitimacy and credibility – and
they are a cause of further unstructured and unpredictable political and
economic changes. Russia, Turkey, India (with its economic transition),
the Philippines, Thailand, and Ghana are possible examples of this sort.
Finally, undemocratic regimes by definition are marked by political
opportunities that are few in number and tightly controlled (indeed,
that often become the stakes of corrupt deals). But in part because of
international pressures economies in many such countries have been
liberalizing over the past generation, even if they are nowhere near fully
open or competitive, with the result that growing economic opportunities
can be exploited by a powerful few. Political institutions in systems ruled
by a few are likely to be weak; parts of the state or a dominant party may
well be coercive and widely feared, but that is not strength in the sense
outlined above. Strong economic institutions are also uncommon
because of the nature of political power, a general lack of accountability,
and (as above) the scope of recent economic change. Institutional weaknesses both reflect and abet the power of rulers and their favored interests. In this last group we might find countries such as China, Indonesia,
many but by no means all sub-Saharan African states, and Middle
Eastern countries such as Jordan and the Emirates.

These are intentionally very general categories; at the same time there
will be some countries that fit none of them. A later section of this chapter
will, as noted, use statistical indicators to test whether such groupings
make empirical sense. But what might they have to do with corruption? In
the remainder of this book I suggest that they correspond to four major
syndromes of corruption: Influence Markets, Elite Cartels, Oligarchs
and Clans, and Official Moguls. The proposed connections are summar-
ized here, in Table 3.1, and brief descriptions of each corruption
syndrome follow.

Influence Market corruption Influence Markets deal in access to, and influence within, strong state institutions; often politicians serve as middlemen, putting their connections out for rent in exchange for contributions both legal and otherwise.

Mature market democracies offer extensive political and economic opportunities. They are undergoing only slight liberalization, as there is not much left to be done, and generally have strong, legitimate institutions. They resemble each other in important ways, which may help explain why they are often held up as reform ideals. Legitimate constitutional frameworks, political competition, free news media, strong civil societies, and open economies do help check abuses. But many of these countries have not so much "solved" the corruption problem as they developed states and political systems accommodating to wealth interests, fitting the rules to the society as well as persuading people to follow the law. Most economic dealings take place entirely within their private sectors under rules much less demanding than those of the public sector, while the political influence of wealth follows well-established channels.

Corruption in well-institutionalized market democracies – or at least, the high-level bribery that tends to influence corruption index scores – will be the exception, not the rule, and is unlikely to thwart development (although it is hardly cost-free: see chapter 4). But these societies still have corruption problems worth worrying about. Some are global: banks and investment markets in Influence Market countries are often the repositories, or participate in the laundering, of corrupt gains from elsewhere, and their multinational businesses have made illicit deals in many other societies. Most, however, are domestic, and can at times be quite serious. Influence Market corruption revolves around access to, and advantages within, established institutions, rather than deals and connections circumventing them. Strong institutions reduce the opportunities, and some of the incentives, to pursue extra-systemic strategies, while increasing the risks; moreover the very power of those institutions to deliver major benefits and costs raises the value of influence within them. The role of competitive politics in this variety of corruption is complex. It can allow citizens to oust a corrupt government, but the costs of running for office create incentives for politicians to put their connections and expertise up for rent, and for parties to keep competition under control.

Influence Markets thus work mostly "within the system," another factor contributing to the relatively favorable corruption scores these societies receive. Power-oriented corruption will focus on winning offices and influencing those who hold them; corruption in pursuit of wealth will target government contracts, the implementation of policies, or specific aspects of legislation, rather than creating black markets or parallel economies. Some major channels may be legalized and regulated (such as the financing of campaigns) while in others, rules and expectations can be unclear ("constituent service" by legislators). Public *or* private parties may take the initiative, or be prime beneficiaries, but given the affluence of most societies in this category wealthy interests seeking political influence will dominate Influence Markets.

Further, a significant portion of the damage done by Influence Market corruption is *to* the system. In chapter 4 I will suggest that the primary costs of current political finance arrangements in the United States are not that policies and roll-call votes are bought and sold – there is little solid evidence that they are – but rather come in the form of reduced public trust and widespread perceptions of abuses of power and privilege. Such costs may be intangible, but over time they do little for the legitimacy and responsiveness of democratic politics. Power- and spoils-sharing among German political parties may make for a less responsive policy and legislative process. Japan's Influence Markets have involved much more illegal dealing, but for many years also helped underwrite modified one-party politics in which key competition took place among factions rather than different interests in society, and in which policy adaptations took a back seat to keeping key supporters happy. Influence Market societies do experience straightforward, transgressive corruption, to be sure, but as suggested in chapter 1 the main concern is their systemic corruption problems.

Elite Cartel corruption In other market democracies institutions are weaker, politics and markets are becoming more competitive, and networks of elites use corrupt incentives and exchanges to shore up their positions.

The market-democratic model may not be as resistant to corruption as we sometimes suppose, particularly where institutional frameworks are weaker. New or reconstituted market democracies – South Korea, Chile, Poland, Hungary – are still consolidating in important ways. Others pass through times of crisis: Italy's *mani pulite* and *tangentopoli* scandals of the early 1990s, for example, were not a surge of new corruption but rather consequences of the unraveling of collusive networks of party elites and greater pressures from within and without for accountability. In those kinds of cases power and its links to wealth are in flux, creating new opportunities and risks for elites. For them, corruption may be defensive in nature, protecting existing economic, political, or policy advantages, preempting competitors, and strengthening connections with allies and backers. Those involved can have a variety of power bases, such as business, the military, the bureaucracy, a political party, or ethnic or regional social ties. Official positions will be particularly valuable, but less secure than in Influence Market cases because of more rapid liberalization, growing political competition, and weaker institutions. Elites' corrupt linkages will often bridge the public–private gap.

A mature political machine offers an instructive example of Elite Cartel corruption. Shefter's (1976) account of the rise of Tammany Hall in New York City describes a phase during which segments of the political and business elite virtually merged at the top of the organization. Tammany welded city government and entrepreneurs' wealth into a formidable combine strong enough to limit political and, in sectors dominated by business-politicians, economic competition. The Tammany leadership was smaller and more monolithic than the elite cartels of whole countries, and many societies in this group will not be as turbulent as nineteenth-century New York. But I will suggest in chapter 5 that two generations of power- and spoils-sharing among Italy's non-communist parties prior to the early 1990s, and the networks of presidents, politicians, business leaders, military figures, and families that dominated Korea from the 1960s through at least the mid-1990s, illustrate how interlocking networks of elites can use corrupt as well as legitimate influence to maintain control.

Official institutions that are only moderately strong will both facilitate and (from the elites' standpoint) necessitate such linkages. Moreover they weaken anti-corruption efforts and make life more difficult for would-be political and economic competitors. These systems will not be wholly undemocratic or uncompetitive, and in some respects Elite Cartel corruption will be a stabilizing force. But corruption in these cases plays a different role, and has different uses, from the Influence Market variety. Instead of dealing in access to well-institutionalized decisionmakers, corruption in these cases is a systemic mechanism of control, often defensive in nature.

Oligarch and Clan corruption In other societies major political and economic liberalization – in some cases, simultaneous if poorly integrated transitions – and weak public–private boundaries have put a wide variety of opportunities in play in a setting of weak institutions. The dominant form of corruption here will consist of a disorderly, sometimes violent scramble among contending elites seeking to parlay personal resources (e.g. a mass following, a business, a bureaucratic fiefdom, judicial or organized crime connections, or a powerful family) into both wealth and power.

Unlike the Elite Cartel syndrome, in which relatively established elites collude within a moderately strong institutional framework, oligarchs are free agents unlikely to cooperate for long. These elites are oligarchs in the sense that much of the most significant competition takes place – often in intensely personal terms – among relatively few players. But they and their gains are insecure because of the pace and scope of change, the unstructured nature and sheer scale of the stakes of contention, and recurring violence. Weak institutions are a particular problem: inability to enforce contracts or defend property through courts and law enforcement increases the incentive to resort to violence (Varese, 2001), making police and military muscle all the more marketable – and leading, in the worst cases, to reliance upon *mafiyas* or private armies. Scott (1972) and Knack and Keefer (1995) have pointed out that insecure elites will be particularly rapacious.

As in the Elite Cartel syndrome, corruption will take place in pursuit of both political and economic stakes, and will focus only partially upon formal roles and policy processes. But in an Oligarchs and Clans situation it may be difficult to say just what is public and what is private, who is a politician and who is an entrepreneur, or even who is clearly corrupt and who is an innovator. State officials and civil society will be ill-equipped to resist or check abuses. The former will have few effective powers and will be exposed to illicit pressures from within their agencies and without; the latter, particularly in post-transition states, will likely be weak and divided, its potential leaders intimidated or compromised. Those parts of the news media not dominated by oligarchs themselves may well lack the independence and resources needed to be effective watchdogs.

There is considerable political competition in this type of case, but it can be unpredictable and may have shallow social roots. Contending oligarchs building mass followings will find material rewards valuable but difficult to come by; followers, for their part, will have many political options. Political factions will thus be unstable and poorly disciplined. Leaders, needing to pay for support again and again, will exploit any fragments of government authority that may come to hand. Business people may spend large sums for influence but get little from politicians who cannot "deliver." Where elections are rigged and political competition unstructured and personal, reform-minded voters will find it difficult to oust the corrupt or to reward good government. Anti-corruption efforts in this setting will often be smokescreens for continued abuse or ways to put key competitors behind bars. Privatization can become a legalized carve-up of state resources or outright theft; regulatory and legal functions will not only be moneymakers for poorly paid officials, but may also be hijacked by oligarchs. Tax collections and payments are likely to be sporadic, manipulated, and ineffective, as will be the payment of official salaries and other government obligations.

The result is corruption that is extensive, linked at times to violence, and above all unpredictable; it is thus particularly damaging to democratic and economic development (Campos, Lien, and Pradhan, 1999). Much of the economy may be an off-the-books proposition; outside investors will find it prudent to go elsewhere, while those who do venture in will focus on short-term rewards rather than sustained growth (Keefer, 1996). Opposition and reform groups will enter the political arena at their own risk; most citizens will leave politics to others. Those who do win office will find themselves in a framework where formal checks and balances amount in practice to fragmentation of authority creating access points for oligarchs.

Russia is a high-profile case of this sort; Mexico and the Philippines offer other variations on these themes. As we will see in chapter 6 the Oligarch and Clan syndrome is not just "more corruption" than other places; rather, it has a logic and implications all its own.

Official Mogul corruption In a final group of countries institutions are very weak, politics remains undemocratic or is opening up only slowly, but the economy is being liberalized at least to a degree. Civil society is weak or non-existent. Opportunities for enrichment, and new risks for the already wealthy, abound – but political power is personal, and is often used with impunity.

Here, the entrepreneurs with most leverage will be top political figures or their clients. Officials may become economic moguls; would-be moguls need official backing. Once the political connections have been made they face few constraints from the state framework or from competitors. There is a risk – and in some cases the reality – of *kleptocracy*, or rule by thieves (Andreski, 1968). Of our four corruption syndromes this one is least focused upon influence within official state processes: institutions and offices may be merely useful tools in the search for wealth. Ironically, however, such situations are not necessarily stable: those who hold power without rules may face foes who are similarly unconstrained, save by the threat of violence. Neither rulers nor counter-elites (if any) are likely to enjoy much sustained popular support or credibility beyond that created through patronage or intimidation. In the worst of these cases one person, a family, or a small *junta* enjoys unchecked rule. Military leaders may be partners, and in some cases are dominant, in such regimes, often using past corruption as a pretext for taking power. Even where the soldiers have returned to their barracks top brass may be businessmen and politicians too, backed by the threat of military intervention. Development of civil society will be inhibited as elites' personal followings cross-cut or supplant "horizontal" self-organization, and people will thus have little recourse in cases of official abuse.

While mature market democracies resemble each other in many ways, in Official Mogul cases much depends upon the personalities and agendas of those in power. Some may back economic reform or at least refrain from full exploitation of corrupt opportunities, and where that is the case considerable growth may occur. Others ruthlessly exploit both state and economy with devastating results. Corruption-and-development connections within this group of countries will vary widely as a consequence. Many of these countries are poor, though corruption is scarcely the sole cause of poverty. Often they depend upon primary exports such as oil and minerals, a situation known to distort development and encourage corruption (Mauro, 1998; Barro, 1999; Leite and Weidmann, 1999; Sachs and Warner, 2001; Dietz, Neumayer, and de Soysa, 2004; Papyrakis and Gerlagh, 2004). But even in poor countries a political monopoly can be a very efficient way to extract wealth, both from the domestic economy and from any aid, loans, and investment flowing in from outside. Where several factions contend matters may be even worse: weak institutions can mean that wealth for oneself and rewards for backers are best had by exploiting some fragment of state power – in effect, creating a series of independent monopolies tapping into various parts of the economy. That state of affairs is like a highway on which independent operators collect tolls with each running a monopoly – pay up, or passage is denied (Shleifer and Vishny, 1993). Tolls may become so high that traffic declines or ceases. Coordinated monopolies – cooperation to set more bearable rates – would be more profitable and less disruptive in the long run, but unless a particularly strong and insightful leader holds power that may not be possible.

Liberalization, too, has complex implications where institutions are weak and politicians enjoy impunity. Integration into the world economy may check corruption (see, for example, Sandholtz and Koetzle, 2000; Treisman, 2000; Larraín and Tavares, 2004) for several reasons, ranging from the influx of advanced management techniques to the growth of alternatives to doing business with official moguls. But poor, undemocratic countries just beginning to open up markets – especially those dependent upon the export of basic commodities – are likely to be only weakly integrated into the world economy, or to be integrated in disadvantageous ways. That makes it easier for authoritarian rulers to monopolize cross-border flows of goods and capital, particularly early in the process of liberalization.

In many ways then this is the most diverse of our four groups of countries. Several Middle Eastern states may fit this pattern, to varying degrees, along with a number of African countries (particularly those marked by military rule and internal strife). China's economic reforms and spectacular growth are well known, but as we shall see in chapter 7 they have been accompanied by extensive corruption, often driven by officials exploiting segments of an increasingly fragmented party and state apparatus. In Kenya and Indonesia powerful elites have engaged in rapacious corruption that has been exacerbated, if anything, by the launching of competitive elections without the supporting institutions they require. Other countries in which strong elites have pursued reforms may be about to escape a high-corruption/low-development trap (Johnston, 1998): Uganda is no democracy as yet, but it has implemented important anti-corruption measures and increased opportunities for popular participation (Ruzindana, 1997). Even during periods of reform, however, the state (or fragments of it) may remain handy for exploitation by rulers accountable to no one.

These four corruption syndromes remain ideal types at this point, meant to describe (and highlight contrasts among) corruption problems I suggest we will find when participation and institutional factors combine in certain commonly observed ways. No country will have just one kind of corruption, and no syndrome will fit any one case in every detail. All are grounded in the notion that political and economic liberalization has placed stresses upon institutional frameworks, which themselves vary considerably in strength.

A few overall contrasts are worth noting too. As we move from Influence Markets toward Official Moguls we shift from corruption structured along lines of official roles and processes to that which is scarcely institutionalized at all. The former seeks to convert wealth into bureaucratic influence or electoral success, while the latter is the open exploitation of power, and of the weak by the strong. Influence Market and Elite Cartel corruption involve repeated transactions and influence or access usable over a long term; indeed, Elite Cartel corruption may be used primarily to forestall or at least control change. In Oligarch and Clan and Official Mogul cases, however, corruption is less predictable, often involving targets of opportunity in rapidly changing societies or the whims of leaders acting with impunity. Where institutions are stronger opponents of corruption can organize, relying upon relatively sound civil liberties, legal frameworks, and civil societies; where they are weak anti-corruption activity becomes increasingly risky. Finally, in the latter sorts of cases corruption may be not the exception but the norm, at least in certain segments of politics and the economy. More than any other, that contrast suggests the contrasting expectations, relationships between wealth and power, and reform challenges to be found among the world's cases of corruption.

Four groups of cases

Our four categories of countries are suggestive, but do they have anything to do with reality? In this section I present statistical evidence suggesting that these groupings are sufficiently coherent to merit further study. Using country-level indicators of participation and institutional strength and a K-means cluster analysis, I identify four groups of countries that generally fit the categories and inhabit different sections of the corruption-and-development scatter plot in chapter 2. Other indicators also support the descriptions above. Statistics at this level cannot, by themselves, give details of corrupt processes *within* societies, but they allow us to select countries for the case-study chapters that will be the real test of the syndromes argument.

Clusters of countries

The results that follow are based upon a 168-country dataset I assembled using a variety of existing indicators of corruption, development, political and economic liberalization, and institutional quality.[1] The main statistical technique is K-means cluster analysis. It is a bit like factor analysis stood on end: where factor analysis begins with a correlation matrix and groups *variables* in terms of their fit on particular dimensions or factors, cluster analysis uses a set of variables to identify *groups of cases*. Those variables and the number of clusters sought are specified in advance by the user; thus, cluster analysis is simply a way of asking, "If we were to define N groups of countries using variables X, Y, and Z, what would those groups look like?" If the analysis were to show that statistically significant clusters could not be identified, or the clusters do not fit expected patterns, then we would need to rethink the expected relationships between participation and institutions. If, as is the case below, the results *are* consistent with expectations we will have shown only that our groups of cases are worth further study.

The data Performing this analysis requires statistical indicators of participation and institutions. The time period to include affects not only the scope of development trends to be considered but also the number of societies we can include: data on most post-Soviet states, for example, have become available only relatively recently. Other sections of the world, such as the Middle East, are less well represented in datasets

---

[1] The data and documentation are available at http://people.colgate.edu/mjohnston/personal.htm.

than we would wish. Moreover, not all sorts of indicators have been gathered in comparable ways over the same periods of time. Thus, the analysis that follows involves unavoidable compromises. For trends in political participation I turned to the Polity IV dataset,[2] which features a composite Polity indicator ranging from plus ten ("strongly democratic") to minus ten ("strongly autocratic"). Using 1992 as a baseline allows the inclusion of many post-communist states, and 2001 will be the end date because that is consistent with the most recent data available on several other indicators to be considered. On the economic side I used 1990 and 2001 scores from the Economic Freedom in the World (EFW) index compiled by the Fraser Institute,[3] which ranges from zero to ten and assigns higher scores to economies rated as more free. There are no EFW scores available for the years between 1990 and 1995, nor do other indicators of liberalization fill that gap; using 1990 as a beginning point still includes some post-communist states in the analysis.

Institutional quality is also a complex issue, and has only been estimated quantitatively more recently. Institutions include not just the official state apparatus and political bodies but also a wider range of institutions that affect an economy. Fortunately, on the political side, an excellent composite measure of "institutional and social capacity," touching upon both state and civil society, is included in the World Economic Forum's 2002 Environmental Sustainability Index.[4] This index, drawing upon data from as late as 2001 but not yet available as a time series, rates countries from zero to one hundred in terms of institutional and civil-society capacity to debate and address public policy issues. As a proxy for the quality of economic institutions I used the index of the security of property rights compiled by the Heritage Foundation for the year 2002;[5] it ranges from one to five, giving *lower* scores where property rights are more secure. Secure property rights depend upon a range of institutions and policies; thus, while this index scarcely measures all aspects of the economic system it should reflect the soundness of the overall framework.

Results of a cluster analysis that employed these variables to search for four groups of countries appear in Table 3.2.

---

[2] Data and codebook available at http://www.cidcm.umd.edu/inscr/polity/polreg.htm; the data employed were from the revised 2002 version of the dataset.

[3] Data available at http://www.freetheworld.com/.

[4] World Economic Forum, Yale Center for Environmental Law and Policy, and CIESIN (Columbia University), *2002 Environmental Sustainability Index* (http://www.ciesin.columbia.edu/), February, 2002.

[5] The 2002 data were taken as indicative of conditions for our end-date year of 2001, as the Heritage Foundation gathers data and publishes its index for the coming year: for example, the 2003 index was published in the Fall of 2002. See http://www.heritage.org/.

Table 3.2: *Results, K-means cluster analysis*

Cluster/group[6]	1	2	3	4
Polity score 1992				
(High = more dem.)	10	8	6	− 6
Polity score 2001	10	9	7	− 2
Institutional/social capacity	77.9	57.1	39.0	37.2
Property rights 2002				
(low: secure)	1.28	2.43	3.40	3.72
Econ. freedom 1990				
(high: more free)	7.83	5.60	4.79	4.49
Econ. freedom 2001	7.58	6.74	5.92	5.69

Analysis of variance	Cluster mean square	Degrees of freedom	Error mean square	Degrees of freedom	F	Signif.
Polity 1992	1280.245	3	6.179	94	207.192	.000
Polity 2001	771.888	3	9.810	94	78.914	.000
Inst./Soc. Cap.	7791.871	3	35.885	94	217.133	.000
Property rights	26.411	3	.572	94	46.191	.000
Econ. fr. 1990	47.321	3	1.452	94	32.591	.000
Econ. fr. 2001	16.137	3	.493	94	32.747	.000

Cases in each cluster/group:

1	18
2	21
3	30
4	29
Total	98

A full listing of the countries in each cluster appears in appendix A, pp. 221–224.

Four statistically significant clusters were found, and they generally fit the categories discussed earlier. Figures at the top are values on the six variables for each cluster taken as a whole. Group 1 (N = 18) countries, including Austria, Canada, Germany, the Netherlands, Norway, Sweden, the United Kingdom, and the United States, have long since been liberalized for the most part, and thus there is little recent change in Polity or Economic Freedom scores. This group also has strong institutions, as suggested by the institutional and social capacity, and property

---

[6] In the actual analysis, SPSS labeled Group 1, above, as Group 4, Group 2 above as 3, 3 as 1, and 4 as 2. The groups are renumbered hereafter to correspond to the order in which they are discussed in this chapter.

rights, variables. Group 2 (N = 21), including Argentina, Belgium, Chile, Italy, South Korea, Poland, Spain, and Zambia among others, is broadly democratic (and becoming somewhat more so), if not quite as highly rated as Group 1; similarly, the economies in this group are relatively liberalized but also becoming more so. New political and economic opportunities are likely emerging in these societies, but institution scores are lower than those for Group 1. Group 3 (N = 30), exemplified *inter alia* by Albania, Colombia, Ecuador, Malaysia, Mexico, the Philippines, Russia, and Venezuela, is still democratizing as a whole. Economies in this group continue to liberalize too, and these changes have taken place in a setting of weak social/institutional capacity and somewhat uncertain property rights. Finally, Group 4 (N = 29), which includes, for example, Algeria, Chad, China, Indonesia, Jordan, Nigeria, Syria, Tanzania, and Zimbabwe, is marked by rather rapid liberalization in both the political and economic arenas, but remains largely undemocratic and suffers from weak institutions. As the analysis of variance shows, the differences in variable scores defining these four clusters are statistically strongly significant.

The cluster results correspond reasonably closely to the patterns proposed earlier, although statistical clustering does not mean we have "discovered" these groups out in the world. Data limitations mean that many countries of interest could not be classified; further, mean polity scores for Group 3 show less change, and for Group 4, more change than we might have expected. Group 3, however, includes several transitional post-communist cases where rapid political liberalization came just before 1992, and Group 4, while less authoritarian in the aggregate by 2000 than in 1992, remains on the undemocratic side of the scale.

Do these groupings correspond to contrasts in corruption? The scatter plots in figures 3.1–3.4 suggest that they may. There is one plot for each group of countries, and axes are the same as in figure 2.1: HDI scores from the 2003 report, covering 2001, are plotted against "inverted" TI scores for 2003. Earlier caveats about the TI index remain very much in force; the question at this point is only whether grouping countries by participation and institution measures begins to sort out some of the complexities we found when we looked behind the basic corruption–development connections that figure so strongly in the consensus view. Means for the four groups on those indices are presented following the plots.

The plots and data are generally consistent with the idea of differing corruption–development connections among the four groups. Group 1 countries (fig. 3.1) – most of them established market democracies – enjoy high levels of development and are perceived as having moderate to low amounts of corruption (though that notion will come in for critical examination in later chapters). Most Group 2 countries (fig. 3.2) are

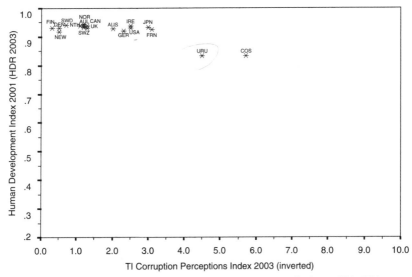

Note: For a list of countries and their abbreviations, see appendix A, pp. 221–224.

Fig. 3.1: Corruption and development indices for Group 1 – Influence Markets

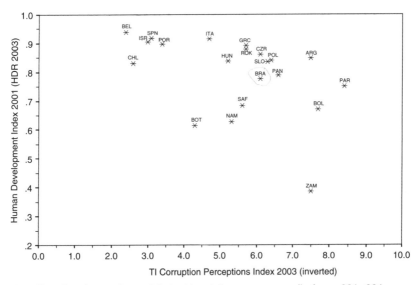

Note: For a list of countries and their abbreviations, see appendix A, pp. 221–224.

Fig. 3.2: Corruption and development indices for Group 2 – Elite Cartels

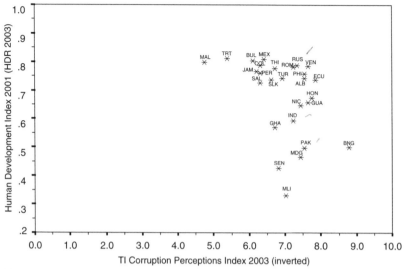

Fig. 3.3: Corruption and development indices for Group 3 – Oligarchs and Clans

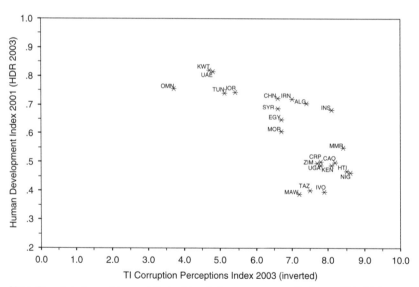

Fig. 3.4: Corruption and development indices for Group 4 – Official Moguls

Table 3.3: *Corruption and development indicators*

Country Group	1	2	3	4	
Corruption type:	**Influence Markets (18)**	**Elite Cartels (21)**	**Oligarchs and Clans (30)**	**Official Moguls (29)**	**Analysis of variance**
Indicator (range) (Source):					$p =$
TI Index 2003 (inverted: 0–10) TI	1.9	5.4	6.9	7.0	.000
Human Development 2001 0.0–1.0 (HDR 2003)	.92	.80	.65	.57	.000

Sources:
1. **TI** = Transparency International Corruption Perceptions Index for 2003 **http://www.transparency.org/**
2. **HDR** = UNDP *Human Development Report 2003* **http://www.undp.org/**

market democracies too but are perceived as more corrupt, and as a group
have lower (and more scattered) human development rankings. Group 3
(fig. 3.3) is more tightly clustered with the majority (notably, non-African
cases) gathered in a moderately high-corruption/high-development
region. Group 4 (fig. 3.4), while not significantly worse on the TI index
than Group 3, scores lowest in terms of human development and – likely
in part because of the varying agendas of undemocratic leaders – is the
least tightly clustered. That group displays an intriguing division between
a group of several Islamic societies with more moderate corruption and
development scores (China is in that region too) and another, tighter
group in the lower right area that includes a number of African states.
That contrast too will also be a focus of discussion later on.

In a perfect world these clusters would be tighter and more clearly
distinct from each other. But the goal here is not to explain variations in
corruption indices as such; rather it is to suggest that knowing something
about participation and institutions in a country adds to our understanding of corruption – or, at least, sharpens our questions. The *qualitative*
contrasts not captured by the indices are the major concern of this book
and will be brought out in chapters 4–7.

Contrasts in other development indicators also support that view.
(Tables A–C, presenting the data on which the following discussion
is based, appear in appendix B, pp. 225–227). Group 1 countries
("Influence Markets"), in aggregate, are stable, well-institutionalized
democracies with free economies; governments are rated as effective and
as intervening in the economy relatively judiciously. Rule of law is firmly in
place, leaders face significant political competition and constraints on their
powers, and critics are able to demand accountability effectively. These are
prosperous societies providing a high quality of life; they enjoy a favorable
position in world markets, and their experiences thus differ considerably
from those of societies more exposed to outside economic interests. While
none of these indicators sheds light directly upon corrupt *processes*, they are
broadly consistent with the "Influence Markets" scenario: wealth interests
are powerful, but the state is well-institutionalized and corruption does not
seem to undermine the system. That regulatory activities are relatively
narrow in scope and comparatively high-quality suggests that officials are
less likely to use such powers arbitrarily.

The suggestion here is not that these societies have solved the corruption problem: the United States in particular has experienced a rash
of regulatory failings linked to private-sector fraud. Instead, Group 1
corruption seems relatively contained both within the institutional framework and in its consequences. The longevity of these systems suggests
both that they have developed a working balance between wealth and

power and that, unlike developing countries today, they had a long time to institutionalize and adapt those sorts of agreements – a point to which I will return in discussing reform.

In Group 2 ("Elite Cartels") there are more uncertainties and fewer restraints upon political and economic elites. Political systems and markets are relatively open and stable (though less so than in Group 1), and these societies are moderately affluent. But elites face significant competition in a setting where institutions are more problematic: political rights, civil liberties, and the rule of law are less secure, government and corruption controls less effective, regulation somewhat more extensive and of lower quality, and black markets more pervasive than in Group 1. The relatively constrained political leaders in this increasingly competitive but less stable institutional environment might find alliances with business, media, military, and other elites particularly useful. For some countries in this group this state of affairs is the result of successful democratic and market transitions (Chile, Hungary, Poland, South Africa, South Korea), but others (Argentina, Belgium, Italy) have experienced crises or deterioration in existing institutions and political settlements. Those countries might present comparable statistical profiles at a given time, but be changing in different ways – an issue for the case studies to come.

Group 3 countries ("Oligarchs and Clans") present an even more complex, and in many ways pessimistic, picture. Political and economic liberalization have come a long way but underlying institutions are problems. Political competition is extensive but political rights, accountability, civil liberties, and the rule of law are markedly less secure than in our first two groups. Both political and economic actors will find it difficult to protect their positions in such systems, and potential anticorruption forces are weak. Leaders face fewer political constraints and regimes are less stable. Government is ineffective, regulation extensive and of dubious quality, and corruption controls are weak. Economic opportunities are growing but relatively few seem to benefit (Gini scores in table B, appendix B, p. 226, suggest high levels of inequality), and black markets are extensive. Further problems grow out of the disadvantageous place these countries occupy in the world economy. They are, on the whole, poor societies in need of international capital, but foreign domestic investment is weak and there is moderate to heavy reliance upon primary exports (ores, minerals, food, and the like). Officials must deal with international economic interests who, facing weak institutions and unstable regimes, are likely to seek short-term returns rather than longer-term engagement (Keefer, 1996) and to circumvent taxation and regulation in any way they can. Local entrepreneurs' positions are no more secure, and they too may amass as much wealth as they can, as quickly as they can take it. Corruption is both a cause of this economic situation, discouraging investment and long-term partnerships, and an effect as well, as political and economic interests scramble to protect their gains.

Group 4 ("Official Moguls"), judged by statistical indicators, shares many characteristics with Group 3: poverty and black markets are extensive, corruption controls are ineffective, and government is ineffective. Countries in this group are distinctive, however, in the impunity enjoyed by political elites. Leaders in this group face less political competition, fewer political constraints, and far less effective demands for accountability than those elsewhere. Despite an overall trend in democratic directions civil liberties and political rights are still weakest, government intervention in the economy the most frequent, the quality of these interventions rated the lowest (suggesting that they are most likely to be abusive), and political and regime stability the shakiest, of all four groups. Foreign direct investment is nearly non-existent and dependence upon primary exports is great. Politically connected individuals who seek wealth corruptly will likely encounter few obstacles; international aid and such investment as does enter a country can be skimmed by top figures or diverted to more secure banks and markets elsewhere. For the rest of society there seem to be few economic alternatives.

Too much should not be made of these results. Cluster results, a scatter plot, and mean values on development indicators cannot tell us about the presence or absence of a particular kind of corruption. Moreover, corruption is not the sole cause of any of these contrasts: Group 4 countries, for example, are poor in part because of corruption, but they have the corruption they do in part because they are poor, and both connections are shaped by other factors. The statistical indicators suggest some surprises too, such as the extent of black markets in Group 2 and the weak state of rights and liberties in Group 3. Still, these indicators offer more evidence that the difference among these countries, in corruption terms, is not just a matter of having less or more of it. The idea of four qualitatively different syndromes of corruption reflecting contrasting experiences of political and economic development clearly merits further testing against case-study evidence.

Conclusion

In the next four chapters I turn to that sort of evidence, using cases from three countries in each group to put the projected corruption syndromes to a detailed test. The expectation is not that we will find identical patterns of corruption among all countries in a grouping, nor that any one country will exhibit corruption of just one variety. Rather, we are

Table 3.4: *Countries included in case-study chapters*

Group/syndrome	Cases
1 Influence Markets (ch. 4)	USA, Japan, Germany
2 Elite Cartels (ch. 5)	Italy, Korea, Botswana
3 Oligarchs and Clans (ch. 6)	Russia, Mexico, Philippines
4 Official Moguls (ch. 7)	China, Kenya, Indonesia

testing the notion that patterns of corruption vary in ways symptomatic of deeper processes and problems – a notion that applies to advanced societies just as much as to their poorer and less democratic neighbors. If case-study evidence supports those arguments we can then understand the roots and significance of corruption – and propose reforms – in terms appropriate to diverse societies.

In the chapters that follow I seek to identify, explore, and account for the major corruption issues of twelve countries. These issues will not be identical within any group; indeed, some are included because they challenge the distinctions among syndromes in useful ways. The goal is to know whether a given corruption syndrome exists, how it works, how it reflects the interaction of participation and institutions, and how it affects democratic and economic development. The four groups of countries represent those corruption syndromes rather than "system types." They illustrate what is at stake in a country's corruption, how people and groups pursue, use, and exchange wealth and power, and how those processes are abetted or constrained by institutions and contending interests. Relative *amounts* of corruption, to the extent that they are even knowable, will be a secondary concern; longer-term effects are a more important theme, as are the sometimes perverse effects of reforms.

To select any cases for detailed study is of necessity to limit the analysis: the groups of countries, and most of the societies within them, embody considerable diversity in their own right. Those selected from each cluster were chosen for several reasons including their inherent importance, the goal of covering as many regions as possible, and the extent of case-study information available for each: chapters 4–7 put the idea of contrasting corruption syndromes to a more detailed test. If the existence and nature of those syndromes can be established with reasonable confidence, then the discussion of reform in chapter 8 can draw upon both the breadth of evidence underlying cross-sectional research, and the depth of detail and sensitivity to context found in good descriptive case studies, to develop ideas about the best ways of dealing with contrasting corruption problems in diverse social settings.

4   Influence Markets: influence for rent, decisions for sale

The value of access

Influence Market corruption revolves around the use of wealth to seek influence within strong political and administrative institutions – often, with politicians putting their own access out for rent. In market democracies many people have interests to pursue and the means with which to do so, and points of public–private access proliferate. Where institutions are strong and credible the overwhelming majority of advocacy takes place within accepted limits, but Influence Market societies also have evolved in ways accommodating to political and economic elites. This corruption syndrome thus does not ordinarily threaten the viability of institutions or the broader system; indeed, to do so would devalue the access at stake.

The stakes are the *details* of policy – whether a program will be funded, a contract awarded, a group declared exempt from a tax, or the rules of a program changed. Private parties do offer bribes and officials practice extortion, but in most Influence Market countries such actions are the exception, not the rule, or are confined to specific agencies and decisions. At times it can be difficult to distinguish legal political contributions and routine "constituent service" by elected representatives from corrupt dealings, a fact contributing to market democracies' favorable scores on indices that emphasize outright bribery. That does not mean bureaucrats in Influence Market countries never collude with elected officials and interest groups. But it is usually easier and less risky for a private interest to curry favor through political donations than to seek out biddable bureaucrats. That service is part of what a corrupt politician offers. For bureaucrats clearly illicit deals can be risky; friendships with powerful politicians or the hope of moving into business in the future may be the preferred path to wealth.

The argument of this chapter is emphatically not that political money is inherently corrupting: in democracies donations are a legitimate form of advocacy, and competitive mass campaigns cost money. But even if all funds flow through legal channels there can still be major corruption concerns. The *perception* that abuses are common, and the citizen disillusionment that can result, are pressing corruption issues in most Influence Market systems. So is a lack of political competition – among parties, or between incumbents and challengers. Even where economic effects appear to be modest, Influence Market corruption can undermine the vitality and competitiveness of political life.

Three market democracies

Japan, Germany, and the United States are three of the world's wealthiest and strongest democracies. Their powerful corporations, the global reach of their policies, and the roles their banks and markets play in safeguarding (and at times laundering) the proceeds of corrupt dealings elsewhere all have major implications for our other three groups of countries. Much the same is true in terms of reform: the United States in particular advocates standards that, for better or worse, dominate the international anti-corruption agenda. All have experienced major scandals during recent decades, ranging from Watergate in the United States to Germany's Flick and Elf/Acquitaine cases, to the Lockheed, Recruit, and Sagawa Trucking episodes in Japan. Still, in none of the three has corruption threatened basic political or economic arrangements. Major scandals in Japan led to a political shakeup in the early 1990s, temporarily ending Liberal Democrat Party (LDP) dominance and bringing new campaign styles, changed relationships between politicians and bureaucrats, and legal efforts to regulate "money politics." In most respects, however, politics and policymaking in contemporary Japan continue as before. What is distinctive about these systems is not that they have avoided corruption – they have not – but rather that strong institutions, together with long-liberalized politics and economies, influence the form corruption takes and enable them to withstand its effects.

These broad characterizations are reinforced by table 4.1, which presents many of the statistical indicators discussed in chapter 3. In Germany, Japan, and the US political and market liberalization are a *fait accompli*; while the data suggest some pulling back on the economic side, property rights are secure, intervention in the economy is selective, and officials are generally held accountable. All three countries have high scores on institutional and social capacity and overall development. Japan ranks somewhat lower than Germany and the US (but still well above the median) in terms of government effectiveness and regulatory quality. It is rated as having somewhat more corruption, and less effective controls, than Germany and the US, though again all three countries compare very favorably to the medians.

How valid are the corruption comparisons? It is hard to say: index scores are approximations at best. Many Japanese scandals take place at the peaks of a centralized political system and closely watched economy and are thus

Table 4.1: *Statistical indicators for "Influence Market" countries*

Indicator (units/range) and source	Germany	Japan	United States	98-Nation median*
Polity Score 1992 (Hi = more dem./0 thru 10) **P**	10	10	10	7.0
Polity Score 2001 **P**	10	10	10	7.0
Institutional/Social Capacity 2002 (0 thru 100) **WEF**	75.6	75.1	74.2	44.7
Property Rights 2002 (Low = secure/1 thru 5) **HF**	1.0	2.0	1.0	3.0
Econ Freedom 1990 (hi = more free/0 thru 10) **FI**	8.08	8.14	8.76	5.15
Econ Freedom 2001 **FI**	7.30	7.10	8.30	6.45
TI CPI, 2003 (0–10/inverted) **TI**	2.3	3.0	2.5	6.3*
UNDP Human Dev Score 2001 (0–1.00) **HDR 2003**	.921	.932	.937	.75
GDP per capita, 2001 **WB**	$25,350	$25,130	$34,320	$5,940
Corruption Control 2002 (−1.89 thru 2.39) **KKZ**	1.82	1.20	1.77	−.22
Gov't Effectiveness 2002 (−1.64 thru 2.26) **KKZ**	1.76	1.07	1.70	.10
Government Intervention 2001 (1 thru 5) **HF**	2.0	1.5	2.0	3.0
Government Regulation 2001 (1 thru 5) **HF**	3.0	3.0	2.0	3.0
Regulatory Quality 2002 (−2.31 thru 1.93) **KKZ**	1.59	.97	1.51	.06
Voice/Accountability 2002 (−2.12 thru 1.72) **KKZ**	1.51	.99	1.32	.05

*Medians for the 98 countries classified in statistical clusters (ch. 3); for TI CPI 2003, median is for the 89 countries included in the CPI and in clusters. Unless otherwise indicated, high scores indicate high levels of an attribute.

Sources:

FI = Fraser Institute **http://www.freetheworld.com/**

HDR = UNDP *Human Development Report 2003* **http://www.undp.org/**

HF = Heritage Foundation Index of Economic Freedom reports **http://www.heritage.org/research/features/index/**

KKZ = Kaufmann, Kraay, and Zoido-Lobatón, "Governance Matters III" dataset, 2002 **http://info.worldbank.org/governance/kkz2002/tables.asp**

P = Polity IV dataset, 2002 update **http://www.cidcm.umd.edu/inscr/polity/polreg.htm**

TI = Transparency International Corruption Perceptions Indexes for 2001 and 2003 **http://www.transparency.org/**

WB = World Bank Data Query online data source (GDP and population used to calculate GDP per capita) **http://www.worldbank.org/data/dataquery.html**

WEF = World Economic Forum, Yale Center for Environmental Law and Policy, and CIESIN (Columbia University), *2002 Environmental Sustainability Index* **http://www.ciesin.columbia.edu/**

highly visible. The US, by contrast, is a federal state with multiple branches of government, decentralized political campaigns, and thousands of local jurisdictions. Important decisions are made at all levels and access points proliferate, yet dealings between local mayors and contributors are unlikely to figure in international rankings. Germany too is a federal state whose *Land* and city governments spend major sums on construction; bribery and extortion have been problems at that level (Seibel, 1997: 85–86). All three have active private economies and civil societies comparatively free from intervention by, or dependence upon, government. Most decisions and transactions in these countries are private, and politics and legal systems reflect that fact. American scandals like Enron, WorldCom, and other corporate fraud, sexual abuse of children within the Roman Catholic Church, diversions of funds and dubious accounting by United Way charities (*New York Times*, January 23, 2003), conflicts of interest among top leaders of the US Olympic Committee (*New York Times*, January 26, 2003, 2 March 2003), and abuses in the world of intercollegiate athletics involve mostly private dealings. While these three countries probably do have more success at controlling corruption than many others, it is difficult to say how large the difference is.

A focus on elections

Influence Markets do not rely on any one technique, nor do societies in this category have just one form of corruption. The targets can include electoral, legislative, judicial, and bureaucratic officials and processes; private or public figures may take the initiative. Germany, Japan, and the US have a variety of corrupt practices in common, such as abuses in local contracting and (less often in Germany) police corruption. But the funding of political campaigns is the most widely debated corruption concern in each and will be our primary focus in this chapter. It raises critical participation and institutional issues: what constitutes fair and responsive politics in competitive market societies? Can abuses be restrained without threatening important values? Influence Market dealings – some of them legal – can threaten the vitality and competitiveness of politics, the openness of economies, and the accountability of institutions. Reforms can at times make such problems worse.

Financing campaigns in the United States: who has the upper hand?

Concern over the role of money in American politics pre-dates the republic. Campaigns for the Virginia House of Burgesses by such luminaries as

George Washington featured widespread distribution of food and spirits (Thayer, 1973; Troy, 1997), which some saw as vote-buying. The Bank of the United States helped underwrite Henry Clay's 1832 presidential campaign, giving Andrew Jackson an issue he used effectively in winning re-election (United States, Federal Election Commission, 1995: 1). The first federal law on political finance, enacted in 1867, protected Navy Yard workers from demands for contributions (United States, Federal Election Commission, 1995: 5). Political machines in the late nineteenth and early twentieth centuries shook down local businesses for funds, and then engaged in vote-buying and paid "floaters" to vote many times. In the 1896 presidential election financier Mark Hanna and his friends raised an unprecedented $3.5 million (about $77.5 million in 2005 dollars) on behalf of William McKinley (United States, Federal Election Commission, 1995: 1; Inflation Calculator, 2005). That led to the first serious proposal for public funding of federal elections, advanced by Theodore Roosevelt in 1905. The 1907 Tillman Act barred contributions by corporations and national banks; in 1910 House campaigns were required by law to disclose financial information, a requirement extended to the Senate in 1911 (United States, Federal Election Commission, 1995: 1).

After the Harding scandals Congress enacted the Federal Corrupt Practices Act of 1925, imposing strict spending limits upon House and Senate campaigns. But they were so low that there was little chance they would ever be obeyed. Moreover, they applied only to campaign committees operating in two or more states, with no limit upon the number of committees a candidate could have. Provisions for disclosure were weak, and candidates could exempt themselves altogether by claiming they had no knowledge of expenditures on their behalf. The law did not apply to primary elections at all – a major drawback where the dominant party's nomination was tantamount to election (Johnston, 1982: ch. 6). Despite its weaknesses, or perhaps because of them – no candidate was ever prosecuted under its provisions, and no less a political operator than Lyndon Johnson termed it "more loophole than law" (Lukas, 1976: 186) – the 1925 Act stayed on the books for nearly half a century.

The rules of play

The current federal system of campaign finance in the United States began to emerge in 1966, when Congress enacted legislation providing for public funding of presidential general election campaigns through payments to parties. This law was repealed a year later, but its provision for a check-off box on federal tax forms inviting individuals to earmark a portion of their tax to fund campaigns was reinstated by the Revenue Act of 1971. That same year Congress enacted the Federal Election Campaign Act (FECA). It mandated extensive disclosure of contributions and expenditures in all federal campaigns, both primary and general; placed limits upon spending from candidates' personal funds; and repealed the 1925 law. The Watergate scandal of the early 1970s spurred another round of legislation in 1974; the Supreme Court's ruling in *Buckley v. Valeo* (424 US 1 1976) which, among other things, invalidated campaign spending limits on First Amendment grounds, led to more amendments in 1976. Court decisions and legislation in the late 1970s and 1980s made way for "soft money" – unlimited contributions to parties for organization-building and get-out-the-vote activities – and changed the process by which the Federal Election Commission issues regulations (United States, Federal Election Commission, 1995: ch 1). Major revisions, however, did not come until the Bipartisan Campaign Reform Act of 2002 (BCRA), to be discussed below.

Contribution limits and public disclosure of data make up the core of the system. Public funds are available only to presidential candidates in the form of limited matching funds for individual contributions in the pre-nomination phase and block grants for major-party nominees (limited public funding is also available to parties to pay a portion of their nominating convention costs). Those accepting public funds must abide by spending limits, but candidates may reject public funds and thus raise and spend as much as possible, a choice that is becoming increasingly common. No public funds are provided for House and Senate races, and thus no limits apply – a situation that, as we shall see, tends to help incumbents. The 1974 amendments created Political Action Committees (PACs) to encourage citizens to pool voluntary contributions, but not surprisingly they are used primarily by organized interests. The 2002 law capped individual contributions at $2,000 per campaign, restoring about half the purchasing power of the old 1974 $1,000 maximum donation, and a total of $95,000 over a two-year election cycle. PAC donations are limited to $5,000 per campaign but not *in toto*. Contribution and expenditure data are regularly reported and easily accessible (United States, Federal Election Commission, 2004a, 2004b), although as we shall see disclosure too can work against challengers.

How well have the laws worked?

Taken on its own terms the system works well: contribution limits and disclosure are widely accepted and obeyed, although they were increasingly *circumvented* from the late 1980s by "soft money." The FEC administers the laws effectively despite periodic assaults upon its budget by Congress, and its political independence has never been seriously questioned. Campaign spending has grown in real terms: total congressional campaign spending in constant 2000 dollars increased from $647.9 million in 1981–2 to $1.006 billion in 2000, the most recent cycle for which full data are available (Federal Election Commission, 2001a; Inflation Calculator, 2005). But the trend has not been uniform: House spending tends to increase significantly in presidential-election years, and to decline slightly during off-year campaigns. Senate spending has remained fairly constant: if two unusually expensive open-seat races in New York and New Jersey are factored out of the 2000 totals, successful candidates spent about the same amounts, adjusted for inflation, as in 1986 (Ornstein, Mann, and Malbin, 2002). Congressional campaign spending *per capita* has increased even less dramatically – from $3.81 for each person of voting age in 1981–2 to $4.89, in constant dollars, in 2000. Add in presidential spending, and per capita spending for federal campaigns in 1999–2000 amounted only to $8.22 (United States, Federal Election Commission, 1996, 2000, 2004b). Similarly, the number of registered PACs – often described as proliferating in dangerous ways – was about the same in 2000 (4,499) as in 1986 (4,596), and has actually decreased significantly in the corporate and labor categories. In the 1999–2000 election cycle, a full third of all registered PACs contributed only $5,000 or less to federal election candidates, and about one in six contributed nothing at all (United States, Federal Election Commission, 2001b). Indeed, spending increases arguably have less to do with corruption than with incumbent insecurity – with changes in campaign rules, in the partisan balance of the electorate, or, in any year, the presence of a strong challenger (Ornstein, Mann, and Malbin, 2002).

In many ways the current system decisively benefits incumbents. Incumbents benefit from name recognition and established networks for financing and running campaigns. Full-time, publicly funded staff members in Washington and in constituency offices perform casework for constituents. Incumbents have access to free television and radio studios, free mailing privileges, and federally subsidized Internet sites. These advantages are part and product of representing constituents, and in no way are they corrupt. Still, an incumbent and a challenger spending exactly the same amounts of money are running an unequal race. The law too favors incumbents. Public funding or rules allowing one or two large individual "startup" contributions could help challengers launch credible campaigns and raise further donations; spending limits could prevent incumbents from massively outspending challengers. But public funding does not apply to Congressional races, identical contribution limits apply to all candidates, and *Buckley* forbade spending limits for candidates not accepting public funds. Disclosure has more subtle effects: under the pre-1970s system many donors, while giving the bulk of their funds to incumbents, also gave at least small amounts to promising challengers, ensuring access no matter who won. With contributions a matter of public record many donors now find it prudent to give to incumbents only. Incumbents also use disclosure to discourage potential challengers by raising and reporting large amounts of "early money."

A sense of exclusion

Many Americans believe "money politics" is corrupt. In a 1997 Gallup survey more respondents said elected officials in Washington are influenced by pressure from contributors (77 percent) than by the best interests of the country (19 percent), and more said elections are "for sale to the candidate who can raise the most money" (59 percent) than "generally won on the basis of who is the best candidate" (37 percent) (Gallup, 1997). In 2003 *Newsweek* asked whether the political system "is so controlled by special interests and partisanship that it cannot respond to the country's real needs"; 70 percent agreed (Pollingreport.com, 2004). A 2004 Harris survey on "power and influence in Washington" found that 83 percent of respondents said that "big companies" have too much power and influence; 81 percent said the same of political action committees, and 72 percent for political lobbyists, respectively. Just 18 percent said public opinion had too much influence, and 72 percent said "too little" (Pollingreport.com, 2004) – responses consistent with results from previous years.

In a January, 2000, *Newsweek* survey 58 percent said that "Good people being discouraged from running for office by the high costs of campaigns" was a major problem for the country, and 57 percent said that "Political contributions having too much influence on elections and government policy" was a major problem; for both items only 10 percent responded "Not much of a problem" (Citizens Research Foundation, 2002). ABC News and the *Washington Post* asked, in 2001, whether "politicians do special favors for people and groups who give them campaign contributions"; 80 percent said "yes, often," and 13 percent said "yes, sometimes." Among those giving either response 67 percent said such favors are "a big problem." In that same group an interesting contrast emerged: 74 percent judged such favors "unethical," but only 46 percent saw them as "illegal," and 48 percent said "legal" (Pollingreport.com, 2004). A significant share of the population believes the current system fails to prevent, or even permits, unethical behavior.

A rogues' gallery

Should they be so concerned? A degree of skepticism is a healthy thing in a democracy, and bribery has often figured in American political history. Until 1912, for example, Senators were chosen by state legislatures and payments by aspirants to lawmakers were frequent in some states. In 1912 Illinois Senator William Lorimer's 1909 election was invalidated by the US Senate on grounds of bribery (US Senate, 2004). More recent examples include James Traficant (Democrat – Ohio), who was expelled from the House in 2002 for trading official services for donations and bribes, extorting salary kickbacks from employees, taking steps to conceal those kickbacks, filing false tax returns, and lying to a grand jury (Your Congress, 2004). The "Keating Five" were Senators John McCain and Dennis Deconcini (Republican and Democrat, respectively, Arizona), Alan Cranston (Democrat – California), Donald Riegle (Democrat – Michigan), and John Glenn (Democrat – Ohio). They were accused of providing illicit favors for major donor Charles H. Keating Jr., the owner of a failed California Savings and Loan, in 1987, including arranging meetings with key regulators handling the "bailout" of his business (Thompson, 1993). Donald E. "Buz" Lukens (Republican – Ohio) was convicted in 1996 of bribery and conspiracy while a Member of the House; Lukens had been voted out of office in 1990 in the aftermath of a sex scandal (United States Department of Justice, 1995; Political Graveyard, 2004). Rep. Jim Wright (Democrat – Texas), Speaker of the House, resigned in 1989 following an investigation of book royalties he received and a job that had been offered to his wife by a private businessman; the investigation was spearheaded by future Speaker Newt Gingrich (Republican – Georgia) who himself became the focus of ethics allegations in the mid-1990s (Williams, 2000: ch. 5). The FBI's 1978–80 "Operation ABSCAM" (bureaucratese for "Arab Scam") videotaped politicians accepting cash from agents of a fictitious Arab sheik in a rented Philadelphia townhouse. Four Representatives were convicted of accepting bribes, Rep. Michael "Ozzie" Myers (Democrat – Pennsylvania) was expelled from the House, and Senator Harrison Williams (Democrat – New Jersey) was also convicted and resigned (Greene, 1981).

Other recent cases include Rep. Albert Bustamante (Democrat – Texas), convicted in 1993 for racketeering and bribery, and Rep. Jay Kim (Republican – California), who pleaded guilty in 1997 to receiving over $230,000 in illegal campaign contributions. Rep. Nicholas Mavroules was sentenced to prison in 1993 for tax fraud and accepting gratuities; Rep. Dan Rostenkowski, a powerful Illinois Democrat, was indicted in 1994 for offenses including embezzlement of public and campaign funds, and served over a year in prison (Morris, 1996). Other cases have involved bribes passed off as campaign contributions, outsized honoraria for speeches (now outlawed for Members of Congress), gifts to politicians' friends, family members, business associates, or even favored charities, and gifts in kind such as vacations, flights on corporate jets, and choice seats at sporting events. Private-sector job offers following an official's departure from government could be the "back end" of a *quid pro quo*.

It's good to be an incumbent

Federalism and relatively weak political parties in the US foster free-standing election campaigns, each responsible for its own organization and nearly all of its funding. Given the cost of campaigns and the policy benefits at stake, and in light of the rapid growth of soft-money contributions beginning in the late 1980s, it might seem surprising that outright bribery is not more common. But donors are not as powerful, nor are candidates and elected officials as vulnerable, as is commonly thought. Money, by itself, usually does not determine election outcomes; rather, it tends to flow to those, usually incumbents, who are likely to win anyway. Total spending is generally driven by how much challengers are able to raise, with incumbents easily outspending them in response. Contributors (particularly PACs), seeing challengers as unlikely to win, give them little "hard money" and create a self-fulfilling prophecy: in 2000, 63 percent of all PAC Congressional donations went to House incumbents, and just 8 percent to their challengers; 14 percent went to Senate incumbents, and 3 percent to their challengers (Ornstein, Mann, and Malbin, 2002). Such incumbent advantages will likely increase under BCRA, which is aimed at creating an all-hard-money system.

Thus the average House incumbent spent $985,461 during the two-year 2004 electoral cycle; challengers spent an average of $283,134 (a drop of about 25 percent from the 2000 cycle). In the Senate, incumbents spent an average of $6,137,988, and challengers $2,182,732 – again, down by a quarter from 2000. (Senate spending is less comparable from one election to the next because states' populations vary, and only a third of the seats are elected in each cycle.) Measured against such totals, even the maximum hard-money donation from an individual ($1,000, at the time of the 2000 race) or a PAC ($5,000) is small change – and most individual and PAC donors contribute less than the maximum.

Most incumbents seeking re-election win easily. Between 1980 and 2004, the share of House incumbents seeking re-election and winning ranged between 90.5 and 98.8 percent, and the share winning with at least 60 percent of the vote ranged between 65.2 and 88.0 percent. In 2004, only five incumbents were defeated (redistricting forced two other incumbents to run against each other). Nearly a quarter of House incumbents, in most years, face token opposition or none at all. In the Senate, re-election rates are only somewhat lower: in 1980, the year of a Republican landslide large enough to oust an incumbent President, 64.0 percent of Senators running for re-election won, 40 percent taking six votes out of ten, or more. Between 1982 and 2004 the percentage of incumbents winning their re-election campaigns ranged between 75.0 and 96.9. In 2004, 25 of 26 Senators seeking re-election were victorious, and 69.2 percent of them topped 60 percent of the vote (Common Cause, 2002; Ornstein, Mann, and Malbin, 2002; Campaign Finance Institute, 2004).

Incumbent advantage is less decisive in presidential races, which attract politically established challengers and major donors, and where incumbents are limited to two terms. Here the law does not so much enshrine incumbents as prop up the present party system. New parties and independent candidates face a high threshold (5 percent of the popular vote) to qualify for even a fraction of the public funding given to candidates of the two established parties, and of course can only claim such funds after the election. Had today's rules been in place in 1860, Abraham Lincoln might well have run as a Whig.

Incumbent success may reflect effectiveness at working for a state or district, good constituent service, and the accumulated name recognition that flows from incumbency itself. But if challengers so rarely win and are unlikely to attract contributions that will discourage all but the wealthiest would-be legislators from mounting a serious run. Campaigns offering a wide range of viewpoints offered by viable candidates have become the exception. The role of contributors is also affected: incumbents know they can win with or without a given contributor, can outspend most challengers with ease, and therefore owe that contributor nothing. Seasoned lobbyists and individual contributors virtually never make *quid pro quo* offers, and scorn anyone who would. Indeed, one study concluded that incumbents' security is so extensive, and donors' leverage is so slight, that contributions more closely resemble protection payments than legalized bribes (Keim and Zardkoohi, 1988). Many donors are critical of the current system and the relationships it creates (Green, 1998) – not a result one would expect if donations simply bought favorable policy. The real corruption risk may be extortion by top legislative leaders; in recent years their power to rewrite bills late in the lawmaking process has grown significantly (Sinclair, 2000).

Scholars have found little clear evidence that contributions buy roll-call votes (Snyder, 1992; Wright, 1996; Wawro, 2001). This may seem counterintuitive in light of cases such as the "bankruptcy reform" bills that followed a campaign marked by unusually large donations by banking PACs (Opensecrets.org, 2001), or pharmaceutical PACs' contributions preceding the Medicare prescription drug legislation of 2003 (Opensecrets.org, 2004a; Opensecrets.org, 2004b). But to attribute the legislation solely to contributions is to ignore wider political dynamics. In the bankruptcy case a pro-business Republican administration had taken office and Republicans held majorities in both houses. Prescription drug legislation treats the pharmaceutical industry very well indeed, but senior-citizen groups were powerful advocates too. In both cases opposition was weak and poorly organized. Contributors have more clout at less visible levels – for example, as subcommittees mark up bills, and as politicians interact informally among themselves and with other officials on small policy details about which neither the legislator nor constituents have strong sentiments (Etzioni, 1984: 9; Denzau and Munger, 1986; Gierzynski, 2000: 9; Levine, 2004). But opportunities to provide such services arise only from time to time. Many groups give to candidates and officials who are receptive to their interests to begin with; while a representative of a dairy-farming district may receive money from dairy PACs he or she has sound electoral reasons to support their interests anyway. Conversely, many well-connected interests are not so much seeking change as hoping to prevent it, and it is impossible to identify things that *did not* happen because of donations. Wealth interests have always been powerful in American politics, and contributions are made with expectations that ordinary citizens are unlikely to have. But those interests would be powerful under any system of campaign finance we might imagine, and their ability to mobilize large contributions is at least as much a *result* of their power as its cause.

Lobbyists, contributors, and candidates generally agree that while donations do not buy legislative votes they do buy *access* – the opportunity to make a case on a given issue. Access is limited and does not guarantee favorable outcomes, but little can be accomplished without it. That is why it is worth paying for. Still, the market for access raises questions about the vitality of politics: a pervasive concern with fundraising can divert attention from groups and issues, and from the constituency work, that should be top priorities. The cumulative effects of spending most of one's

[Institutionalized crupt]

one effect

quote

spare time in the company of wealthy people and their particular view of the world, and corresponding expectations among the wealthy that they have special claims, likewise do little for the quality of representative democracy. //

The corruption problem: not bribery but bad politics

The United States has a systemic corruption problem involving political finance, but not necessarily the one much of the public thinks it has. Bribery of federal elected officials is uncommon, and there is little evidence that large donors can buy Congressional votes. More bribery and extortion occur at lower levels, but again its scope is relatively limited: the US fills over half a million public offices by elections, all but 537 of them through state and local elections. At issue, instead, are the vitality and credibility of electoral politics. Popular majorities *believe* the campaign finance process is corrupting, and there is a significant gap among laws, social values, and the elite political culture regarding acceptable behavior. Further, campaign finance laws protect incumbents, thereby (in conjunction with other developments) reducing political competition and the apparent value of voting as a mechanism of accountability. The institutions regulating the connections between wealth and power in the American electoral process have serious credibility problems, and voter participation takes place in a setting of little real competition for many offices. Those add up to a systemic corruption problem in the sense spelled out in chapter 1.

"Reform"

The new BCRA will likely add to incumbents' advantages. Whatever its other drawbacks "soft money" could be used by party leadership to help challengers via get-out-the-vote activities and party advertising. The new law restricts fundraising and spending to hard money only, an arena in which incumbents fare far better than challengers. Similarly, "issue advertising" – in the past, used more by national groups seeking change than by backers of incumbents – may now be funded by hard money only, and is therefore banned for advocacy groups, in the final phases of campaigns. Perhaps the most incumbent-friendly part of BCRA is its "Millionaire Opponent" provision. For House and Senate candidates limits on individual contributions are raised, and ceilings on party spending on their behalf are removed, as opponents' expenditures from personal funds exceed a series of thresholds. While the law applies to all candidates, self-financing is much more essential to challengers than incumbents: in most years House challengers (many of them political newcomers) raise between 15 and 25 percent of their campaign money from their own funds (Ornstein, Mann, and Malbin, 2002). Even if they spent vast sums of their own to win the first time, incumbents can easily fund re-election campaigns with hard money. Now, when facing well-heeled challengers, such hard-money fundraising will be even easier.

A question of trust?

The American campaign finance system may do tolerably well at inhibiting outright bribery, but it does far less to encourage open, competitive politics or a popular sense that participation is effective. Disclosure of contributions and spending – intended to encourage voters to punish miscreants at the polls – more likely creates images of a flood of special-interest money. A widespread, if diffuse, perception that electoral politics has been captured by wealth may be the most significant legacy of past reforms. A CBS News poll, in 2000, found that 11 percent of registered voters believed only "minor changes" were needed to improve "the way political campaigns are funded in the United States," while 43 percent backed "fundamental changes" and 42 percent said that "we need to completely rebuild it" (Pollingreport.com, 2004). Further reform attracts surprisingly little public backing: in 2000, for example, only 1 percent of a Fox News national survey named campaign finance reform as one of "the two most important issues for the federal government to address" (Citizens Research Foundation, 2002), and 59 percent of those responding to a 1997 Gallup Poll said that even if major reforms are enacted "special interests will always find a way to maintain their power in Washington." When the question was repeated in 2000 the share saying "special interests" would maintain their power had risen to 64 percent (Pollingreport.com, 2004).

The Influence Market described here and its consequences are legal for the most part, which may say as much or more about the way laws accommodate behavior as about any inherent morality in the process. Yet it fits our notion of systemic corruption problems. An older way to think about corruption – one we could broadly call classical – is helpful here. Corruption in that view is not a characteristic of a particular person or deed, but a collective state of being – in effect, a deterioration of a state's capacity to elicit the loyalty of its citizens (Dobel, 1978; see also Euben, 1978). If politics has become a mere extension of markets – or, if a substantial proportion of people *believe* that it has – the system risks losing the trust of citizens and its ability to draw upon private participation and preferences to make legitimate, genuinely *public* policies. The core problem is not lawbreaking as such, but rather the widespread perception that the whole system, and with it the opportunities and guarantees supposedly provided to citizens, has become an Influence Market corrupted by collusion between wealth and power.

Germany: sharing the spoils

Like the United States, Germany has a federal system, democratic politics, and a highly developed economy. It receives favorable corruption rankings, although it too has problems at local levels and is home to international businesses whose dealings have led to scandals. Its corruption differs from the American example to a degree because of the country's party system, conceptions of democracy, and the role of the state in the economy. Still, Germany fits solidly within the Influence Market syndrome.

Seibel (1997: 98–99) notes that the post-unification era has been marked by numerous small scandals, and that small-scale affairs often attract press and public interest while more important cases go nearly unnoticed. He attributes this pattern to long-term weaknesses in democratic values. Germany acquired a powerful modern bureaucracy and state before it liberalized its political system; democracy was eventually handed down from above rather than built from the grassroots. The German *Rechtsstaat* at its legal-administrative core has not been totally incorruptible, but citizens have long regarded it as relatively clean (Seibel, 1997: 86, 90–92). More problems arise, however, in the *Sozialstaat* – that part of government that handles major revenues and delivers significant benefits. In 1999 *The Economist* (December 9) reported that over the previous year German police had investigated 2,400 cases of corruption, double the figure for 1996. Corruption is fairly extensive in local government construction contracting, for example (Seibel, 1997). A variety of interests contend for contracts and other benefits, and Germany's decentralized political system offers a wide range of access points at which parties and politicians can stand as middlemen.

Three large, well-financed and well-organized major parties dominate German politics and link those interests to policy processes. From left to right they are the Social Democrats (SPD), the Free Democrats (FDP), and the Christian Democratic Union, known in Bavaria as the Christian Social Union (CDU/CSU). Also significant, though smaller and often fractious, is the Green Party. These parties provide a variety of connections: vertically, among levels of government; horizontally, among the *Länder* (states) and their subdivisions; and sectorally among contending social and economic interests. As in the US, Influence Markets also work to reduce political competition. Germany's federal and parliamentary system encourages – indeed, necessitates – party coalitions at all levels. Major parties are rarely wholly out of power; even after defeats and scandals they and their leaders retain political leverage. Thus, leaders of several parties are friends worth having. Moreover, despite generous public funding German election campaigns remain expensive business, and the highest-profile scandals have revolved around political fundraising (Seibel, 1997: 86; Alemann, 2002). These are often cross-party affairs: sharing out benefits, both legitimate and otherwise, among parties in proportion to their strength is reflected in longstanding practices known as *Proporz*. At the *Land* and municipal levels *Proporz* is an unwritten law, and even in the most significant scandal at the federal level – the Flick affair – all major parties except the Greens were cut in on the spoils. Some of these characteristics can be seen in a few of the major scandals in the Federal Republic (the following cases draw upon Glees, 1987; Glees, 1988; Seibel, 1997: 87–90; Alemann, 2002).

Federal purchases of armored vehicles in the 1950s, and of Lockheed fighter bombers in the 1960s, were facilitated by Otto Benz, a center-right *Bundestag* (lower house) member linked both to the auto manufacturer and to the Minister of Defense. He paid significant sums for political influence, in the form of unusually large party contributions rather than bribes. Both vehicles and aircraft turned out to be faulty, and the latter eventually figured in the international Lockheed scandal of the 1970s.

In the mid-1970s the Flick industrial combine sold a major block of shares in Daimler-Benz, creating a potential tax obligation of DM1 billion or more. Flick sought a special tax exemption that could legally be given if funds were reinvested in beneficial ways. Two FDP Ministers of the Economy, Hans Friedrichs and his successor, Graf Lambsdorff, granted the exemption; later it emerged that they had received large payments from Flick managing director Eberhard von Brauchitsch. Those funds were part of a much larger scheme, totaling perhaps DM25 million, of contributions to the three big parties and their leaders. While the Flick scandal hastened the fall of the SPD/FDP coalition government in the early 1980s, legal repercussions were few: cases against SPD president Willy Brandt and CDU/CSU president Helmut Kohl (former and future Chancellors, respectively) were dropped. Von Brauchitsch, Friedrichs and Lambsdorff were convicted only on tax offenses, and Lambsdorff eventually served as FDP president into the early 1990s.

In 1999 a former CDU treasurer was arrested on charges of receiving DM1 million from a defense contractor, Thyssen-Henschel, which had sought to sell tanks to Saudi Arabia at the time of the first Gulf War. Thyssen claimed the funds were a party donation; the CDU denied receiving the cash. Subsequent investigations revealed an extensive network of secret party accounts financed by inflated prices charged to the Saudis. CDU parliamentary Secretary of Defense Agnes Hürland-Büning was paid several million DM as a consultant to Thyssen after leaving office. She also helped the Kohl government arrange a deal between Thyssen and French oil giant Elf-Aquitaine to take over an aging refinery at Leuna, in the old East, and market its products. Payments to Kohl skimmed from such dealings amounted to DM2 million or more; his refusal to disclose their sources led (after Kohl's election loss in 1999) to his resignation as CDU honorary chairman, and to major investigations. All three major parties received payments; one account put the total at DM100 million while one "bagman" claimed that DM85 million went to one party alone.

Take the money and run

These sorts of dealings are aided by relatively weak legal and political constraints. Germany did introduce new controls on party contributions in the 1980s, but there are no limits and no bar against contributions by corporations or in cash (Alemann, 2002). Bribery of *Bundestag* members is a legal offense, but the law is not vigorously enforced. Bribery of or through parties is illegal, with parties obliged to repay illegally received funds plus penalties to the Presidium of the Bundestag, which will then turn such sums over to charity (Alemann, 2002). Most of the burden for monitoring such contributions, however, falls upon the parties themselves (Germany's anti-corruption laws and their enforcement are analyzed in GRECO, 2004). Finally, as the cases above suggest, top figures often enjoy *de facto* immunity (Seibel, 1997: 89, 94–96): jail terms are rare, criminal charges are likely to deal with tax evasion rather than bribery, and political careers may continue with little loss of standing. Edmund Stoiber, CSU Interior Minister in Bavaria, who admitted in the early 1990s to receiving personal favors from businesses, went on to become Prime Minister of Bavaria and, by 2002, CDU/CSU leader and candidate for Chancellor. The dynamics of German democratization noted above may have devalued democratic accountability while emphasizing the mere distribution of social benefits (Seibel, 1997: 96–99); in any event, the resentment of Influence Markets evident among American citizens is not apparent in Germany.

Germany thus shows how Influence Markets adapt to political realities. A US Senator or Representative has more policy leverage than an individual *Bundestag* member, but in the German system major influence can be had at higher levels – often, among the leaders of more than one party. Those leaders and their parties have a common interest in a political and electoral system in which they often share power, and in continuing to distribute material benefits. Germany's economy, too, is distinguished by the presence of very large private corporations, labor unions, and other groups with major funds at their disposal. The result is an Influence Market that flourishes at high levels, crosses party lines, and involves relatively few risks.

What of the longer-term consequences? Germany's political processes are fluid and competitive, and yet in recent years it has been slow to adapt to new realities, especially as regards the affordability of the extensive social benefits that are so central to public acceptance of the *Sozialstaat*. Absorbing the old East has been a major burden and has given rise to a variety of resentments. Repeated revelations of influence-dealing at high levels (and at high prices) together with weak legal restraints and public tolerance or resignation suggests that here too Influence Markets extensively accommodate elite interests, but at considerable cost in terms of political responsiveness. Indeed, whether Germany can make needed economic and social policy adaptations over the next decade may tell us, in large part, just how extensive those costs have been.

Influence markets in Japan: leaders, factions, and tribes

Japan too has Influence Markets in which political figures help connect private interests, many of them businesses, to decisionmakers within a strong, well-institutionalized state. Here too political contributions, some of them legal, are integral to that process. But there are important contrasts too. Japan's Influence Markets have produced extensive, lucrative, and factionalized corruption. A strong, centralized, and remote bureaucracy has raised the value of mediation by political faction leaders who cultivate their own bureaucratic and parliamentary networks. Factionalism in the Diet dates back to the rise of electoral politics in the 1890s (Mitchell, 1996: 131), and in society at large far longer than that. But for many years modified one-party rule and an unusual electoral system that forced candidates within a given party to compete with each other encouraged "money politics" on a spectacular scale. Japan illustrates key elements of Influence Market corruption and also tests the boundaries of this syndrome, showing us ways in which Influence Markets reflect variations in participation, institutions, and historical-cultural characteristics.

Corruption is nothing new in Japan. Mitchell (1996) shows that it was as much a fact of political life in pre-modern days as during the current era. In 1914 a major scandal involved the Siemens industrial combine and naval procurement decisions (Johnson, 1995: 194; Mitchell, 1996: 28–31). Nine of the fifteen LDP Prime Ministers elected between 1955, when the modern party system was established, and the political breakup of 1993 were implicated in major scandals (Boisseau, 1997: 132); national scandals surfaced almost annually during that period (Mitchell, 1996: 109). Police corruption has been a continuing concern, extensive wrongdoing can occur at the local and prefectural levels, and some observers spot a worrisome trend toward more wrongdoing by bureaucrats themselves (Johnson, 2001: 1–2; Berkofsky, 2002). But a high-priced market in national bureaucratic influence has been so much a fact of national political life that many observers term the problem "structural corruption" (*kōzō oshoku*) (Mitchell, 1996: 139–140; Johnson, 1995: 15, and ch. 9 and 10, accepts the term "structural" but challenges the "corruption" idea).

Influence-dealing – Japanese style

Japan fit the syndrome particularly well between 1955 and 1993. LDP and other politicians traded influence and access to the workings of a well-institutionalized bureaucracy for money from business (Johnson, 1995: 202). They used the funds thus obtained for their campaigns; for their supporters within party factions, in the Diet, and in home constituencies; for the wining and dining required to cultivate clients in the bureaucracy – and, of course, for self-enrichment.

But Influence Markets are by no means alike, and Japan's version reflects a variety of influences. The pervasiveness of corruption, the large financial stakes involved, and cultural dimensions too (such as norms of exchange and attitudes toward authority, the latter shaping both factionalism and responses to scandals) set Japan apart. The amounts of money involved can be astonishing: when former LDP Deputy Secretary General Kanemaru Shin was arrested for tax evasion in 1993, the valuables seized from his home were worth an estimated ¥3.6 billion, or roughly $30 million. Boisseau (1997: 133–135) conservatively estimates that toward the end of LDP dominance in the early 1990s the party was spending about $8 billion *annually* to keep its machine running; some of those funds were raised legitimately but much was not. Kickbacks to LDP politicians from the winners of public works contracts ran a flat 3 percent of the total value of the contract (Johnson, 1995: 208). When we consider that in the mid-1980s domestic construction outlays in Japan totaled ¥53.6 trillion yearly (Woodall, 1996: 1) – around $225 billion at then-current exchange rates – or that in the early 1990s around 15 percent of the LDP's reported contributions come from real-estate and construction interests, with many more kept secret (Woodall, 1996: 11), we get a rough sense of the scale of the process. Major post-war cases include the following (these descriptions draw upon Johnson, 1995: 194–201, 218–225; Mitchell, 1996: 109–130; Pascha, 1999: 3–5; Blechinger, 2000: 8–9; Johnson, 2000: 60–62, 64–68; Samuels, 2001: 13).

The Shipbuilding scandal began in 1953 with legislation granting shipbuilders the right to borrow capital at below-market interest rates. The following year it was revealed that lobbyists backing that law had paid large bribes to politicians and some bureaucrats. The Yoshida government fell in the wake of the scandal, but two other consequences were equally important. Extensive political intervention halted prosecutions, beginning a pattern of weak enforcement of bribery laws and large numbers of suspended sentences. The scandal also hastened the consolidation of feuding conservative parties into the LDP, a move backed by business leaders wishing to avoid the high cost of influence seen in the Shipbuilding case. The *Kuro Kiri* ("Black Mist") scandal of (1966–7) involved not only specific abuses, such as bribes paid by Kyōwa Sugar to LDP politicians for help in obtaining government loans, but also to the general atmosphere of the Satō Eisaku government: bribery was said to envelop politics like a black mist. Eventually the term included bribery in Japan's major baseball leagues. Shigemasa Seishi, former Kyōwa chairman and former Minister of Agriculture, received large sums, as did many Socialist and LDP figures. While the opposition and LDP dissidents used the issue to push for a national election, Satō's faction campaigned on the strong economy and won.

Best-known of Japan's corruption cases was the Lockheed scandal that began in 1976. Lockheed made payments of around ¥500 million (about $1.6 million in 1976) to Prime Minister, and longtime LDP faction leader, Tanaka Kakuei. Tanaka was convicted of corruption in the 1980s, but because of appeals served no jail time; the case effectively ended with his death in 1993. Another 460 persons were questioned and seventeen Diet members were named in connection with payments, but no other charges were filed. In the US Lockheed was the subject of Congressional hearings that spurred eventual passage of the Foreign Corrupt Practices Act.

During the 1980s Recruit Cosmos, a real-estate and investment combine, issued stock to top politicians, bureaucrats, and other VIPs in advance of the shares' appearing on the market, frequently offering no-interest financing via funds diverted from government subsidies. Those stocks could then be sold for large profits. Political and bureaucratic favors were given to various Recruit units in return. A major scandal beginning in 1988 eventually revealed that such deals extended to most top political figures in Japan. In 1991 it was revealed that Kyôwa, a steel-fabrication and construction firm, made large payments to Abe Fumio, leader of an important LDP faction and former head of two regional development agencies. Abe used political contacts, including former Prime Minister Suzuki, to win permission for Kyôwa to build a golf course (a major real-estate undertaking in Japan). Abe eventually was sentenced to prison.

The Sagawa Kyûbin case of 1991–3 did more than any other to bring down the LDP in 1993. Sagawa, a trucking and delivery firm seeking permission to expand nationally, gave large sums to LDP politicians with interests in transportation matters. A particularly ominous note was that payoffs also went to organized crime factions. Kanemaru Shin was dealing with Sagawa while working to elect Prime Minister Takeshita. Revelations of his political, business, and organized crime connections both undermined public trust in the LDP and worsened resentments among younger and rural candidates who were cut out of the spoils, yet had to compete with fellow LDP politicians backed by Sagawa money. Kanemaru was also involved in extensive tax evasion and personal enrichment.

For years it was thought that top bureaucrats – high-status figures in society as well as within the state – were generally honest. By the end of the 1990s, however, an important official in the Ministry of Health and Welfare was found to have taken both payments and extensive hospitality from construction firms. Others in the Bank of Japan and Ministry of Finance took money in exchange for information on "surprise" regulatory inspections. In 2000, Nakao Eiichi's close ties to a Tokyo construction contractor during his short stint as Minister of Construction (May–November, 1996) became the subject of an investigation. Wakachiku Construction paid Nakao over ¥60 million for help in designating the company as a bidder on public works projects. Wakachiku's generosity extended to other politicians including then-current, and former, cabinet members.

Behind the scandals

Blechinger (1999: 57) has described Japan's party–business links as a kind of mutual services agreement, with the LDP dealing in access and business providing contributions. Modified one-party politics (Pempel, 1998) created enough political competition to make it worthwhile for backers to put up cash to keep the LDP in power, *and* a near-monopoly over access that gave factional leaders leverage over donors that no American politician could begin to exercise. That, together with the sheer scale of the expenditures and contracts on offer, helps account for the level and scope of illegality. Such corruption did not prevent a four-decade economic miracle; indeed, it fed upon prosperity. But Japanese Influence Markets have had significant *political* costs, aggravating the factional splits that brought the LDP down (temporarily) in 1993 and perhaps contributing to Japan's ineffective economic adaptations over the past fifteen years. Woodall (1996: 3) calls the contrast "first-rate economy, third-rate politics."

Two layers of formal and informal institutions influenced political and economic participation in critical ways, setting the stage for the marketing of bureaucratic influence at very high prices. One is the "1955 system" of

political parties dominated by a unified LDP, built out of formerly
squabbling parties on the right, and including a unified (if much less
effective) socialist opposition (Johnson, 1995: 214; Mitchell, 1996: xvi,
109). The other is the "1941 system" of "bureaucracy-led industrial
cooperation" (Johnson, 1982; Johnson, 1995: 226) dominated by presti-
gious, remote, highly able officials – a system that not only survived war,
devastation, and reconstruction but also guided Japan's emergence as a
world economic power. The 1941 system made bureaucratic access and
influence essential, while the 1955 system turned them into marketable
political commodities. Together the 1955 system overlaid on the 1941
allowed top politicians with bureaucratic connections to offer credible
commitments (Woodall, 1996: 20; Pascha, 1999: 10).

The strength of bureaucratic institutions raised the ante – important
decisions were made by high-status bureaucrats who followed through
with great efficiency. A lack of access could mean not even being invited
to bid on construction contracts, for example, or – for an aspiring local
politician – not being able to take credit for projects or subsidies in a
constituency. Trading in influence at a high level required a *zoku*
(Johnson, 1995: 209–210; Blechinger, 2000) – a network or political
tribe. A *zoku* linked Diet members sharing an interest in a particular
kind of policy or sector of the economy to businesses and bureaucrats;
some *zoku* members became virtual industry spokespersons (Blechinger,
2000: 3).

If the LDP held a near-monopoly, why was electoral politics so expensive? The answer has to do with both factionalism and the way Diet
members were elected before 1994 (Christensen, 1996; Seligmann,
1997). Most districts elected between two and six Diet members on a
ballot on which parties did not designate an official list of candidates. Real
political influence depended upon being an LDP Diet member, but
various factions' candidates had to run against each other. Unable to
differentiate themselves on policy issues, candidates had to buy electoral
support. This they did by attending weddings, funerals, and other family
occasions (or sending one of their dozen or more local agents to such
affairs) and giving cash, often enclosed in an ornate gift card, to those
involved (Pharr, 2005). Over time politicians built *koenkai* – local support
networks of people sharing a recreational or cultural interest as well as a
political commitment – through such contributions. One "W. T.," a
rank-and-file Lower House member, reported in 1976 that he gave out
ninety-three such gifts in a typical month, the costs of which could easily
exceed $1 million annually (Iga and Auerbach, 1977). Finding money on
that scale meant backing an LDP faction leader whose prestige within the
party was enhanced, in turn, by a large and active following. "Money

politics" of this sort pre-dates 1955: Johnson (1995: 188–189) and Samuels (2001) date it as far back as the early post-war Kishi government, and Mitchell (1996: xvi) traces "structural corruption" back to the 1930s. But the 1955 party system, meshing with the 1941 bureaucratic system, encouraged an influence market that was active, lucrative, and essential to financing a highly factionalized and personalized style of electoral politics.

Weak constraints

Those incentives were exacerbated by weak anti-corruption responses (Castberg, 1997; Castberg, 2000: 437; Johnson, 2000: 64–76). From the Shipbuilding scandal onwards corruption investigations were routinely constrained or ended on political grounds. Prosecutors, who enjoyed considerable prestige and had wide discretion in most other cases, treated corruption allegations with caution, particularly when high-level figures were involved. Lengthy court appeals could stretch a corruption case out for decades: Tanaka Kakuei's Lockheed convictions were still under appeal when he died in 1993. In 1978, nearly nine out of ten corruption convictions led to suspended sentences (Mitchell, 1996: 135). Before 1993, politicians who elsewhere might have been disgraced by scandal could reclaim their power and prestige once they had spent some time tending to the home constituency, and had been re-elected (Blechinger, 1999: 48–49).

Many reasons lie behind these weak restraints. At the elite level Japan's political culture encourages harmony and in some cases deference while discouraging confrontation (Johnson, 1995: 8). Among citizens traditional acceptance of authority, an emphasis upon personal connections rather than upon formal roles, and the notion that favors (including political support) deserve an equal return (such as gifts and local pork-barrel projects) fostered tolerance for corruption (Mitchell, 1996: 135–137). And the post-war state *worked*, rebuilding a devastated country and delivering unprecedented standards of living.

Legally Japanese political parties were long regarded as private organizations, and their financing and internal dealings were normally private concerns too. Moreover, convictions in bribery cases bear a high burden of proof: it must be shown not only that payments were made and received, but also that the recipient knew they were bribes *and* had the authority to deliver what was being paid for (Johnson, 2000: 68–72). A politician can thus claim he thought payments were campaign contributions, or say he had no way of providing the benefits expected, and thus stand a strong chance of acquittal or a suspended sentence. Political interventions to halt or divert investigations reflect the fact that the Prosecutor General is appointed by the Prime Minister. Prosecutors must keep their superiors informed of plans and progress; at times they make decisions in anticipated reaction to political pressures (Mitchell, 1996: 114–115; Johnson, 2000: 64–68). For many years a politician caught in an investigation could turn to faction leaders for protection, a fact that only reinforced the value of *zoku* membership.

The 1993 crisis

By 1993, however, structural corruption seemed to be collapsing under its own weight. The scandals of the late 1980s and early 1990s had damaged public perceptions of the LDP, a problem made worse when the Sagawa case revealed links to organized crime, and by perceptions that corruption was reaching into the central bureaucracy. The cost of "money politics" was also rising rapidly, fueled both by affluence and factional competition. In July a badly split LDP was narrowly defeated at the polls for the first time since its formation (Boisseau, 1997: 142–146). It is tempting to see that as a political turning point, but defeat grew less out of national revulsion against "money politics" than from factional infighting (Boisseau, 1997: 143–144). Younger politicians, and those from poorer and rural areas, rebelled against the high costs of campaigning – particularly because many felt they were not receiving their share of their factions' money – while conflict at the top over issues dating back to Lockheed and before had become particularly bitter (Johnson, 1995: chs. 9, 10). But no opposition party could convincingly claim the moral high ground, as all (save possibly the communists) had engaged in "money politics" and lacked the strength to govern on their own. By 1994 the LDP was back as part of an uneasy coalition, and it has stayed in government ever since. Factional conflicts remain, however (Cox, Rosenbluth, and Thies, 1999), and indeed are built into the LDP's internal culture.

Reforms enacted in 1994 created 300 single-member parliamentary constituencies – a measure intended to curb ruinously expensive intra-party competition – and left 200 seats to be filled by proportional representation. New limits and disclosure rules for contributions were imposed, and limited public funding of parties – which were accorded a new quasi-public status – was implemented over a five-year period (Mitchell, 1996: 128; Christensen, 1998: 987–989; Blechinger, 2000: 1). Reformers hoped the new system would check *zoku* factionalism, make it more difficult for leaders to accumulate influence and manipulate campaign funds, and reduce incentives both for businesses to pay up and for individual Diet members to buy voter support. The effects of these reforms will take some time to assess: public funding provisions took full effect only at the beginning of 2000, for example. The hoped-for transition to more unified party competition revolving around clear policy choices has been slow to materialize (Christensen, 1998), and pork-barrel politics shows few signs of fading away, particularly at the local level (Fukui and Fukai, 1996). Meanwhile scandals continue, at times involving top bureaucrats in ministries such as Foreign Affairs (Berkofsky, 2002).

The systemic political costs of corruption have been considerable, however. Surveys in 2001 found that only 9 percent of Japanese adults had confidence in the Diet and only 8 percent in the central bureaucracy (Johnson, 2001: 4); as recently as 1994 trust in bureaucrats was as high as 44 percent (Tachino, 1999: 14–15). Such results must be viewed in the context of Pharr's (2000: 174–175) evidence that political satisfaction and trust in modern Japan have never been particularly high compared to other democracies. Still, Pharr shows that misconduct in office, and not economic problems, poor policy performance, or any fundamental weakness in civil society, is a primary cause of political disenchantment in Japan.

There have been some changes in politics, and in the ways scandals are dealt with, since the 1993 crisis. Single-member constituencies with new boundaries have weakened ties between some politicians and local supporters' groups (*koenkai*), leaving the latter up for grabs in some places. Factional leaders are somewhat less able to control individual Diet members or local voters (Cox, Rosenbluth, and Theis, 1999: 56). Individual politicians dispute corruption allegations more vigorously, at times taking legal action, and try to distance themselves from the wrongdoing of others. Cabinet members are more likely to take responsibility for bribery within their ministries, and may resign in the wake of revelations. Disgraced politicians now find it harder to make a comeback (Blechinger, 1999: 46–53). But Influence Market corruption has in no way come to an end; instead, it has adapted somewhat to reform legislation and the realities of post-1993 politics.

Influence markets in Japan: alternative futures

The effects of corruption over the past half-century in Japan are not easy to assess. As recently as the mid-1990s Johnson (1995: 202; see also Pascha, 1999: 8–11) could argue with justification that its economic costs had not been extensive. As in the American case, much of the damage has been political, and therefore less easily measured. Competition was largely confined to elite and intra-LDP arenas; voters had choices, but holding the party accountable at the ballot box was nearly impossible. But that lack of accountability may have indirect economic costs to the extent that governments find it difficult (or unnecessary) to change policies in response to economic change (on Japan's political and economic prospects see Mann and Sasaki, 2002; Katz, 2003). As long as growth was rapid and living standards continued to rise, voters may have concluded that their bargain with the state, and with the LDP that mediated between it and society, was a good one. But as Japan's economic tides have rolled out in the past decade resentment of corruption has grown. Mitchell (1996: xvii, 157) is undoubtedly correct in arguing that genuine reform will require not just new electoral laws, but rather fundamental changes in relationships between wealth and power.

The future of Japanese corruption is difficult to predict. Weaker factions and a more pluralistic pattern of influence within the LDP, enhanced inter-party competition, and more decisive national elections could produce a more decentralized Influence Market – perhaps like that of the United States. The frequency of bribery and the amounts changing hands might remain high by American standards, but individual politicians – most with little bureaucratic clout to put on the market – running against real competitors from other parties in single-member districts would not command bribes on the scale seen before 1993. LDP and *zoku* membership would be less saleable assets. If people and businesses in Japan are now less dependent upon the state (Schoppa, 2001) that too might check Influence Market corruption. Japanese politics will remain factionalized, and the power of the central state bureaucracy will continue to be a fact of life, but corruption may come to look more like that of other Influence Market countries (Cox, Rosenbluth, and Theis, 1999: 56).

But another, more pessimistic scenario is also possible. Mishima (1998) argues that the high status and remoteness of the bureaucracy helped "discipline" policies during the LDP's years of dominance, but notes that bureaucrats are now somewhat more accessible and "conciliatory" to the political world. As a consequence, Mishima argues, the bureaucracy has also become less effective in making and implementing policy. Enhanced bureaucratic transparency, we might speculate, could make such a situation worse – particularly if such efforts multiply the points of access to officials and policy processes, and if an increasingly competitive political process creates more intermediaries seeking to cultivate bureaucratic friendships. At worst, Influence Markets could turn into a disjointed set of uncoordinated monopolies (Shliefer and Vishny, 1993) – potentially far more unpredictable and harmful in economic terms than the pre-1993 model (see also Campos, Lien, and Pradhan, 1999; Pascha, 1999: 16). While it is hard to say how likely that outcome is, it would ironically be partly a consequence of the post-1993 reforms.

Influence market corruption: more than meets the eye

Political contributions and influence processes are not inherently corrupt, but they pose major questions about relationships between wealth and power in democracies. Most Influence Market societies have reached legal and political accommodations that check the worst excesses while not greatly restraining political and economic elites; still, many citizens of those societies regard "money politics" as a broadly corrupting influence. Clearly, established democracies have not solved the corruption problem despite often depicting their own systems as standards of reform. A more accurate statement would be that they have a syndrome of their own that is more threatening to the values and vitality of politics than to economic development, one likely to attract less attention from organizations and interests accustomed to thinking about the costs of corruption primarily in economic terms. It is still a syndrome that is worth considerable concern.

The scope of Influence Market corruption is difficult to specify. Corrupt contributions and influence can be difficult to distinguish from legitimate varieties; costs are long-term, widely distributed, and take the form of reduced vitality of electoral politics and quality of public policy, rather than damage done by a few specific deals. Wealth interests may have so much political clout that more extensive corruption is unnecessary; alternatively, they and their political clients may have become adept at covering their tracks or at putting an acceptable public face on activities. If either (or both) are true, Influence Market democracies will have legitimated, privatized, or decentralized connections between wealth and power that in other societies take on clearly corrupt forms. That point is relevant not only to the relatively favorable corruption scores most Influence Market countries receive, but also to the longer-term implications of viewing economic liberalization as an anti-corruption strategy. Possible economic effects are also hard to judge. We will never know whether these three economies might have grown faster, or in more equitable or desirable ways, without Influence Market corruption. Germany and Japan are finding it difficult to adapt to the new world economy, a problem that might be traceable in part to the role of Influence Markets in preempting political competition and change. Further, we should not forget corruption involved in the international dealings of corporations that call market democracies home. Such cases will emerge, in chapters to come, as problems in less-developed countries.

Influence Market cases share many attributes, but they are far from identical. Economic and political participation factors specific to these countries introduce variations; so do institutions, including not just anti-corruption laws and their enforcement but also party systems, the legal foundations of markets, electoral systems, and the rules of political finance. Cultural factors, which are more often invoked in the countries that inhabit our other three clusters, are important too: liberal outlooks on politics and the economy are a political and social culture, after all. Behavior within Influence Markets is influenced by conceptions of citizenship and authority, of mutual exchange and obligation, and of course of right and wrong – values and judgments influenced by the sorts of everyday experiences and home truths that comprise culture everywhere (Johnston, 1986b, 1991). Finally, as Theobald (1990) reminds us, patrimonialism and the pull of kinship, ethnicity, and other kinds of primary ties are far from absent in liberal systems. Influence Markets will continue to evolve in both legitimate and illicit ways.

One final question is worth posing: does Japan really belong in this group? The frequency of scandals and the scale of money involved were, for many years, much greater than that seen in the US and Germany, while the factionalism within the LDP and the corruption-aided hegemony of that party are reminiscent of the Christian-Democrat dominated political cartel that dominated Italy until 1993 (Johnson, 1995; see also chapter 5 of this book). Both parties, in fact, suffered major defeats in that year. But Italy's corruption crisis was driven in part by the rise of an aggressive new generation of jurists and, perhaps, the accumulating effects of economic liberalization and EU policies upon businesses (Golden, 2002). Once underway it disrupted key business–political connections and shattered the old party system. The LDP, by contrast, was back in government within a year as a coalition partner, and it has stayed there ever since. Japan's political class and national business leadership were stirred up but hardly displaced (Boisseau, 1997: 132).

Boisseau also draws a parallel between Japan and Germany's path to democracy, noting (as did Seibel for Germany) that a modernized state administrative core came well before democracy and was the spine of the system. As in Germany, he argues, democratic processes are less valued than the material goods the state can dispense (Boisseau, 1997: 135). Competitive political parties, when they arose, were less the voice of contending segments of society than elite gatekeepers to bureaucratic influence. Similarly, in Germany Seibel (1997: 92) notes an emphasis on outcome – who gets what – over democratic process as a value in itself, and suggests that notions of public office as impersonal power held in temporary trust are only weakly developed.

Another comparison is relevant to Japan. Its "money politics" outwardly resembles that found in Korea. Given regional similarities and the complex, intertwined histories of those two countries, putting them into separate categories may seem an error. But there are important contrasts too. For most of the post-war era Japanese politics revolved around competitive elections – even if the competition was as much within the LDP as between it and other parties – while Korea remained a dictatorship. Korea is still consolidating democratic political processes and key regulatory institutions. Japan's bureaucracy was widely regarded as independent – even remote – but of high quality for most of that period, while Korea's was more politicized – colonized in important respects by the personal networks of top national figures. Both economies are dominated by huge industrial combines, but Japan's were not the objects of manipulation by political leaders in the ways Korea's *chaebols* were for many years. Japan's national political elite is larger and less tight-knit than Korea's. Korean corruption was shaped much more by collusion among a tight-knit national elite – one that for many years possessed a political monopoly sustained partly by coercion but also by the shared spoils of corruption. More recently Korean elites have used corrupt influence as a kind of rearguard action against rising political competition and economic liberalization – unlike their Japanese counterparts who found the threat of political competition quite useful as a way to extract money from businesses.

"Money politics" has indeed been the style of corruption in both Japan and Korea, but the alignments of interests it served, its relationship to political competition, and the role played by strong (Japan) versus weaker (Korea) state institutions, have differed considerably for most of the past half-century – enough so to justify the two countries' places in different categories of corruption. These contrasts reflect combinations of participation and institutions that differ from the Influence Market syndrome. They will become clearer as we look at Korea, along with Italy and Botswana, in our discussion of Elite Cartel corruption in chapter 5.

5   Elite Cartels: how to buy friends and govern people

Introduction

Sometimes corruption is less a matter of influence than of control. Where interlocking groups of top politicians, business figures, bureaucrats, military and ethnic leaders share corrupt benefits among themselves they can build networks and alliances that solidify their power and stave off the opposition. Corruption of this sort may well be highly lucrative, but it is also a strategy for forestalling political change.

These Elite Cartel practices may outwardly resemble Influence Markets: money and favors change hands, with benefits flowing to favored people and businesses. Most societies involved are relatively stable, middle-income or affluent democracies, or are well along in the consolidation process. Perceived levels of corruption, while higher than in Influence Market societies, remain lower than in Oligarchs and Clans, or Official Moguls, cases. Civil society and for accountability, while weaker than in Influence Market societies, are far from negligible.

But differences become apparent at the level of Elite Cartel countries' institutions. Political regimes have been in place for shorter periods of time, and institutions are weaker, than those of Influence Market societies. Inequality is more pronounced, and economies are more dependent upon primary exports, and thus upon global commodity markets. Leaders in these societies face political competition that is growing faster, is less institutionalized, and is thus comparatively unpredictable. Judiciaries are weak and often compromised, making contracts more difficult to enforce and property rights harder to protect. Political parties have shallow roots – often embodying contending elite followings rather than representing major segments of society – and political competition both at and between elections can be treacherous. Bureaucracies are large and permeable – in some cases, extensions of political factions – and are uncertain agents of policy implementation. Elites thus face many risks and uncertainties.

For those reasons the core function of Elite Cartel corruption is to protect, as well as to enrich, networks of higher-level elites. Deals take

89

place not only between public officials and private interests, or between political leaders and mass followers, but also among hegemonic political, bureaucratic, and business figures. The point is not to influence specific policies (although that can certainly be the immediate reward) but rather to stymie or co-opt competitors, amass enough influence to govern, and insulate economic and policy advantages from electoral and social pressures. Even where Elite Cartel corruption is extensive, the state may be neither wholly "captured" nor predatory (see, for Korea, Cheng and Chu, 2002: 57), for the emphasis is upon integrating political and economic power rather than upon giving either a decisive advantage over the other. Elite Cartel societies may have significant anti-corruption activity: indeed, the political opposition may essentially consist of those excluded from corrupt dealings, and *vice versa*. And there will be no shortage of official anti-corruption proclamations and campaigns, though often they will be used to punish dissidents or rivals rather than to pursue reform as such.

Elite Cartel corruption is centralized, organized, and relatively predictable in its scope and processes. Paradoxically, where Elite Cartels are strong the breadth or frequency of corrupt activities (difficult as such judgments are) may be somewhat reduced in favor of fewer, larger, high-level deals reflecting and sustaining elite cohesion. For these reasons among others Elite Cartel corruption can coexist with rapid economic development, at least for a time. On the democratic development side, however, the damage is significant: the point, after all, is to stave off competition, demands for accountability, and the possibility of losing power – even when the votes go the wrong way.

Elite Cartel corruption is thus an illicit substitute for weak institutions – one with potential uses to be examined in our discussion of reform in chapter 8. But it is an imperfect substitute at best, often depending upon other forces – coercion, shared group identity, or a perceived threat from without – for some of its cohesion. The political and policy alignments it sustains can become rigid and out of step with changing realities; and when Elite Cartel networks do change, it is often sharply and discontinuously. The outcome may be greater democracy – or disruption and renewed oppression.

Three cases

In this chapter I will examine Elite Cartel corruption in Italy, Korea,[1] and Botswana. In Italy two generations of political collusion, bound together by a pact to bar the Communists from power, built a multiparty electoral

---

[1] For reasons of convenience the term "Korea" refers here to the Republic of Korea, or South Korea.

hegemony anchored by the Christian Democratic Party that extended into the bureaucracy and business as well. Elections and governments came and went, often in quick succession, but networked elites fed upon, and provided political cover for, extensive illicit dealings. Italy experienced significant, if uneven, economic development, but a weak yet heavy state resisted reform. When change came early in the 1990s, the old party system collapsed. In Korea an elite network led by the President, but including top business and military figures (many of whom came from a particular region of the country), practiced "money politics" with a vengeance. Democratic pressures were headed off while access to capital and foreign exchange went to businesses that paid "quasi-taxes" to presidents and their pet projects. Parties were weak and shifting organizations, usually the personal creations of leading politicians. From the mid-1980s onwards, democratization and global economic liberalization placed the Elite Cartel system under new stresses, driving "money politics" to new highs. Still, Elite Cartel corruption has proven remarkably durable in Korea. In Botswana corruption has helped a modernizing traditional elite maintain its internal ties and authority. There have been significant scandals, but the elite has absorbed or seen off many political challenges. It has governed effectively and produced impressive economic growth in what was once one of the world's poorest countries. Elite Cartel corruption is by no means "functional" in itself, but it helps elites retain power. What they *do* with that power is of course a major question.

In differing ways Italy, Korea, and Botswana reflect the sorts of system characteristics discussed at the beginning of this chapter. Table 5.1 presents statistical indicators comparable to those shown for our Influence Market cases.

Italy and Botswana are established democracies, as reflected in Polity scores for 1992 and 2001, while Korea continues its democratizing path. The three countries are rated nearly identically in terms of economic liberalization ("Economic Freedom"), with Italy remaining a market-oriented society while Korea, and more notably Botswana, shifted toward the market during the decade. In all three political and economic competition are extensive. But institutional frameworks, while stronger than those found in Groups 3 and 4, are considerably weaker than those of Influence Market cases. Institutional and social capacity scores in table 5.1 range from 58.1 to 60.6, compared to 74.2 to 75.6 for Germany, Japan, and the United States. Corruption control scores, which range between 1.20 and 1.45 for the three Influence Market cases in chapter 4, fall between .33 and .80 for these three cases. The security of property rights, government effectiveness, and regulatory quality are generally

Table 5.1: *Statistical indicators for "Elite Cartel" countries*

Indicator (units/range) and source	Italy	Korea	Botswana	98-Nation median*
Polity Score 1992 (Hi = more dem./0 thru 10) **P**	10	6	9	7.0
Polity Score 2001 **P**	10	8	9	7.0
Institutional / Social Capacity 2002 (0 thru 100) **WEF**	58.1	58.6	60.6	44.7
Property Rights 2002 (Low = secure/1 thru 5) **HF**	2.0	1.0	2.0	3.0
Econ Freedom 1990 (hi = more free/0 thru 10) **FI**	7.21	6.33	5.73	5.15
Econ Freedom 2001 **FI**	7.00	7.10	7.00	6.45
TI CPI, 2003 (0–10/inverted) **TI**	4.7	5.7	4.3	6.3
UNDP Human Dev Score 2001 (0–1.00) **HDR 2003**	.916	.879	.614	.75
GDP per capita, 2001 **WB**	$24,670	$15,090	$7,820	$5,940
Corruption Control 2002 (−1.89 thru 2.39) **KKZ**	.80	.33	.76	−.22
Gov't Effectiveness 2002 (−1.64 thru 2.26) **KKZ**	.91	.84	.87	.10
Government Intervention 2001 (1 thru 5) **HF**	2.0	3.5	4.0	3.0
Government Regulation 2001 (1 thru 5) **HF**	3.0	3.0	3.0	3.0
Regulatory Quality 2002 (−2.31 thru 1.93) **KKZ**	1.15	.86	.81	.06
Voice/Accountability 2002 (−2.12 thru 1.72) **KKZ**	1.11	.63	.73	.05

*Medians for the 98 countries classified in statistical clusters (ch. 3); for TI CPI 2003, median is for the 89 countries included in the CPI and in clusters. Unless otherwise indicated, high scores indicate high levels of an attribute.

Sources:

FI = Fraser Institute **http://www.freetheworld.com/**

HDR = UNDP *Human Development Report 2003* **http://www.undp.org/**

HF = Heritage Foundation Index of Economic Freedom reports **http://www.heritage.org/research/features/index/**

KKZ = Kaufmann, Kraay, and Zoido-Lobatón, "Governance Matters III" dataset, 2002 **http://info.worldbank.org/governance/kkz2002/tables.asp**

P = Polity IV dataset, 2002 update **http://www.cidcm.umd.edu/inscr/polity/polreg.htm**

TI = Transparency International Corruption Perceptions Indexes for 2001 and 2003 **http://www.transparency.org/**

WB = World Bank Data Query online data source (GDP and population used to calculate GDP per capita) **http://www.worldbank.org/data/dataquery.html**

WEF = World Economic Forum, Yale Center for Environmental Law and Policy, and CIESIN (Columbia University), 2002 *Environmental Sustainability Index* **http://www.ciesin.columbia.edu/**

lower than for the three cases considered in chapter 4. Too much should not be made of these measures by themselves, but in these societies elites face considerable political and economic competition within a weaker framework of institutions.

Italy: politics visible and invisible

Images of Italy and its politics have long been at odds with underlying realities. Its First Republic, lasting from the end of World War Two until the early 1990s, had over fifty governments, some of them short-lived, and yet there was considerable underlying stability. A broad, if sometimes shifting, coalition of parties led by the Christian Democrats (DC) held power throughout that era, with electoral results and a roster of top political figures that was remarkably consistent over time. A "weak but heavy" state[2] intervened extensively but incoherently in the economy (Colazingari and Rose-Ackerman, 1998: 448–449). Public administration was of very low quality (Golden, 2003); laws often had little moral or practical force, tax evasion was the rule rather than the exception, and successive governments ran up massive debts. Still, Italy rose from military defeat and traditional poverty to global economic importance by the 1980s. In the Italian *partitocrazia* or "partitocracy" (Calise, 1994; Bufacchi and Burgess, 1998: 4–5) national parties dominated governments, policy, business, communications media, and much of civil society to a remarkable extent. But those parties were ineffective at such basic functions as selecting personnel for political roles, integrating citizens and their views into politics, and forming public policies (Della Porta and Vannucci, 1999, 2002). As the 1970s and 1980s wore on they became weaker as organizations too.

Corruption too was a matter of appearance versus reality. That it was extensive was never in doubt; still, the revelations of the early 1990s, in the course of the *tangentopoli* ("bribe city") scandal and *mani pulite* ("clean hands") investigations, were on a scale few had anticipated. By the time the scandals broke, *partitocrazia* and the parties themselves had been "hollowed out" by corruption and organizational decline; revelations of bribery and kickbacks would discredit major business firms and executives too. In 1994 virtually the entire political class and party system of the First Republic were swept away by voters. But the particular kind of corruption that had been practiced had given the First Republic much of

---

[2] Thanks to Paul Heywood for suggesting that term.

its *de facto* structure, contributing to its stability and accomplishments as well as to chronic weaknesses and ultimate collapse.

Italy as an Elite Cartels case

Elite Cartel corruption can bridge public and private sectors, political and economic power, and political parties. Such was the case in the *partito-crazia* of Italy's First Republic. A weak executive (Colazingari and Rose-Ackerman, 1998: 460) wrangled with a parliament whose powerful, party-dominated committees wrote legislation that was complex, vague, oriented toward local or sectoral interests, and frequently allowed wide discretion. Implementation was the task of a large, ineffective bureaucracy which, through patronage and *de facto* lines of influence, was "colonized" by the major parties (Waters, 1994: 175; Bufacchi and Burgess, 1998: ch. 4). The state's credibility suffered not only because of the gap between formal institutions and political reality, but also because of history and culture. For many Italians Catholicism or Marxism provided a more compelling framework of allegiances and values than the Constitution or the civil state (Waters, 1994: 176). In the south, organized crime was often the strongest organizing force of all. Party spoils systems extended into civil society (Golden, 2003); voluntarism, and social and political trust, were weak (particularly in the south), with traditional clientelism taking the place of more civic ties and modes of action. Indeed, Pizzorno (1993, quoted in Hine, 1995) has argued that the parties played a major role in "socializing" both elites and their clients into patterns of illegality. In the economy, many enterprises wore invisible "party labels" (Della Porta and Vannucci, 1999: 191–192, 2002: 722) and obtained credit, contracts, and favorable bureaucratic decisions on political grounds (Waters, 1994: 176). Boards of directors at times resembled caucuses of the various parties' representatives. Business and politics were increasingly fused – a good working definition of Elite Cartel corruption.

Golden (2003) argues that the parties deliberately created a system of poor governance in order to maximize the value of their bureaucratic interventions. That state of affairs might seem to be just another Influence Market case, but there are important differences. One was the weakness of the bureaucracy, as noted; another was that political interventions into that bureaucracy were systematic, continuous, and pervasive, as the notion of colonization implies, rather than discrete deals. Most important, the parties themselves engaged in extensive collusion. Electoral politics, on the surface, was strongly ideological and competitive, but in reality political risks were managed for half a century by a

DC-led coalition that shared power and a pervasive spoils system. A coalition party could lose a few parliamentary seats at the polls – though in fact electoral results remained remarkably consistent through most of the First Republic era – but still have a place at the trough (Calise, 1994; Hine, 1995: 193; Buffachi and Burgess, 1998: 5, 11, 87–88; Colazingari and Rose-Ackerman, 1998: 457–462; Della Porta and Vannucci, 1999, 2002; Della Porta, 2004). After the late 1940s the Communists (PCI) were an ineffective opposition at the national level, but their presence, along with anticipated US reaction should they win power, helped bind the coalition together and enabled it to put pressure upon business contributors (Rhodes, 1997: 66–72).

Extortion of business by party cashiers was common, though often bribes and kickbacks were given as a matter of course. Some payments were for specific benefits; more often they were informal "taxes" paid in anticipation of the protection the parties could afford, be it against the actions of the state or corrupt demands from competing politicians. Kickbacks on construction contracts of 10 percent were a *de facto* standard. Party leaders who brokered favorable decisions for businesses could expect a substantial cut. In an ordinary year during the late 1980s the DC took in around 60–65 billion Lire (approximately US$40 million), a figure that rose to around 80–85 billion Lire in election years. Of that total 16–17 billion Lire was illicit income, some of it from business speculation but much of it from bribes (Colazingari and Rose-Ackerman, 1998: 457–459). Corruption may have been made worse by "reforms" in 1974 that barred contributions from public corporations, effectively compelling parties to seek out illegal contributions (Waters, 1994; Rhodes, 1997; for a dissent see Colazingari and Rose-Ackerman, 1998: 459).

Business politicians and their clients profited personally from corruption, but through most of the First Republic corrupt revenues were used more to cement party hegemonies and elite networks than for self-enrichment (Hine, 1995: 182). Proceeds were shared among the parties, and even at times with the Communists, in order to buy cooperation; party shares of major construction contracts were often negotiated in advance. Parties carved out bailiwicks in the public, private, and Italy's large parastatal sectors roughly in proportion to their national power but also based on local and regional power bases (Golden, 2003: 189–202; Della Porta, 2004). Through a process of *lottizzazione* ("allocation") jobs at many levels, including major policy and management positions, were divided up among parties (Hine, 1995: 185; Bufacchi and Burgess, 1998: 95). Della Porta (2004) describes a similar *partitizzazione* (partitioning) process for appointments in the public bureaucracy that extended party-based clientelism.

The real political competition took place behind the party façade among political factions increasingly dominated by business politicians (Della Porta and Vannucci, 1999, 2002; Della Porta, 2004). The pre-1993 party-list system, in which voters expressed preferences among various candidates, exacerbated intra-party contention by forcing competition among politicians of the same party. Campaign finance was channeled through the parties legally and through faction leaders illicitly. Competing factions bought support with extensive local patronage (Moss, 1995; Golden, 2003: 198–204), further driving up the appetite for cash (Golden and Chang, 2001; Della Porta, 2004). Factions and the distribution of spoils extended across party lines (Della Porta, 2004) as a way of minimizing the risks of losing office. Left–right distinctions became mostly *pro forma*; broad policy initiatives were absent and would have had little credibility. Elections served to preserve the status quo and to define the parameters of the next rounds of *lottizzazione*, rather than to oust ineffective governments or reward success. At times, the DC coalition functioned almost as a national "super-party" (Della Porta and Vannucci, 2002: 726).

Corruption ultimately led to the downfall of the First Republic. But in other ways the elite linkages it reflected and sustained were the skeleton and nerves of the system. Corruption eased conflict, controlled the scope and risks of electoral competition, and made unworkable laws and agencies at least somewhat effective. It both thrived upon, and partially compensated for, the weakness of state institutions, political parties, and popular allegiances. Italians would have been better served by genuinely competitive parties rooted in real social interests, and by a less-politicized economy. But given the weakness of the state and the persistence of factionalism it is unclear how real those alternatives were.

Secret networks and failed reforms

Corruption has long been a fact of Italian life (Waquet, 1996, discusses the sixteenth and seventeenth centuries; on corruption as a continuing presence in the post-World War Two era see Chang and Golden, 2004). The practices that ultimately led to *tangentopoli* and *mani pulite*, however, were of relatively recent origins. Much of the wrongdoing in the early First Republic was non-systematic and relatively modest in scale; one of the most notable 1960s scandals revolved around the import and sale of bananas, for example. Beginning with the "petrol scandal" of 1973, however, corruption grew dramatically in frequency and scope, and became more systematic (Hine, 1995: 185–186; Rhodes, 1997: 56; Della Porta and Vannucci, 1999; Golden and Chang, 2001: 595).

The rapid rise in oil prices that began in that year spurred laws aimed at energy conservation, the development of alternative energy sources (particularly nuclear), and limiting price increases. All were threats to petroleum refiners and marketers, and Unione Petrolifera, their business association, went on the offensive by paying bribes (*tangenti*) to the governing parties. ENEL, the state electricity combine, engaged in similar activities. Some of that money reached party treasuries, but more stayed with party leaders and top bureaucrats.

While investigations revealed bribery reaching higher into the party and state hierarchies than many had realized, the scandal might have been "more of the same, only more so" had it not been for the reform response. In 1974 Law number 195 (also boosted by revelations of bribery by Lockheed, which sought to sell C-130 military transports to Italy) outlawed contributions from public-sector corporations to parties and instituted a new combination of public funding and disclosure of private contributions. But the public funding was vastly inadequate, voluntary private contributions were low, as always, and disclosure was widely ignored. Moreover, the law did not change Italy's longstanding policy of parliamentary immunity to criminal prosecution. Deprived of legitimate funds from public corporations, faced with insufficient public and private contributions, and guaranteed immunity, party and faction leaders turned to illicit funding. Many observers date the expansion and increasing organization of corruption in Italy from this legislation (Hine, 1995: 185–186, 191; Rhodes, 1997: 56–65; Golden and Chang, 2001: 595–597; Pujas and Rhodes, 2002: 745; Golden, 2003: 208–209).

The activities of Michele Sindona and the P2 Masonic Lodge in the 1970s and early 1980s revealed extensive links between corruption and violence, implicating not only organized crime but also terror cells and state security forces. Sindona was an international private banker whose fortune was built partially upon political bribery and shady capital, and partly upon his role as the Vatican's banker. When his empire collapsed in 1978 he was jailed and his businesses went into liquidation. The official overseeing that process was murdered, however, and Sindona himself died in prison under suspicious circumstances – a suicide, according to security forces. A series of political murders during the late 1970s raised further suspicions, as did investigations of the P2 Masonic Lodge, a largely secret body whose membership included not only police, security, and party officials, but also suspected fascists. P2 was implicated in the 1982 collapse of Banco Ambrosiano, Roberto Calvi's financial conglomerate, which also involved suspicious deaths and had financial repercussions reaching from London to the Vatican. Subsequent tax scandals, the murder of an investigating journalist, and oil-related bribery and kickbacks were also linked to P2. In the end almost a thousand people, including politicians, security officials, and top business figures were linked to secret networks practicing corruption and violence (Hine, 1995: 186–187; Della Porta and Vannucci, 1999: 168–170).

Larger and more systematic *tangenti* became common during the 1980s. Italy's economy included major state-owned enterprises, as well as a range of public–private joint ventures, that often competed with private businesses; many enterprises had been colonized by political parties. Moreover, *partizzazione* of the bureaucracy among the governing parties continued apace. The results were often complex financial dealings, legal and otherwise, among convoluted networks of bureaucrats, party officials, and "business politicians." ENI, the state hydrocarbon enterprise, had become a kind of subsidiary of the Socialist Party (PSI) by the end of the 1970s; yet it helped bankroll all major parties (at times in conjunction with ENEL) through kickbacks exceeding 1 billion Lire annually. In the chemicals sector the Montedison and Enimont combines, along with ENI, shuffled major assets between state and private hands, aided by payments as large as 75 billion Lire to Socialist leader Bettino Craxi and 35 billion to DC Secretary Arnaldo Forlani. The result was a lucrative nationalization of chemical production while most competing countries were pursuing privatization. In Milan, contractors building a new Metro line were assessed at 4 percent of the value of their contracts, payments shared among political parties in proportions agreed in advance (Rhodes, 1997: 68–70; Colazingari and Rose-Ackerman, 1998; Della Porta and Vannucci, 1999: 97–99).

Tangentopoli, mani pulite, *and the fall of the First Republic*

The scandal that ultimately brought down the First Republic began with a single arrest in Milan, but ultimately reflected the rise of a new generation of judges in the late 1980s, political fissures revealed by the 1992 general election, and Italy's changing place in the European and world economies (this discussion draws upon Hine, 1995, 1996; Buffachi and Burgess, 1998; Burnett and Mantovani, 1998; Della Porta and Vannucci, 1999, 2002; Della Porta, 2004). The young jurists combined a new commitment to fighting corruption with the considerable powers and independence of the Italian judiciary, and used such tactics as extended detention without trial to extract information from suspects. The 1992 elections – the country's first since the fall of communism (Pasquino and McCarthy, 1993; Buffachi and Burgess, 1998: chs. 2, 3) – revealed the weakness of *partitocrazia*. The old PCI had become the Democratic Party of the Left (PDS), depriving the DC-led coalition of the symbolic threat that was part of its *raison d'être* (Waters, 1994: 180). Anti-coalition parties won nearly 32 percent of the vote, while the DC, which had never won an outright majority, fell below 30 percent (Buffachi and Burgess, 1998: 41) and unusually large numbers of voters stayed home.

Tangentopoli and *mani pulite* began quietly enough: an investigation in Milan led to the arrest of Mario Chiesa, a mid-level PSI figure, on charges of receiving bribes while managing a state-run senior citizens facility. Luca Magni, a small business operator weary of paying kickbacks on cleaning contracts, had gone to the police with his evidence. Chiesa was jailed, refusing at first to cooperate with investigating judges, but perhaps because of pressure from his wife, who was making an issue of Chiesa's inexplicable wealth in the course of divorce proceedings, he began to talk. Soon the judges had solid evidence of a network of bribery, business politicians, bureaucrats, and inter-party collusion running right through city and regional government. Surprisingly large numbers of businessmen gave evidence to the judges, implicating others who then found it prudent to talk in order to avoid (or shorten) imprisonment. Judges filed 228 requests for waivers of parliamentary immunity – a necessary first step in investigating any sitting member – in connection with over 600 crimes; eventually parliament accepted 111 of those requests. Major bureaucrats were likewise investigated, tried, and jailed. Judges in effect decimated the nation's political class and their networks of corruption. Voters helped too: in March, 1994, they effectively ended the First Republic by voting the old party system out of existence. The results were partially shaped by 1993 electoral reforms ending the party-list/"preference vote" system and party-based financing arrangements that had made party cashiers and factional leaders so powerful, but they were also a massive rejection of the old political elite (Golden, 2002: 4).

Why the sudden collapse? One answer is that it was not so sudden at all. In part because of corruption, the parties had been faltering electorally and organizationally for a generation. By the 1990s party memberships had fallen by half or more (Della Porta and Vannucci, 2002; Della Porta, 2004), ideology and policy commitments had given way to mercenary motivations, and "business politicians" were extending their dominance. Parties had to buy services and loyalty they had once commanded on ideological grounds, thereby driving up the cost of politics and the need for sizeable kickbacks (Della Porta and Vannucci, 1999, 2002; Della Porta, 2004). They were not only more vulnerable in the open political arena; behind the scenes party leaders were less able to serve as guarantors for corrupt deals or provide protection for those involved. Economic changes further weakened the corrupt system: Golden (2002) argues that gradual reductions in state spending, under pressures from the EU and global economic trends, were drying up the pool of patronage that had sustained corrupt networks (see also Guzzini, 1995). Party cashiers were demanding ever larger sums from business people who found it harder to pay, and all but the most prosperous began to drop out of the game. Most business people who talked to the judges were second-rank figures or lower (Golden, 2002: 49); the bribe-payer whose testimony started the *tangentopoli* avalanche ran a local cleaning service in Milan. The young judges' new aggressiveness contributed to the collapse of a system that had been hollowed out over two decades.

Holding the deals together

Parties had been critical to Elite Cartel corruption not only because of the state benefits they could distribute, but also because they were the guarantors of the deals that built and sustained elite networks. Those networks were highly factionalized and contentious, but they shared an interest in retaining the political power that was the source of all good things. Collusion was sustained by corrupt deals. But given their illegality, and the low levels of trust that often existed among factions and their leaders, how could those deals be enforced?

While corruption was scarcely a secret, the illusion of electoral competition was important, and the constitutional independence of the Italian judiciary meant that specific deals and spoils-sharing agreements had to be concealed. Pizzorno (1993) argues that the parties functioned much like credit bureaus, providing information on the dependability of various politicians and factions. They also enforced *de facto* codes of silence and honor; those who revealed abuses or failed to carry out their end of a deal could be dropped from the party list, cut out of the spoils, or handed over to the judiciary – the latter, perhaps, even doing the party's image some good. Parties also negotiated the terms of *lottizzazione* and shares of contracts, again reducing conflict and penalizing defectors. At times political notables were recruited, and paid, to serve as enforcers and monitors of corrupt agreements (Della Porta and Vannucci, 1999, 2002: 723). In the south, the role of enforcer was often taken over by organized crime.

Such machinations helped DC elites and their partners share the spoils and hold on to power, but they also diverted energy and resources from the parties' broader political functions. Memberships declined; those who remained active did so for mercenary reasons, or out of loyalty to a patron, rather than to fight for a cause. The parties became less rooted in organic segments of society and on the left–right spectrum, and more like overlapping bands of business-politicians. In effect they became "cartel parties" in which state and party extensively interpenetrated while real competition withered away (Katz and Mair, 1995; Rhodes and Pujas, 2002). When change came it was abrupt and devastating; interlocking networks of mutually guaranteed deals may have helped control electoral competition for quite some time, but they were poorly adaptive in the face of accumulating pressures for more basic political and economic change. Variations on that theme also became apparent a few years later in Korea's economic crisis, as we shall see.

In several respects Elite Cartel corruption in Italy may seem a reprise of Japan. Major business payments to parties in exchange for policy favors sustained an electoral hegemony that lasted nearly half a century. The two countries' dominant parties eventually suffered unprecedented electoral defeats at about the same time. But the similarities are limited. Italy's bureaucracy was not nearly as autonomous or effective as Japan's, and its business sector was dominated by political parties to a far greater extent. In this sense the reach of money politics was more pervasive than in Japan (Buffachi and Burgess, 1998: 85). The LDP dealt in access to a strong, autonomous bureaucracy, but Italian parties permeated the state such that bureaucrats and state agencies were often the intermediaries *between business and the parties* (Waters, 1994: 171; Della Porta, 2002: 721–722). Italian parties took advantage of the weakness of the state, but the DC stayed in power only through extensive collusion with the PSI and other parties, making use of a Communist opposition whose threat was more illusory than real. When the LDP lost it was in an election, and via the electoral system the party was back in power within a year. When the DC-led party cartel collapsed, the First Republic and its entire political class collapsed with it.

In fact the political implosion of 1992–4 illustrates some implications of Elite Cartel corruption. Elite networks based on corruption may be informal substitutes for state, political and social institutions, but over time they can become inflexible and thereby fragile (Nelken, 1996). They are built upon deals that can be difficult to enforce. Over time, instabilities can arise: leaders may keep too large a share of the spoils, and the price of politics may rise faster than the supply of corrupt incentives. For insiders political change can (and in 1994 did) mean not just temporary defeat but the loss of everything. Thus, Elite Cartels will not necessarily adapt to new political realities or internal tensions. In the face of a major external shock – *tangentopoli*, in the Italian case – Elite Cartels may not so much bend as break.

Past tense, or present?

A decade after *tangentopoli* it is still unclear whether we should discuss Italy's Elite Cartel corruption in the past or present tense. Today's

Second Republic is dominated by media magnates and new-model candidates contending beneath different party banners. Business payments to parties declined significantly in the wake of the scandals and the costs of some public contracts dropped by half (Buffachi and Burgess, 1998: 97). European Union policies and global economic change (Guzzini, 1995) likely have contributed to the decline in state contracting that Golden (2002) argues left many middle-level and small-business operators unable to pay up, and thus willing to talk with the *mani pulite* judges. But administrative corruption persists (Golden and Chang, 2001: 622). The new electoral and party system produced results that were novel but not necessarily more decisive in terms of encouraging or rewarding good government: the first government of media baron Silvio Berlusconi, who became Prime Minister in 1994 at the head of his Forza Italia party and a center–right coalition, dissolved amidst corruption allegations before the year was out. By 2001 Berlusconi was back as Prime Minister at the head of a new coalition; in late 2004 he was acquitted in a Milan court of a bribery charge dating from the 1980s, and another charge was dismissed (*New York Times*, December 10, 2004), but this is scarcely a new era of genuinely clean hands. Reforms could not change the underlying culture of clientelism or, by themselves, strengthen the state or civil society (on the latter point, see Della Porta, 2000). Some measures, such as a tax check-off intended to fund individual candidates' campaigns, failed outright, and subsequent measures moved back toward older practices of routing funds through the parties (Pujas and Rhodes, 2002: 747).

Reforms may have changed formal institutions and public aspects of politics and business, but Elite Cartels never depended upon those visible parts of the system alone. Deeper dynamics of Elite Cartel corruption – only moderately strong institutions and significant competition in politics and the economy – remain in place. Those factors are not just analytical abstractions: corruption in Italy has long been a systematic response to political opportunities (Kitschelt, 1986; Pujas and Rhodes, 2002) and to specific weaknesses in the state (Hine, 1995: 199). *Lottizzazione* and *partitizzazione* are ways of managing political risk. Such incentives may become all the more compelling to the extent that economic liberalization and the evolving role of the state limit the range of policy alternatives open to parties, making it harder to rebuild real social constituencies. A political culture in which the law and state have a normatively ambiguous status, boundaries between public and private (and thus, between what can and cannot be bought and sold) are indistinct, and in which private loyalties and secret societies play major roles, did not vanish with the elections of 1994 (Hine, 1995: 194–200).

Korea: "money politics" and control

Governing Korea has often been lucrative, but it has never been easy. With a "strong state" ruling over a "contentious society" (Koo, 1993: 231–249; Clifford, 1994: 11) of 48 million citizens on the southern portion of a rocky peninsula, a heritage of colonial domination and civil war, few natural resources, and a national capital just forty miles from the world's most tensely guarded border, the Republic of Korea has spent the past half-century in a state of crisis (Clifford, 1994: 7; Kang, 2002a: 50). Its successes therefore are all the more remarkable: from desperate poverty after the armistice of 1953 the country has climbed into the first rank of the world's economies. Authoritarian government backed by violence and a tightly integrated national elite kept civil society, political parties, and electoral politics weak for three decades, yet gave way to democratic forces in 1987. Out of unpromising circumstances Korea has launched an increasingly competitive and legitimate democracy, so that by now there seems little threat of a relapse into authoritarianism. Corruption has been integral to all of these developments, supporting a hegemonic elite, aiding early economic development, and exacerbating deferred economic risks and political resentments. It remains a serious concern today.

Korea's Elite Cartel corruption outwardly resembles the "money politics" seen in Japan (chapter 4). Very large payments by businesses to political elites – sometimes as "contributions" to parties or foundations, often as outright bribes – bought major policy favors. Despite Korea's many similarities to Japan, however, I will argue that its money politics was simpler, more centralized, and helped maintain tightly integrated state–business–military networks of elites. Korean corruption took place in a setting of weaker institutions, and was less a system of specific exchanges between business and political sectors than a continuous incentive system integral to rule by a political–business–bureaucratic network (Tat, 1996: 50; Moran, 1999: 582; Steinberg, 2000: 209). Elite networks included, at various times and in differing kinds of balance, top state officials (notably, presidents, their families, and their personal entourages); the heads of the *chaebols* (huge family-controlled industrial conglomerates); segments of the bureaucratic elite; and military leaders as well. These networks were bound together in part by corrupt incentives, but also by regional and family loyalties, the threat from the North, and a continuing need to stave off political and economic competition. A weak civil society and traditional attitudes toward power and authority facilitated this style of regime; so did its ability, from the mid-1970s onwards, to deliver economic development and rising living standards on a breathtaking scale.

Money politics is not the whole story of corruption in Korea: the country has more than its share of bureaucratic corruption (Kim Yong Jong, 1994, 1997), and bribery covering up shoddy construction practices contributed to the collapse of several large buildings and a major bridge in Seoul during the 1990s. Moreover, elite alliances have had their internal tensions, and as the country has changed they have evolved in important ways (Kim Joongi, 2002: 174). Since democratization began in 1987 political competition has intensified, but bureaucracies have remained only moderately effective and political parties and civil society have shown continuing weakness. Economic growth has created a business elite no longer content to be a junior partner, but has also been marked by crises – notably, but not only, in 1997. Still, the notion of Elite Cartels does help us understand the tenacity of Korea's corruption and explains its role in the country's development.

An uncertain hegemony: origins and influences

History, state, and society combined in Korea to produce regimes that until 1987 were authoritarian – at times, brutally so – yet faced continuing opposition, and an economy dominated by giant economic combines dependent for many years upon political patrons. Democratization brought an end to the worst repression, more meaningful elections, and the beginnings of strength in civil society; by 1997 an opposition candidate, Kim Dae Jung, won the presidency, and another peaceful handover of power took place after the 2002 race. Still, money politics continues, now in more competitive and costly ways, and in early 2004 Korea was embroiled in a presidential impeachment controversy.

Two historical influences, among many, stand out in this story. First, Japanese colonial rule during the first half of the twentieth century created a powerful, centralized, indeed "overdeveloped" state apparatus (Moran, 1998: 163). Chalmers Johnson (1987: 137–138) has contrasted the "soft authoritarian" style of post-war Japan with the "hard state" of pre-democratic Korea – a view of Korea that still retains some relevance. State dominance under the Japanese substantially eroded the influence of the landlord class (*yangban*), a process that was completed by wartime devastation and land reforms at mid-century. The Korea that emerged from the war had strikingly low levels of inequality – though at first it was the kind of equality that results from pervasive poverty – and a kind of government without politics in which the state, confronted by few countervailing forces, ruled by domination rather than administrative capacity.

Second, traditional attitudes including deference and a sense of duty toward higher powers fostered conformity, low levels of trust and civility, a personalized view of authority often structured by patron–client relationships, and a view of the individual as acting within a defined place in a larger social matrix. These values – more deeply entrenched than in Japan (Pye, 1997: 221) – discouraged broad social initiatives to check the state and perpetuated a "zero-sum" conception of power (Clifford, 1994: 14; Neher, 1994; Steinberg, 2000: 212–213, 221, 231; Koo, 2002: 45; Chang, 2002) in which the gains of any one person or group were seen as coming at the expense of all others. For thirty-five years, therefore, successive governments faced little sustained political opposition yet had tense relationships with society. Governments did not represent or draw upon support from society but rather contended with it, seeking to retain control (Koo, 2002: 42). Strong, if diffuse, resentments of government, and among citizens themselves, could break out in unpredictable ways. President Rhee Syng Man was toppled in 1960 by massive student demonstrations and critical news reports; Park Chung Hee, his eventual successor, held occasional elections in part to placate his American backers but his victories were not particularly decisive.

To complicate matters, many key institutions were weak. Korea has had six republics since independence in 1948, each with its own Constitution. Political parties have been organized or reconstituted by successive presidents and their rivals, rather than emerging out of ideologies or major segments of society (Park Byeog-Seog, 1995: 166). There have been over 100 active parties since 1948, and the 1990 merger of three conservative parties into the Democratic Liberal Party – an attempt to replicate Japan's LDP – did not last (Tat, 1996: 53; Cheng and Chu, 2002: 43–44). When Kim Young Sam relaunched an inherited party, *en route* to the presidency in 1992, it was the tenth different party membership of his career (Steinberg, 2000: 224–225). The national bureaucracy attracted increasing numbers of able and educated civil servants after 1960, but key segments were controlled by presidential patronage (Johnson, 1987: 154; Kang, 2002a). The military's officer corps was riven by secret societies. One – *Hanahoe*, or the "one mind society" – was powerful enough to help put Chun Doo Hwan into the presidency in 1980 (Moran, 1998: 164). For years official institutions and duties have contended, often at a disadvantage, with the influence of "blood, region, and school" (Hwang, 1997: 100) – loyalties to family and clan, to one's part of the country and the leaders who came from there, and to one's university (see also Kang, 2002a: 53–55).

Presidents could rule through the threat of force, but governing was difficult. Rhee ran Korea for over a decade in an autocratic fashion, financing his regime in part through business "contributions" (Woo, 1991: 65–69). Yet parts of his government were captured by rent-seeking business interests (Cheng and Chu, 2002: 32–33), and a short-lived alliance of students, newspapers, and opposition groups proved more than his regime could withstand in 1960. Presidents had to reward and restrain economic, administrative, and possibly military elites, and control political competitors. They would also have to attack the pervasive poverty creating a desperate and unstable social situation. Support from a strong network of supporting elites and the military was essential, and constructing that sort of network was not easy.

Bringing power and money together

"Money politics" was the usual response to this dilemma, and in this as in so much else about Korea we must examine the era of Park Chung Hee (1917–1979). Park's military career began in the Japanese army during the colonial years, and he rose to the rank of general in the Korean army after independence. He was a member of a *junta* that took power in 1961, and was elected President in 1963, 1967, and 1971 – the last time, after amending the Constitution to allow himself a third term. After declaring martial law in 1972 Park became more brutal; again the Constitution was amended to ratify and extend his powers. Park was assassinated in 1979 by the head of the Korean Central Intelligence Agency. His governments were notable for their repressive techniques, but also laid the foundations for spectacular, *chaebol*-driven economic growth (Woo, 1991; Woo-Cumings, 1999a).

Park's power rested in part on force, but also on money (this discussion draws upon Moran, 1998: 166–173, and Kang, 2002a). His early dealings with business seemed adversarial; at one point top business figures accused of profiteering during the Rhee era were arrested (Woo, 1991: 83–84) and paraded through the streets of Seoul (though promised punishments were never fully carried out). But Park quickly made favored businessmen and *chaebols* junior partners in the regime. In the early years the balance of power clearly favored Park, who favored *chaebols* on the basis of personal loyalty and success in producing growth (Cheng and Chu, 2002: 33). As Korea's dash for growth accelerated, however, the *chaebols* became integral to a growing alliance between official power and family/corporate wealth. By the 1980s political and economic power and interests were virtually unified (Wedeman, 1997a: 470; Steinberg, 2000: 216; Cheng and Chu, 2002: 33–34; Kang, 2002a: 97ff.).

"Money politics" was a powerful combination of political power and wealth that furthered both interests. It was also rather simple: *chaebols* made payments to political leaders, their parties, or their pet "foundations" and charities. During the 1980s and early 1990s, such contributions ran as large as 22 percent of net profits (Woo, 1991: 9). This immense cash flow helped maintain party and legislative organizations and rewarded key bureaucrats and military figures for their loyalty. A significant portion also underwrote the cost of *huwŏnhoe* or "personal vote" practices (Kang, 2002a: 99) – gift-giving and vote-buying similar to those seen in Japan (Park Byeog-Seog, 1995: 168–172 describes a typical National Assemblyman's political income and outlays). Some money stayed in the pockets of top politicians, although in the Park years it seems personal enrichment was secondary to building an elite network strong enough to hold power and to pursue growth (Kang, 2002a). Later, as democratization proceeded, some of the funds were slipped to opposition parties and leaders in order to keep them compliant (Pye, 1997: 220). In return for their money *chaebols* got access to capital and foreign exchange on preferential terms, light or non-existent regulation, and labor peace guaranteed by state repression. Until 1993 assets and property could be held under fictitious names or those of relatives, and money borrowed at preferential government interest rates could be re-lent at much higher rates. Favored *chaebols* pursued their own collusive economic practices such as underwriting each others' debts (Beck, 1998). These exchanges took place within political and business strata smaller and more tight-knit than Japan's; moreover, as Khan (2002: 480) notes, given the weakness of civil society there was no need to share the spoils with "intermediary classes," as was the case for many of the business-political networks of South Asia.

The resulting Elite Cartel was a device of political control. *Chaebol* leaders who did not "contribute" – or, later on, those who showed signs of political independence – not only had to seek credit on the far more expensive "curb market," but also found themselves targets for hostile and arbitrary bureaucratic and legal proceedings. Business failure was a real possibility for those who fell out of favor. Whether by calculation or as a byproduct of political control and predictability – there is disagreement on this point – elite networks built partly on corruption also proved very effective at producing economic growth (Woo, 1991). Park rewarded development "winners," making productivity and export growth important criteria for admission to the cartel.

Corruption at work: major cases

During his presidency Park Chung Hee raised large sums for his Democratic Republican Party's operations and vote-buying (estimated to have cost $40 million in the 1967 campaign). DRP officials cultivated specific firms, collecting *chaebol* contributions that came to be known as "quasi-taxes." Construction firms routinely kicked back between 2 and 10 percent of major contracts' value. Some of these funds went to Park's personal projects, such as the "New Village Movement" which nominally improved the quality of rural life but in reality was a Park slush fund. The Blue House – Korea's presidential residence – became the national clearing house for political money; during the 1970s as much as 10 billion *won* per year passed through its money machine. There is disagreement over the extent of Park's self-enrichment; during much of his era he was portrayed as resisting the temptations of money politics (Cheng and Chu, 2002: 34). After his assassination about $500,000 was discovered among Park's effects (Kang, 2002b: 188), but that sum pales by comparison to the fortunes amassed by various cronies. A side-attraction of the Park years was the revelation in the mid-1970s of major sums of political money spent in the United States by agents such as Park Tongsun (Moran, 1998: 166–173; Kang, 2002a, 2002b: 185–189; Kim Joongi, 2002: 172–175).

Kim Young-Sam, winner of the first competitive civilian presidential election, took office in 1993 with reform as a stated priority. Among his accomplishments was "real name" legislation (1993) requiring that financial and real-estate assets be held under actual owners' names. But the most important development was to investigate "money politics" under predecessor Roh Tae Woo, an inquiry that eventually included the leaders of the top thirty *chaebols* as well. Roh had taken in at least $650 million (an average of over $10 million per month), and after leaving office still had about $245 million in hand. The fund was administered by Lee Hyun-Woo, a former bodyguard and later a government intelligence official. The top four *chaebol* contributors had kicked in between $27 million and $33 million. Nine top business figures were indicted, and five convicted; Roh himself was convicted and sentenced to jail. Most sentences were suspended or reduced, but the spectacle of a once-dominant national leader on trial was a shock. Opposition leader Kim Dae-Jung (later the first opposition candidate to become President) accepted $2.6 million from Roh, and suspicions extended to, but were denied by, Kim Young-Sam as well (Park Byeong-Seog, 1995: 172–177; Moran, 1998: 573–574; Blechinger, 2000: 3–4; Steinberg, 2000: 207; Kang, 2002b: 196–197).

Former President Chun Doo Hwan was brought to trial in 1996, convicted, and condemned to death (a sentence later commuted). Corruption was not the only issue; charges included his roles in a military coup in 1979 and the Kwangju massacre of protesting students in 1980. But Chun practiced "money politics" with particular effectiveness during his presidency (1981–87). Contributions from *chaebols* and other sources ran as high as $1.2 billion, with Chun retaining $270 million; some of the proceeds went to buy off opposition figures. Those refusing to play Chun's game were punished: the Kukche conglomerate, whose chairman balked at demands for large contributions, had its credit effectively cut off, went into bankruptcy, and was sold off piece-by-piece to others who had met their political assessments. "Contributions" were demanded for the New Village Movement, the Illhae Foundation, and the 1988 Olympics. By Chun's time, however, the *chaebols* had more leverage since continued growth depended upon their success. Thus, while Chun made some moves to clean up *chaebol* business practices, his initiatives served as more of a disciplinary threat than as real reform (Pye, 1997: 220; Moran, 1998: 171; Moran, 1999: 575; Blechinger, 2000: 4; Steinberg, 2000: 207; Schopf, 2001: 698–708; Kang, 2002a: 96, 2002b: 187–188; Kim Joongi, 2002: 175–177).

Hanbo Steel, a middling *chaebol* at most, had economic – and therefore, political – ambitions, and it too paid a major price. In 1992 it contributed 130 billion *won* to Kim Young-Sam's presidential campaign, winning major favors including permission to build one of the world's largest steel mills. Hanbo's relatively modest assets would have made it difficult to borrow the needed $6 billion had it not continued to buy influence, spreading over $6 million among legislators, bankers, and officials in Kim's administration. Delays raised the cost of construction, however, and by 1996 lenders began to withhold credit; in 1997 Hanbo declared bankruptcy. Investigations uncovered bribery and business irregularities and revealed that Kim Young Sam's youngest son, Kim Hyung-Chul, was taking substantial bribes. The son was sentenced to prison (though later released as a part of an amnesty), a profound embarrassment to the President. The Hanbo episode was a turning point of sorts: it destroyed Kim Young-Sam's reformer image, proved that *chaebols* could collapse, and also showed that democracy by itself was no barrier to corruption. If anything, Hanbo's bribery in the National Assembly showed that demo-cratization could increase the number of figures whose support had to be bought and their appetite for funds (Blechinger, 2000: 4–5; Schopf, 2001: 709–712; Moon and Kim, 2000: 153–154).

The Alsthom case illustrated the role of regional loyalties in the oper-ation of Elite Cartels. Over the years Kyongsang province, in southeastern Korea, has been a privileged place: many top political, bureaucratic, and economic figures hail from there, and they have looked after each other and the folks at home. It was no surprise when Seoul announced in the 1990s that the nation's first high-speed rail project would link the capital with Pusan, one of Kyongsang's major cities. Five rounds of bidding left a

German firm the likely winner of a $2.1 billion contract to provide locomotives and rolling stock, but on the final round the French combine Alsthom won. Investigations revealed large bribes and lobbying expenditures; Ho Ki-Chun, wife of Alsthom's Korean branch manager, was charged with receiving nearly $4 million, and a Los Angeles lobbyist named Choi Man-Sok put his connections in Seoul and Kyongsang to work for a commission of $11 million. The locomotives produced by Alsthom eventually proved unable to perform up to standard (Blechinger, 2000).

Predictability – at a price

Corruption not only enriched key figures in politics, the bureaucracy, and business, but also helped protect their sometimes shaky hegemony. In economic development terms the result was both early benefits and deferred costs. Corruption integrated political and business elites into durable and extensive networks of reciprocities (Cheng and Chu, 2002: 34). Those who cooperated could win power, become wealthy, and reduce political and economic uncertainties for themselves and their followers or businesses. Those who did not could be punished or frozen out. Particularly during the Park years government-aided, *chaebol*-driven growth enabled Korea to lay down an industrial and trade foundation and exploit niche opportunities in international markets. Cheap capital and labor costs and light regulation were available to those who paid up, and the biggest favors flowed to successful exporters. Investors both foreign and domestic could depend upon political continuity.

By the 1980s several *chaebols* had become global economic powers, but capital for diversification, a predictable business environment, and checks upon "excessive competition" still bore price tags. Policy remained politicized and new competitors faced major barriers. As Korea shifted to a more mature economy and took on more global competitors the drawbacks of that strategy became more apparent. Overcapacity and overextension of *chaebols*' product lines were rewarded; environmental and labor regulations were weak and poorly enforced. Corporate governance was opaque (Beck, 1998), with many *chaebols*' balance sheets existing mostly in the minds of family executives. The practice of underwriting each others' loans turned corporate debt – which often exceeded assets by spectacular margins – into a house of cards. These accumulating risks added to Korea's troubles during the 1997–8 Asian crisis.

In politics too Elite Cartel corruption bought predictability but raised problems for longer-term development. Before the transition of 1987 state officials ran dictatorial regimes yet faced periodic challenges to their power; afterwards electoral competition gradually increased. In either phase building a power base while staying within the rules was a doubtful proposition: parties were weak and personalized, society was poorly organized and fractious, and political elites were guided more by personal, regional, and family loyalties than by official duties or policy commitments. Elite Cartel corruption solidified power but reinforced those systemic problems. It likely helped Korea maintain order through the difficulties of political transition, and provided elites with predictability in the early years of the new regime. Business–political–bureaucratic networks evolved over time (Kim Joongi, 2002: 174ff.): as the *chaebols* grew their power within the elite stratum increased, but they never became dominant over the top political figures (Kang, 2002a). Sharing political money with opposition leaders was a way to pacify them in the short term and to accumulate damning evidence for use later on. But building broad-based, competitive electoral politics proved a slow process, and both credible anti-corruption reform (as opposed to spectacular trials of past presidents) and creating a strong civil society remain challenges a generation after the transition.

Much as Elite Cartel corruption enabled Italy to realize impressive growth despite a blocked political system and only moderately effective official institutions, Korea's particular style of corruption likely aided the economic takeoff and underwrote a measure of political continuity through the democratic transition and the aftermath of the 1997–8 economic crisis. This does not mean that corruption is inherently beneficial: particularly in the long run, as chapter 2 shows, the evidence runs strongly to the contrary. Moderate economic policy changes, and measures for political and corporate accountability, that might have staved off the worst of the economic meltdown were not implemented in Korea. The logic of Elite Cartels – rather than aggregate amounts of corruption – preempted economic and political adaptation, turning the need for a variety of small changes into an eventual systemic crisis.

Cheng and Chu's notion (2002: 57) of a state that, in Korea's authoritarian phase, was "neither predatory nor captured," raises one final issue: because of its internal logic Korean corruption might have been self-limiting in important respects (see also Kang, 2002a). Both accounts suggest that those who are strong enough to form cartels are also in a position to check excesses that might undermine their advantages. But the question is complex: if by limits to corruption it is meant that overall amounts were restricted we would need somehow to guess how much corruption would otherwise have occurred – an exercise that is conjectural at best. But limits could also refer to the scope of corruption – who could participate – or to the kinds of practices involved, and here the case is stronger. Elite Cartel corruption included a few people while excluding many more in part because limits upon economic – and later, political – competition were a major purpose of the whole process. Had policy benefits been spread much more broadly they would not have been worth the large prices they commanded. While the vehicles of corruption – foundations, charities, and the like – did change, and the amounts of money grew considerably, Korean corruption stayed focused upon a relatively narrow stratum. Those sorts of limits distinguish Korea's case both from more open Influence Markets and from many of the wilder practices we will consider in later chapters.

Just another Japan?

Korea's past and present are closely intertwined with Japan's (Tat, 1996: 545). "Money politics" in Korea outwardly resembles that of Japan too. Yet the two countries fall into different clusters in our statistical analysis (chapter 3), and the argument here is that they embody differing corruption syndromes. Is there really such a difference?

I argue that there is a difference, less of form – practices of corruption – than of function: the sort of response corruption embodies to deeper dynamics of participation and institutions. ("Function" as used here should not be confused with the old claims that corruption was "functional" for development.) In Korea as in Japan "money politics" was a critical prop to the regime; but Pye (1997: 214, 228) argues that the implications of such processes depend upon the kinds of elite networks and agendas that are being sustained. Japanese political figures positioned themselves as middlemen between business interests and farmers, on the one hand, and a strong, remote bureaucracy on the other. Influence dealing of that sort helped the LDP build an electoral monopoly lasting forty years. In Korea, by contrast, the stakes of money politics were not just specific decisions but also the power and sustainability of the regime. Japan's LDP, while a hegemonic and factionalized party, has a real base in society; it also encompassed significant electoral competition – the source of considerable corruption – and its 1993 defeat, while spectacular, was temporary.

Until the 1990s Korea's regimes did not, and could not, depend upon popular support in the LDP manner, even if rising living standards backed up by the threat of coercion kept most citizens compliant. Power in Korea was won and exercised within a comparatively small elite stratum (Hwang, 1996: 319; Tat, 1996: 545) rather than by building a base in society at large. Political challenges were episodic, difficult to predict, and potentially disruptive. Economic competition was a threat to the thirty or so *chaebols* that dominated the economy. In both instances it was the unpredictability of such challenges, more than their absolute strength, that was unsettling; Elite Cartel corruption was a way to buy or rent predictability at a systemic level.

Present and future

Scandals and corruption continue to be facts of life in Korea (Ha, 2001: 33–34), and top political figures, including recently departed President Kim Dae Jung, continue to be viewed with suspicion (French, 2003). But now political competition has broadened in scope, civil society has become stronger (Koo, 2002; Steinberg, 2000), and since 1997 *chaebol* and banking reform have gained considerable momentum (Cho Juyeong, 2004; Cho Myeong-Hyeon, 2003; Woo-Cumings, 1999b). Presidential elections now are civilian affairs; in 1997 Kim Dae Jung, who not only was an opposition leader but hailed from the long-neglected Cholla region, was elected President. The 2002 presidential elections led to another peaceful handover of power – indeed, at the inauguration of Roh Moo Hyun, in February 2003, the disgraced former Presidents Chun and Roh Tae Woo made rare public appearances, perhaps to symbolize continuity. Korean democracy is still a work in progress; by early 2004 Roh was embroiled in an impeachment effort which he survived, thanks to favorable election results (Brooke, 2004) and a subsequent Constitutional Court ruling that while he had violated laws removal from office was not warranted.

Elite Cartel corruption survives in this new setting (Moran, 1999; Steinberg, 2000: 210–211; Kang, 2002b: 193–198), but change is visible too, not all of it reassuring. As in Italy Elite Cartels need ways to guarantee corrupt deals and control factional conflict (Wedeman, 1997a: 474; Schopf, 2001: 708). Coordination was aided by the fact that in Korea's relatively small elite stratum (Tat, 1996: 545; Kang, 2002b: 201) the spoils only had to be divided so many ways. For four decades after independence force was integral to the process too. But democratization has eroded the military presence in politics, enlarged the political elite, and created more divisions and competition within it. The result has hardly been an end to corruption: if anything, the Hanbo case showed that now more officials might have to be bribed, while their ability to deliver is less clear. Democracy strengthened the hand of business while making politicians and the state less effective as risk guarantors (Cheng and Chu, 2002: 57); Tat (1996: 54) sees increased business initiative in offering bribes as one result.

Competitive politics has raised the costs of campaigns, driving demands for cash upwards. Kang (2002b: 195) reports estimates of 200–300 billion *won*, or $266–400 million, for the total expenditures in the 1981 National Assembly election, compared to more than 1 trillion *won* (about $1.3 billion) for the 1996 campaign; total presidential campaign expenditures were estimated at 443 billion *won* ($590 million) in 1987, and 2 trillion *won* ($2.7 billion) in 1997. The 1997 presidential total is roughly on a par with all federal election expenditures in the United States – which has over five times Korea's population – in 2000. Some of these increases reflect the growth of Korea's economy and population, and inflation is a factor too. Moreover, not all of this money came from business; some was raised through legitimate contributions, and other funds have been corruptly diverted from the national budget over the years (Park Byeog-Seog, 1995: 175–176). But pressure upon business for contributions has intensified (Moran, 1999: 573) and businesses will still pay to reduce political uncertainties (Root, 1996: 167–168).

Can Elite Cartel corruption continue on such a scale? There are reasons to think it cannot. Lobbying activities recognizable in any democracy have become more common (Park Byeog-Seog, 1995: 183). As parties and civil society become stronger, political uncertainties may become more manageable: real competition would bring risk of defeat, but a strong electoral system would guarantee opportunities to win future elections. Democracy could weaken the force of clientelism (Kim Joongi, 2002: 184–185) and clan ties may give way to more fluid political competition. Global competition and international pressures to improve both public- and private-sector governance may make *chaebols* less able to pay (and to conceal) the price of political influence, and the state less able to maintain politically protected lending markets and policy favors.

If Elite Cartel corruption should break down, however, the alternative will not be no corruption. Korea might become more like Japan and other Influence Market societies. For that to happen institutions would have to continue to strengthen while the economic and political competition would need to become more predictable. Such trends seem likely and, in the case of institutional development, are already underway. But if those changes are derailed, key figures in a less-unified elite may turn to personal followings, influence within their own segments of the state and economy, and perhaps even violence to protect their interests. While that seems a less likely scenario, our case discussion of Mexico in chapter 6 will suggest that Elite Cartel corruption can change in some very worrisome ways. Governing Korea is a changed task early in the twenty-first century, but that does not mean it has become easy.

Botswana: an Elite Cartel success story?

Nowhere is the need to understand contrasting syndromes of corruption quite as urgent as in Africa. In the face of both continuing scandals and numerous proclamations of reform, and of the political and economic damage corruption can work, it is too easy to ignore qualitative contrasts (Boone, 2003, spells out many variations among African states and their relationships to society). Thus, we are often told that there is something distinctive about "African corruption" (often contrasted to Asian cases) and that there is an immense amount of it. The latter may well be true, but there are variations; the former, while an attractive *ex post* explanation for African troubles and Asian development (Sindzingre, 2005), is unproven. A look at Botswana's Elite Cartel corruption, and at its relatively successful record of development and self-government over the past two generations, makes it clear that we need to re-examine both assertions.

Cattle, diamonds, and tradition

Botswana's 1.6 million citizens are scattered across a dry but diamond-rich land nearly the size of Texas. At independence in 1966 it was one of the world's ten poorest societies; in the decades since, however, it has consistently ranked among the fastest-growing economies (Good, 1992, 1994; Danevad, 1995; Samatar and Oldfield, 1995; Tsie, 1996). Cattle and diamonds have enabled Botswana to climb into the middle-income ranks, and indeed the country has at times experienced social strains resulting from growth (Good, 1992: 69). Indices show that it is widely regarded as an African anti-corruption success story: while measurement issues are as intractable in Botswana as anywhere else, relatively effective state and social institutions apparently help keep the problem under control (Good, 1994). So do political loyalties of several sorts: leaders committed to national development (Rotberg, 2004: 15), with traditional roots in society but also drawn together by corrupt incentives, have been able to govern effectively.

Botswana is of interest not so much because of its amount of corruption – although the country did experience some significant scandals in the early and mid-1990s – but rather because it illustrates both the Elite Cartels syndrome and a case that differs from typical images of Africa. Corruption in Botswana has helped interlink elites in the face of increasing political competition and market activity, and in a setting of only moderately strong institutions. That security, in turn, has helped a development-minded leadership produce rapid and sustained economic growth (Tsie, 1996), a pattern found in Korea. And like pre-*tangentopoli*

Italy, corrupt deals underwrite multiparty political linkages dominated by a core ruling elite (Good, 1992, 1996; Holm, Molutsi, and Somolekae, 1996). If Botswana's corruption has been less pervasive than that of Korea and Italy it reflects similar underlying dynamics of participation and institutions.

A modernizing traditional elite

Cattle breeding, grazing, and marketing not only were the basis of the Botswana economy for many years; they also reflected and perpetuated the influence of local chiefs who exercised considerable social power at the local level, resolved disputes, and dominated village and rural economies (Good, 1992: 69–72). After independence many of those notables became the core of an effective, if paternalistic, political elite – one in which traditional relationships built up through the cattle trade carried over to government and the emerging national economy (Good, 1992: 74; Samatar and Oldfield, 1995: 653). That elite governed with a legitimate authority and an open style (Holm, 2000). Client networks extending to local levels of Botswana's relatively small society enabled elites to extend their influence, gather information, and carry out policy. They became an adaptive and responsive political class, reacting effectively to emerging challenges – more so, in many ways, than their Italian and Korean counterparts – but retaining autonomy that helped it govern. Despite a measure of contention among elite factions, the Botswana Democratic Party (BDP) continues to be the nation's dominant political organization, even though other parties have gradually increased their support.

The elite political style has long been paternalistic; still, the BDP manages to accommodate a range of interests in policymaking and is skilled at containing political contention over many issues (Good, 1992: 85; Danevad, 1995: 381–382, 393, 400). During the 1990s, for example, bureaucrats were able to implement rangeland privatization policies effectively in the face of divided public opinion because competitive local political processes both helped legitimate the process and produced support for the sorts of results the bureaucrats sought (Poteete, 2003). Even potential crises have been turned to the BDP's advantage. In the early 1980s, for example, a temporary slump in the world diamond market threatened a major source of economic development. The government responded with a variety of grants and subsidies; the program was generally well designed and administered, and targeted to real entrepreneurs, but also effectively rewarded the political loyalties of a range of business leaders and rural communities (Danevad, 1995: 390–393).

As in many patronage systems such considerations at times spilled over into corruption. Misappropriation of $15 million intended to provide school supplies occurred when a politically connected firm lacking prior experience in that field was given major contracts. Illegal land sales, fraud in the construction and allocation of housing in and around Gaborone, the capital, and a near collapse of the Botswana Cooperative Bank all involved corrupt dealmaking among elites. The board of the National Development Bank, dominated by bureaucratic protégés of top ministers, turned a blind eye to lax lending, land-titling, and debt collection procedures in a variety of programs benefiting ministers and their allies (Good, 1994: 500–516). During the early and mid-1990s a series of presidential commissions of inquiry were created to look into corruption, and a new corruption control agency, the Directorate of Corruption and Economic Crime (DCEC) was eventually created (Frimpong, 1997).

Hegemonic corruption

The 1990s scandals involved significant misappropriation of resources, and did little good for Botswana's image. But they did not produce anything like a crisis for the system: public protests were broad-based but not confrontational. Opposition parties continued to gain strength, in part through public reactions to corruption. Politics remained largely non-ideological, and the official response to the scandal – presidential commissions, the DCEC – in a sense reflected the same patterns and agendas that had shaped politics since independence.

Botswana, like several other countries in the Elite Cartels group, is a democracy with competitive elections, dominated by a core elite whose legitimate and illegitimate dealings maintain cooperation while controlling political competition. It would not be accurate to say that corruption has been "functional" for Botswana, even given its economic successes. Instead – as in Korea – corruption helped a paternalistic elite stay in power and pursue goals that were development-oriented. The stability and predictability that followed, along with considerable external backing, enabled Botswana to take advantage of liberalizing trends and opportunities in a way that many of its neighbors have not.

Conclusion

In thinking about Elite Cartel corruption, it is tempting to fall into two traps. The first is to conclude that it is a benign, or even beneficial, form of corruption. The second, perhaps less likely, is to emphasize the relative simplicity of corrupt practices – "money politics" exchanges, for example, or sharing of spoils among cartels of party leaders – while understating the complexity of the elite networks that are built up, and of the political and economic implications for society.

Neither view is supported by these cases. While Elite Cartels can compensate for weaknesses in official institutions – an idea with possible reform potential, explored in greater detail in chapter 8 – they are built and maintained, first and foremost, to protect the interests of their members. That those elites and interests may be growth-oriented, as in Korea and Botswana, only reinforces the point: it was not corruption as such that produced growth, but rather an elite whose policies were solidified and made credible in corrupt ways. Others practicing similar corruption might pursue very different agendas. Even when policies are relatively effective the networks backing them up are less likely to adapt to changes, crises, or new opportunities than will genuinely open and well-institutionalized systems. Instead, they will more likely protect the status quo. Corrupt networks can thus help launch positive trends where formal institutions are too weak to do so, but over time they can ossify, or gradually be hollowed out if private partners begin to see alternatives to constantly footing the bill. Eventually such systems, unable to bend, may well break.

Second, maintaining Elite Cartels is not simple. Italy and Korea under-went sequential political and economic transitions: Italy democratized and then developed its economy, while Korea did the reverse. Botswana, a smaller and more organic society, was able to do both more or less simultaneously. In all three societies Elite Cartel corruption helped create makeshift institutions strong enough to manage change. But in Italy and Korea those alignments are undermined by regional differences, factional rivalries, and the unenforceability of corrupt deals. Botswana's elites face a somewhat simpler situation because of their roots in a smaller, more homogeneous society, but they have also been more successful in using political patronage and carefully crafted policies to maintain their base of support. They have thus avoided both the "zero-sum" style of inter-group relations noted in Korea and the low levels of social trust and unwieldy inter-party settlements of Italy. But dealmakers in Elite Cartel systems have a continuing need for guarantors, face an unknown potential for internal competitors or external developments to disrupt their bases of support, and – unlike election losers in a more open and institutionalized democracy – risk total defeat. Like Elite Cartel politics, the aftermath will have much to do with which sorts of interests and elites are there to pick up the pieces.

The countries in this category have weak institutions compared to Influence Market cases, but strong ones when viewed from the vantage-point of many other societies. Growth in political and economic participation has been significant yet orderly. But when rapid democratization and economic liberalization occur in a setting of very weak institutions, corrupt but durable elite networks are far more difficult to sustain. In their place we are likely to find pervasive insecurity and an economically ruinous, even violent scramble: one in which faction leaders can neither make solid alliances nor gain a decisive advantage, and in which political and economic gains are continually at risk. That is a good description of the Oligarchs and Clans syndrome of corruption – the focus of chapter 6.

6 Oligarchs and Clans: we are family – and you're not

Introduction: high stakes, insecurity, and personal power

Oleg Deripaska, one of Russia's most aggressive *biznis* oligarchs, had his eye on an industrial plant in the nation's Far East not long ago. He got what he wanted, not through a buyout but by bringing a low-profile legal proceeding before a friendly judge in a court thousands of miles to the west. The plant's rightful owners, knowing nothing of the case, defaulted on the judgment; equally friendly local police then helped Deripaska seize the plant (Tavernise, 2002a, 2002b; *Agence France-Presse*, 2003). In the Philippines several generations of the Lopez family – landowners, sugar producers, and political figures in the West Visayas region – saw their wealth and power rise and fall depending on who held the nation's presidency. Under Ferdinand Marcos their interests suffered – often, from "reforms" targeted at those Marcos personally opposed. After the Aquino "People Power" revolution, however, the Lopez family reinvented itself as a media conglomerate whose political connections were as essential as its satellite network (McCoy, 1993). In Mexico drug lords and their armed gangs dominate some areas, engaging in legal as well as illicit business, money laundering, and politics. Often they operate with the protection of local police.

In cases like these it is hard to distinguish among organized crime, state officials, and corrupt politicians (Leitzel, 2002: 37). A relatively small number of individuals use wealth, political power, and often violence to contend over major stakes, and to reward their followers, in a setting where institutional checks and legal guarantees may mean little. Their power is neither clearly public nor private – often, it is both – but it is definitely personal. Political and economic opportunities are great and gains can be difficult to protect; those brave (or foolish) enough to investigate or publicly oppose such dealings may pay with their lives.

Opportunity, risk, and violence

If Elite Cartel corruption is about control, the Oligarchs and Clans syndrome is about protection. Countries in this group have experienced rapid and significant liberalization of politics, economies, or both, yet their institutions and civil societies are very weak. There is much to contend over, both in the economy and in politics, but risks can be extreme and there are many unscrupulous competitors. Official powers and institutions are ineffective, unpredictable, and often up for rent. The enforceability of contracts and the security of property and investments are by no means assured; gains often must be protected by further corruption or violence, and wealth may only be secure when sent out of the country to safer havens.

Corrupt activities take place at many levels in such situations, but the most important involve a relatively small number of elites and their extended personal clans. Poverty, insecurity, and the need for protection make followers relatively easy to recruit; unpredictable competition and a climate of uncertainty, however, can make it difficult to reward and retain them, adding to the incentives to corruption and violence. The state can lose much of its autonomy, becoming just another source of protection and of corrupt incentives. Contending clans can extend across business, state agencies and political parties, law enforcement, the communications media, and organized crime, at various times conflicting with each other, colluding, or deepening their domination of economic and political bailiwicks. Such a situation is hardly promising for either democratic or economic development.

Oligarch and Clan corruption can be linked to violence. Parliamentarians, journalists, and jurists opposed to Russian corruption have been murdered; so have businessmen, party officials, and investigating journalists in Mexico, and opponents of local election fraud in the Philippines. Unpredictable contention over large stakes and the weakness of law enforcement contribute to the violence, but equally important is the inability of courts and other state institutions to resolve disputes, enforce contracts, and protect property rights (Varese, 1997: 581–590, 2001; Humphrey, 2002). Where public agencies cannot maintain such basic guarantees active markets in "protection" services emerge (Volkov, 2002). Threats of violence also play a role in disciplining followers who, after all, have a variety of options. Buying their support repeatedly is very expensive; using a bit of "muscle" on the unreliable can have valuable demonstration effects.

Elite Cartel corruption was a source of enough predictability in Italy, Korea, and Botswana to compensate, at least in some ways, for the weakness of formal institutions. But Oligarch and Clan corruption feeds upon and reinforces pervasive insecurity, and unpredictable corruption is the most damaging of all in development terms (Johnson, Kaufmann, and Zoido-Lobatón, 1998; Campos, Lien, and Pradhan, 1999). Investors are likely to insist on short-term gains rather than planning for the long haul – or will stay out of a country altogether (Keefer, 1996). Safer institutions and more sustainable returns abroad encourage capital flight. A lack of orderly development does not, however, mean an absence of politics and markets (O'Donnell, 2001); much activity will take place outside the formal system. Black-market businesses are difficult to tax, to regulate, and to restrain so that legitimate enterprises may flourish; political parties and civil society may be similarly preempted by private followings. Inefficient and undemocratic as those illicit activities may be, they can be more rewarding than legitimate alternatives. Therefore, further economic and political liberalization in the absence of strong institutions may only add more fuel to the fire (Satter, 2003). The rule of law can become a fiction in an Oligarchs and Clans setting, while the expectation of corruption and violence becomes a kind of self-fulfilling prophecy (Leitzel, 2002: 41).

Oligarchs and Clans: three cases

Russia, Mexico, and the Philippines all fit this profile in somewhat differing ways. Russia saw the fall of a dictatorial (if ossified) state and a planned economy that had sustained development in some respects while impeding it in many more. Mexico's most recent liberalization has been political: Vicente Fox's presidential victory in 2000 was the first national defeat for the Institutional Revolutionary Party (Partido Revolucionario Institucional, or PRI) since its founding seventy-one years before. But during the 1980s the state's role in the economy was cut back significantly (Levy and Bruhn, 2001: 165–179). Economic liberalization in the Philippines intensified during the early 1990s (Ringuet and Estrada, 2003: 237–239), although its pace has slowed in recent years (Montesano, 2004: 98–99); political liberalization dates from the "People Power" revolution of 1986. All three countries – Russia most of all – offer major economic opportunities based on natural resources, emergent domestic markets, and, particularly in Mexico, manufacturing. They are middle-income countries (the Philippines perhaps excepted) and their Human Development scores reflect a similar ranking. However, table 6.1 also indicates institutional weaknesses, less pronounced in Mexico (a transitional case in terms of corruption syndromes, as we shall see) but very serious in Russia. Ratings for institutional and social capacity are well below those seen in the Elite Cartel cases – not to mention those for

Table 6.1: *Statistical indicators for "Oligarchs and Clans" countries*

Indicator (units/range) and source	Russia	Philippines	Mexico	98-Nation median*
Polity Score 1992 (Hi = more dem./ 0 thru 10) **P**	6	8	0	7.0
Polity Score 2001 **P**	7	8	8	8.0
Institutional/Social Capacity (0 thru 100) **WEF**	26.8	42.1	42.2	44.7
Property Rights 2002 (Low = secure/1 thru 5) **HF**	4	3	3	3.0
Econ Freedom 1990 (hi = more free/0 thru 10) **FI**	1.51	5.59	6.46	5.15
Econ Freedom 2001 **FI**	5.00	6.70	6.20	6.45
TI CPI, 2003 (0–10/inverted) **TI**	7.3	7.5	6.4	6.3*
UNDP Human Dev Score 2001 (0–1.00) **HDR 2003**	.779	.751	.800	.750
GDP per capita, 2001 **WB**	$7,100	$3,840	$8,430	$5,940
Corruption Control 2002 (−1.89 thru 2.39) **KKZ**	−.90	−.52	−.19	−.22
Gov't Effectiveness 2002 (−1.64 thru 2.26) **KKZ**	−.40	−.06	.15	.10
Government Intervention 2001 (1 thru 5) **HF**	2.5	2.0	2.0	3.0
Government Regulation 2001 (1 thru 5) **HF**	4.0	4.0	4.0	3.0
Regulatory Quality 2002 (−2.31 thru 1.93) **KKZ**	−.30	.10	.49	.06
Voice/Accountability 2002 (−2.12 thru 1.72) **KKZ**	−.52	.17	.33	.05

*Medians for the 98 countries that could be classified in statistical clusters (ch. 3); for TI CPI, median is for the 89 countries included in the CPI and in clusters. Unless otherwise indicated, high scores indicate high levels of an attribute.
Sources:
FI = Fraser Institute **http://www.freetheworld.com/**
HDR = UNDP *Human Development Report 2003* **http://www.undp.org/**
HF = Heritage Foundation Index of Economic Freedom reports **http://www.heritage.org/research/features/index/**
KKZ = Kaufmann, Kraay, and Zoido-Lobatón, "Governance Matters III" dataset, 2002 **http://info.worldbank.org/governance/kkz2002/tables.asp**
P = Polity IV dataset, 2002 update **http://www.cidcm.umd.edu/inscr/polity/polreg.htm**
TI = Transparency International Corruption Perceptions Indexes for 2001 and 2003 **http://www.transparency.org/**
WB = World Bank Data Query online data source (GDP and population used to calculate GDP per capita) **http://www.worldbank.org/data/dataquery.html**
WEF = World Economic Forum, Yale Center for Environmental Law and Policy, and CIESIN (Columbia University), *2002 Environmental Sustainability Index* **http://www.ciesin.columbia.edu/**

Influence Market countries. Property rights, corruption control, regulatory quality, and overall government effectiveness receive mediocre to poor ratings. Ratings for voice and accountability suggest that in the Philippines and Russia, at least, the powerful are confronted by few significant countervailing forces (table 6.1).

Oligarch and Clan "corruption": complex meanings

In rapidly changing societies with shaking institutional frameworks, connections between wealth and power are very complex. Indeed, as we move from Influence Market societies into Oligarch and Clan cases it becomes more difficult to use the term "corruption" in clear-cut ways. Laws and institutions are less clear and credible, and their uses are more arbitrary; state-like functions such as protection of property and contract enforcement are often provided by private figures. Often, the key is not whether a particular action fits formal definitions of corruption devised for societies with stronger institutions, but rather how people pursue and defend economic and political gains in a setting of weak institutions, major opportunities, and significant risk.

It was with those difficulties in mind (among others) that I conceptualized corruption, in chapter 1, as a systemic problem rather than as a discrete category of behavior. This chapter will examine several such problems. For Russia I will focus upon corruption in processes of privatization and economic "reform," but those issues also require discussion of organized crime and other activities that might elsewhere be defined as private. The arbitrary and corrupt ways such "private" domains have been created is a consequence of rapid liberalization and deeper institutional weaknesses. In Mexico we will consider corruption as a force in both legitimate (oil) and illegitimate (drug) markets, as well as in the PRI political machine. In the Philippines the entrenched influence of regional landholders is partly political, but their power and the weaknesses of the state reflect deeper developmental issues and perpetuate specific kinds of corruption. Together these three cases can help us understand a syndrome of corruption quite different from those considered so far.

Russia: risky *biznis*

Corruption in Russia is pervasive, often organized along clan lines, harmful to democratic and economic development, and at times linked to violence. It is not, however, something new – nor are the *mafiyas* and politically wired entrepreneurs who make the headlines. All have been influenced by post-1991 developments, but all have roots in the Soviet past.

Russia has attempted a massive (and massively uneven) dual transition to democracy and a market economy, comprehensive assessment of which lies well beyond the scope of this discussion. I will focus instead on corruption in privatization processes, and on its links to organized crime and violence, from the fall of the Soviet system through mid-2003. That date is somewhat arbitrary, but does bring the analysis up to about the time of the arrest of Mikhail Khodorkovsky, richest of the so-called "oligarchs" – a turning point of sorts whose implications will take some time to become apparent. This first post-communist era saw a run on former state assets, first by members of the old *nomenklatura* and then by powerful oligarchs; declining state autonomy, administrative capacity, and political credibility; and a pervasive climate of insecurity – problems that encouraged further corruption and violence. While privatization issues scarcely exhaust the full range of Russian corruption, they are among the country's most significant corruption problems (Shelley, 2001; Satter, 2003), and vividly illustrate the origins and consequences of Oligarch and Clan corruption.

The sheer scope of Russian corruption is striking. Former Interior Minister Boris Gryzlov estimated state revenues lost because of organized crime at $1.57 billion for 2002, an increase of one-third over the previous year (Lavelle, 2003). In early 2002 Transparency International and the InDem (Information for Democracy) Foundation, the latter controversial in its own right because of its political ties, surveyed citizens and businesses in forty regions about experiences with corruption (Grigorian, 2003). Not surprisingly, they found considerable variation: Arkhangel'sk, Bashkortostan, Karelia, and the regions of Krasnoyarsk and Novgorod reported relatively low levels of corruption while the Altai, Volgograd, Moscow, Rostov, and St. Petersburg ranked at the top of the table. Annual bribe payments by citizens were estimated at 23 billion Rubles (approximately $752 million) in Tambov region and R22.4 billion (about $732.5 million) in Moscow, for example.[1] Business bribery in Moscow alone was estimated at nearly R230 billion (roughly $7.5 billion). Another InDem survey put corruption into comparative perspective: the $3 billion in bribes by citizens are the equivalent of about half of their income tax payments, while the $33 billion paid by businesses equaled half of the federal government's revenues in 2002. Education employees were the biggest takers on aggregate ($449 million in 2002) followed by traffic police at $368 million (Tavernise, 2003a). Irina Hakamada, Deputy Speaker of the State Duma, told a 2003 gathering

---

[1] Dollar figures based on the exchange rate of US$1.00 = 30.58 Rubles as of September 18, 2003.

of economists that Russian businesses pay an average of US$8 billion in bribes annually (Rosbalt, 2003). Such figures are guesses at best, but depict a reality qualitatively different from the cases we have analyzed thus far.

Who are the oligarchs?

"Oligarchs" is more of a popular political term than an analytical concept, and there thus is no consensus as to who does or does not belong in the category. *Forbes* magazine in 2003 estimated that there were seventeen Russian billionaires, but not all would necessarily be oligarchs (*Baltimore Sun*, November 9, 2003). Some accounts (Pribylovsky, 2003) point to four main leaders and clans within the national political and administrative elite and downplay the "financial oligarchs." Others give more credence to economic clan leaders, add Boris Yeltsin's "family" – both relatives and political insiders – to the mix (Bernstein, 2002; but Ryabov, 2003 dissents) and note a political-bureaucratic clan as well (Ivanidze, 2002). Still others point to eight or more business oligarchs and their followings (Freeland, 2000, chs. 6, 7; Hoffman, 2002).

Most lists from 2003, however, included names such as Mikhail Fridman, chair of an oil and banking consortium. Mikhail Khodorkovsky, a former Deputy Fuel and Energy Minister, became Russia's wealthiest individual through aluminum, electricity generation, and mining, and before his arrest in 2003 was emerging as an advocate of corporate transparency. Vladimir Potanin, mastermind of the "loans for shares" scheme (see below), is a banker and owns a large share of Noril'sk Nickel. Vladimir Gusinsky, former owner of the independent NTV television network, is a Putin critic who was forced to sell many of his holdings after an arrest in 2000. Oleg Deripaska was involved in the takeover of the aluminum industry in the mid-1990s. Boris Berezovsky, formerly a mathematician and Yeltsin adviser, once controlled Aeroflot and a television network and has relocated to the United Kingdom, probably to avoid investigations. Also in Britain is Roman Abramovich, a Berezovsky associate, former governor of the Chukotka region in Eastern Siberia, and former owner of Sibneft Oil. Abramovich's latest venture has been the purchase of Chelsea Football Club, now called "Chelski" by some wags. Viktor Chernomyrdin, former Soviet Oil Minister and Yeltsin-era Prime Minister, is a former CEO of, and still deeply involved in, Gazprom, the state natural-gas monopoly. Others sometimes listed as oligarchs include Mikhail Prokhorov, Viktor Vakselberg, and Rem Vyakhirev (Bernstein, 2002; Andrusenko, 2003; Arvedlund, 2003; *Baltimore Sun*, November 9, 2003). The Yeltsin "family" retains great influence: Vladimir Putin's first Presidential Decree granted criminal immunity to Yeltsin and his relatives, a move seen by many as a *quid pro quo* for their backing. Many oligarchs had careers in the Soviet-era *nomenklatura*, and built empires by pushing aside other "red bureaucrats" who dominated the early "unofficial" privatizations; their followings extend into the political, business, and criminal worlds (Satter, 2003: ch. 4).

The clans are made up of personal loyalists, opportunists, would-be tycoons, criminals, and corrupt officials. For those seeking to move up in life, economic and political opportunities outside of a clan are comparatively few and risky (Ryklin, 2003). In exchange for aiding an oligarch's schemes they receive opportunities, money, protection, and a measure of status. Andrusenko (2003) and Coalson (2003) argue that the regime itself has such a stake in the oligarchs, in the profits they can deliver and in the muscle they can use to get things done, that reform efforts from the center lack basic credibility (see also Shelley, 2001: 252).

Just how powerful business oligarchs are is a complicated question, made more so by the Putin government's legal and political offensive against Mikhail Khodorkovsky and his Yukos Oil empire in the late summer of 2003. Selective anti-oligarch initiatives continued into 2004. Those events may mark the opening of a real attack against oligarch-based corruption; conversely, Khodorkovsky's arrest may be punishment for his financing of liberal opposition parties (Mortishead, 2003; Shleifer and Treisman, 2004), or may be an attempt by state officials to cut themselves in on the economic action (Coalson, 2003; Goldman, 2003b; Handelman, 2003; Kagarlitsky, 2003; Kostikov, 2003; Tavernise, 2003b; Weir, 2003).

Oligarchs and Clans in action

How did the oligarchs acquire wealth and power, and how do they use it? More than any other the "loans for shares" episode of the mid-1990s enabled oligarchs to oust many "red bureaucrats" who had taken over industries during the early stage of privatization. In late 1994 the state was desperate for cash and for ways to jump-start private economic development. At the same time a few well-connected bankers and businessmen were looking to take over major firms and natural resources. Vladimir Potanin proposed loans to the state in exchange for the privilege of managing major shares of state enterprises. In theory the deal would end once the state repaid the loans or sold off its interests in the corporations. Not surprisingly, however, the loans were never repaid (it is unclear whether the state ever received significant new revenues, as the bankers simply lent the government's own deposits back to it), and the "auctions" that followed were rigged. Foreign bidders were barred while oligarchs colluded on their bids, dividing major assets among themselves at extremely low prices. The loans were made before the 1996 presidential election, in which Boris Yeltsin faced significant challenges, while the resolution of the scheme took place after. The loans enabled Yeltsin to make good on public obligations, pay some back salaries, and finance his campaign at a level one hundred times higher than the legal limit. The oligarchs, meanwhile, acquired an interest in Yeltsin's re-election so that the scheme could be seen through to conclusion (Freeland, 2000: 169–189, 194–195; Reddaway and Glinski, 2001; Shelley, 2001: 246; Hudson, 2004).

Another more specific scheme involved Russia's aluminum industry. In the mid-1990s a syndicate led by Oleg Deripaska and "Yeltsin family" backers used corrupt influence, rigged bids, and the threat of violence to take over the industry at knock-down prices. Entrepreneurs in other industries, not all related to metals production, have complained more recently of legal and illegal pressures, and outright threats of violence, from those same forces seeking to expand the aluminum empire. Aluminum production requires large amounts of electricity: one reason why Deripaska's clan acquired major influence in the energy sector as well (Ivanidze, 2002; Tavernise, 2002a; Reut and Rubnikovich, 2003).

Evidence of corruption was a saleable commodity in the Soviet era, but now the market is booming. *Kompromat* – a contraction of "compromising materials" – involves the use of evidence of corruption to threaten political and economic rivals as well as uncooperative officials. Journalists, investigators, and politicians amass incriminating information (easily obtainable, but forged if need be) and sell it back to the person involved; if the target will not pay, the evidence can just as well be sold to a newspaper. The effectiveness of *kompromat* reflects the abundance of corruption itself, the ineffectiveness of state investigators and law enforcement, and a climate of lawlessness that makes even fictitious allegations widely believed (Karklins, 2002: 28–32; Szilágyi, 2002).

The Putin government has made tax reform a priority, in part for revenue reasons but also as a way to demonstrate a measure of official credibility. Tax evasion, in itself, is not necessarily corruption, but in Russia it reflects oligarchs' power and the state's ineffectiveness. Simplifications of the tax code enacted in 1999 have increased revenues to some extent and, by limiting discretion in the calculation of taxes owed, may have reduced some low-level corruption. But some oligarchs and bankers continue to enjoy near-impunity regarding taxes, while the state scrambles for revenue and many public servants are paid poorly or not at all. In 2002 the Prosecutor General's Office reported that "problematic bankers" evaded a total of 36 billion Rubles (nearly $1.2 billion) in taxes; evasions in Kalmykia, an emerging internal tax haven, totaled 17.8 billion Rubles. Listed in the same report of lost revenues are a range of privatizers, military officers, and the former Deputy Chairman of the State Fishing Committee, who cost the state 42 million Rubles by issuing fishing quotas illegally (Shelinov, 2003). Perhaps the most serious official credibility problems, however, are with the courts and law enforcement agencies. Oligarchs such as Oleg Deripaska use legal proceedings to justify the seizure of productive assets, as noted above. Similarly, news media frequently report raids by police (called "werewolves in uniform" by some Russian citizens) on the headquarters of some business, ostensibly investigating business misconduct or enforcing the law but in fact helping a powerful rival execute a legally camouflaged takeover (Tavernise, 2002a, 2002b; *Agence France Presse*, 2003; Filipov, 2004).

Organized crime: muscle for hire

Organized crime's power is both a consequence and a sustaining factor of the Oligarchs and Clans syndrome, reflecting the same opportunities, ineffective institutions, and climate of insecurity that shape corruption. *Mafiyas* are often allied with business and state participants in corrupt deals; oligarchs frequently rely on illegal "muscle" to get things done, and organized crime figures are key members of several clans. Imagery borrowed from the Sicilian case abounds in discussions of Russian organized crime, and indeed the imported word *mafiya* makes useful shorthand. But Russian organized crime is decentralized and non-hierarchical: instead of a unified national network thousands of small gangs operate with little or no coordination (Leitzel, 2002: 37). They may cooperate for a time on larger projects, but overall organized crime is a universe of small, shifting groups exploiting whatever illicit opportunities are at hand (Shelley, 2001: 248; Volkov, 2002: 64). Estimates in 1995 had it that 30,000 individuals were involved, 3,000 of them as leaders of their own gangs. Over 1,000 of these groups were thought to link various regions within Russia, and 300 of them to engage in international dealings (Frisby, 1998: 32).

By the mid-1990s, organized crime held substantial influence over half of the Russian economy, and in 1994 paid an estimated 22 billion Rubles in bribes (Frisby, 1998: 34, 37). *Mafiya* figures and oligarchs such as Vladimir Gusinsky were behind some of the worst of the pyramid schemes of the mid-1990s, luring citizens with extravagant promises of returns on their money that, of course, they would never see. The same risks and uncertainties from which the *mafiyas* profit mean that little of their money has been reinvested in Russia (Shelley, 2001: 250–252); instead, organized crime has been a major force contributing to capital flight. Recently there has been some speculation that *mafiya* money is shifting back into Russia in response to more favorable domestic economic trends (Collinson and Levene, 2003; Pribylovsky, 2003; RIA, 2003), but the scale of any such flow has yet to be demonstrated. In any event, major domestic investment controlled by crime figures would be a mixed blessing at best.

Providing protection in a situation of insecurity is the essential activity of most Russian gangs (Leitzel, 2002: 36). Under the Soviet order *protektsia* of various forms was provided by party patrons, state bureaucrats, and law enforcement officials, often corruptly but effectively. In the post-Soviet era, organized crime (sometimes in league with police, sometimes in armed conflict with them) can fill gaps created by the weakness of official institutions. Entrepreneurs put a "roof" (*krysha*) over their enterprises by paying local *mafiyas* for protection against ordinary crime, official harassment, threats from other gangs, and of course from crimes by the very people being paid off (Harper, 1999; Humphrey, 2002). Protection is available from many sources: there is a booming legitimate private security industry (Leitzel, 2002: 42) and corrupt police offer their services too. Organized crime, however, is perceived by many as the most effective source of protection – a view that only adds to long-term insecurity – and *mafiya* leaders aggressively marketed their services during the 1990s (Volkov, 2002: ch. 2). Getting out of such deals can be difficult, however: one can fire a private security firm, but ending a relationship with mafia "protectors" is far more difficult (Leitzel, 2002: 37); for that reason among others gangsters usually have the upper hand in dealing with all but the most powerful business figures (Volkov, 2002: chs. 2, 4).

At other times, though, the point is not protection but violence. Reformers, business rivals, and politicians all too often are assassinated: twenty-seven bankers were murdered during a two-year period in the mid-1990s. In the fall of 2002 Valentin Tsvetkov, governor of the resource-rich Far East region of Magadan and an emerging entrepreneur, was murdered in broad daylight in Moscow's Novyi Arbat district. In August of 2002 alone, murders claimed Vladimir Golovlyov MP, Vice-Governor of Smolensk region; the Deputy Mayor of Novosibirsk; and a prominent Moscow subway and rail transit official (Wines, 2002). One of the most notorious murders was that of Galina V. Starovoitova, a prominent democracy advocate and Member of Parliament, in St. Petersburg in November, 1998. It is unclear whether such killings are carried out by security personnel or by oligarchs' *mafiya* cronies; corruption also ensures ineffective investigations and a lack of prosecution (Birch, 2002; Myers, 2002a; Round, 2002; Weir, 2002; Wines, 2002; Yablokova, 2002).

The Soviet era: order without markets

It is tempting to think of oligarchs, organized crime, and corruption generally as something new, or as outgrowths of post-communist problems and events. But while the post-1991 climate of immense opportunities and weak institutions has helped make corruption particularly disruptive, many of the underlying problems, and some of the key figures involved, have roots in the old Soviet order. A full discussion of Soviet corruption is beyond the scope of this chapter (see Kramer, 1977, 1998; Schwartz, 1979; Simis, 1982; Vaksberg, 1992), but some points are essential to what came next. During that era a bureaucratized, centrally planned economy lacking a price system was ruled by a one-party dictatorship answerable to no one. Bureaucratic corruption was the norm, not the exception, as officials and enterprise managers not only took advantage of illicit opportunities but struggled to keep up the appearance of meeting quotas. A parallel system of corruption for personal gain (Kramer, 1977) helped individuals cope with shortages, obtain better housing, health care, and education, angle for better job assignments, and generally cushion the impact of harsh and arbitrary state policy (DiFranceisco and Gitelman, 1984; Ledeneva, 1998). At the top of the political structure – and occasionally, at key points in the economy – corrupt gains could be spectacular (Simis, 1982). Corruption was no secret during those days, but official acknowledgment of the problem was sporadic and usually served political ends. When a top official was publicly labeled corrupt, that often meant that he or she had come out on the losing side of a factional struggle.

Bureaucratic corruption helped the system survive in a distorted and inefficient form by easing bottlenecks and creating a crude sort of exchange system. By the last decades of the Soviet era it was far less risky for the regime to wink at corruption than to undertake fundamental reform. Corruption was hardly beneficial, but alternatives were few and had huge potential costs. Long-term damage came in the form of lost opportunities to change and adapt, and in a pervasive cynicism about official statements and policies. The result was a system that in the end could not bend, but rather broke.

For our purposes four aspects of the Soviet era are of particular importance. First, the party-state apparatus was large and monopolistic, but in many ways ineffective. The state bureaucracy was slow-moving and deeply politicized; the party ruthlessly punished opponents and offered no legitimate way to influence policy from below. Even had it been spared the worst of the dislocations and dubious policy advice (Stiglitz, 2002) that accompanied the fall of the Soviet order, a state that had ruled by coercion was woefully unsuited to respond to the signals sent by markets and politics, or to sustain open and orderly competition in either arena. Second, even though the state was weak as a whole, groups of officials and managers within it were powerful. Indeed, they were already operating with a degree of impunity as the system began its long collapse under *perestroika*. McFaul (1995: 211–221) argues that officials were acquiring limited *de facto* property rights – of consumption and of profit, if not rights of transfer – in the enterprises they ran. In the chaos that followed 1991, those officials had the means, the motive, and the opportunity to turn major state assets into personal property.

Third, having property rights is one thing; defending them in an insecure setting is quite another (Mendras, 1997: 125). Organized crime's private law enforcement and debt-collection functions quickly became essential (Varese, 1997, 2001) while court, police, and bureau-cratic functions broke down, and here too the Soviet era had set the stage. The forerunners of present-day *mafiyas* began to form in the 1920s, and by the late 1930s were *de facto* partners with the party-state in disciplining inmates of the immense network of prisons (Frisby, 1998). During the stagnation of the Brezhnev era, and to a greater extent during *perestroika*, criminal gangs exploited niches within the shadow economy, particularly in remote areas such as Georgia and the Far East. After 1991 organized crime groups were well-positioned both to extend their influence and to rent out their "muscle" to entrepreneurs. All markets require a level of trust; organized crime and corrupt officials turned trust into a commodity because of the weakness of public institutions and private norms (Varese, 1997: 594–595, 2001).

Fourth, while corruption in the Soviet era was extensive it had a kind of normative framework. Enterprise managers could exploit their economic fiefdoms within limits (McFaul, 1995). More pervasive were practices of *blat* – a term often used to refer to illicit influence but having richer connotations of reciprocity and what we might call networking (Ledeneva, 1998). *Blat* was an aspect of corruption, but it was also a process of mutual aid reaffirming personal relationships. When the Soviet system fell key underpinnings of *blat* went with it: a "shortage economy" and the daily opportunities for personal exchanges it created gave way to markets, state property became private property (often overnight, in obscure ways), and informal solidarity gave way to pervasive insecurity (Ledeneva, 1998: 176). Increasingly relationships were structured by money exchanges, becoming impersonal and limited in terms of mutual obligations (Frisby, 1998: 28–29; Ledeneva, 1998: 178). More or less anything could be bought or sold, but interpersonal relationships, trust, and an older normative framework faded.

After the fall: markets without order

Early on, much post-Soviet corruption was straightforward: in a series of smash-and-grab operations, members of the old *nomenklatura* laid claim to "their" industries, mines, and enterprises. Sometimes these moves were portrayed as privatizations (Varese, 1997: 591–592); other assets were simply stolen (Karklins, 2002: 25–27) and defended by *mafiya* muscle where necessary. Old enterprises, banks, and ministries were simply rebranded as private concerns, often with the same people in the same buildings continuing to run day-to-day affairs (Satter, 2003: 49). In a sense this first "unofficial" round of privatization only ratified trends already taking place during the last years of communism. That meant, however, that the *official* privatization efforts launched in 1992 encountered powerful entrenched interests (McFaul, 1995: 212, 224). Reformers could hardly take back the enterprises that the "red bureaucrats" had seized, and they could make few credible promises to investors in official privatizations. Indeed, later entrants often found it necessary to use corruption of their own to protect against predation by the early movers and their bureaucratic clients (Varese, 1997: 580). The resulting bidding war for official influence seriously undermined the credibility of state institutions just as official privatizations were being launched.

That process was supposed to take place in two phases. "Voucher privatization," launched in October, 1992, gave each citizen a voucher, nominally valued at 10,000 Rubles, supposedly representing one share of the nation's industrial structure (Appel, 1997; Lavrentieva, 2002; Pribylovsky, 2003; Satter, 2003: 49–50). In theory vouchers created broad-based ownership and distributed wealth to those needing it most: as antiquated as Russian industry was, officials still believed the "true" value of one share far exceeded 10,000 Rubles and that citizens would benefit from the difference. In practice, however, the system was poorly understood by citizens who were given little real information and had never experienced legitimate market interactions; converting vouchers into their theoretical full value was impossible. Many sold their vouchers to speculators for next to nothing or lost them in fraudulent "cooperative" schemes. At the program's end in 1994 officials claimed that the overwhelming majority of vouchers had been redeemed; actual benefits, however, flowed to very few.

"Money privatization" began in 1994. In this phase the goal was to auction off state-owned assets, thereby attracting foreign investment and expertise, creating profitable enterprises owned by a range of competing interests, and earning major revenue for the state. The latter, in turn, would narrow public deficits, support the Ruble, and enable state ministries to pay back salaries and improve public services. But foreign investors proved reluctant: even where they were allowed to bid it became clear that asset sales were rigged (Satter, 2003), that prices bore no resemblance to actual values, and that property rights were far from secure (Freeland, 2000; Satter, 2003). The problem with money privatization was not that it failed to put public assets into private hands; indeed, emerging tycoons and their official partners rapidly moved in. By November, 1994, 78 percent of service enterprises had been privatized; by September of 1995, 77 percent of industry, accounting for 79 percent of industrial jobs and 88 percent of production, had moved into private hands by one mechanism or another (Varese, 1997). The problem was that those assets fell into the hands of emerging oligarchs, often at ludicrously low prices. Large factories went, for just a few million dollars each, to those who had bought influence rather than to those best able to improve the facilities. United Energy Systems, which generates virtually all of Russia's electricity (of which more will be said below), was sold for $200 million; a similar firm would have been worth $30 billion in central Europe and $49 billion in the United States. Oil wells went for prices that, based on known reserves, were about one-half of 1 percent of those expected in the West (Satter, 2003: 51). Very little revenue flowed to the state. By early 1995 it was clear that money privatization was failing on virtually all counts; the result was the "loans for shares" scheme, which did more than any other episode to strengthen economic oligarchs.

At a key juncture in Russia's move away from communism, desperately needed resources were falling into the hands of corrupt businessmen and their cronies both in and out of government, while the state remained impoverished. Other resources left the country altogether: one estimate of capital flight during the Yeltsin years pegs the figure at between $220 and $450 billion (Sattter, 2003: 55). State institutions, weak at the beginning of the decade, were further undermined by shortages of both cash and credibility. Between 2000 and 2002 the Putin government announced legal reforms in the corporate sector, but there is little to cheer about in recent events. Yukos and Sibneft, major oil producers, went to oligarchs such as Khodorkovsky through rigged bidding. At the end of 2004 Yuganskneftgaz, Yukos's oil production arm – seized in the wake of Khodorkovsky's arrest – was back in the public sector as the state's oil firm Rosneft quickly bought out the little-known winners of another "auction" (CNN.com, 2004). The 2002 privatization of United Energy Systems was advertised as an example of enhanced transparency, but foreign bidders were again seen off, domestic interests engaged in bid-rigging, and the auction "loser" announced it would join the winner in generating Russia's electricity (Jack, 2002; Karush, 2002; Albats, 2003).

Oligarchs, Clans, and change

Russian corruption differs in kind, and not just in amount, from the Influence Market and Elite Cartel cases discussed in previous chapters. There is no counterpart in the latter cases to the insecurity, or the oligarchic contention, that marks Russia's systemic corruption problems. Violence was part of the pre-1987 Korean Elite Cartel's strategy for retaining power, and organized crime is a part of the corruption story in Italy, but Russia is a case apart.

The contrasts reflect a volatile combination of rapidly expanding political and economic opportunities and a very weak institutional framework – the latter including not only the bureaucracy, courts, and law enforcement, but also political parties, the news media, and civil society (on the latter three see McFaul, Petrov, and Ryabov, 2004: chs. 5–7). Oligarchs moved in on the Russian economy because immense wealth was at stake and there was little to stop them. The old Soviet state had been weak in key respects, and the events of the 1990s undermined the successor state even more (McFaul, 2001). Sometimes that happened through poor policy choices and advice; sometimes it happened through official connivance with criminals and business elements; sometimes it happened as both Russian citizens and international investors took a look at a violent, unpredictable situation and found it prudent not to get involved. However such weakness came to pass, it only enhanced the power of oligarchs while encouraging others to seek protection however they could get it.

For those reasons, Oligarch and Clan style corruption may be more durable and adaptable than Elite Cartels. Oligarchs – unlike Elite Cartels – need not govern a whole country, and are less exposed to scrutiny, external shocks, or internal competition. Indeed, to the oligarchs Russia's troubles often appear as new ways to profit. If private rapaciousness and public institutional weakness are indeed central to this kind of corruption, then further liberalization or decentralization without close attention to the state, political, and social foundations such changes require will only pour more gasoline on the fire. Russia needs stronger institutions first (Popov, 2002) – credible political parties, bureaucracies, tax collection, and law enforcement; improved banking and intermediate economic institutions such as bond and equity markets; and a strong, active, engaged civil society. Recent reforms in taxation, the criminal code, and land and property laws may have borne some fruit (Cottrell, 2001; Myers, 2002b; Dettmer, 2003; Farquharson, 2003), and a new Anti-Corruption Council headed by former Prime Minister Mikhail Kasyanov may (or may not) be a positive step (Alyoshina, 2004). But corruption continues in high-stake business (*arbitrazh*) court cases (Burger, 2004); a culture of impunity is alive and well among state officials, and Putin himself has conceded that anti-corruption measures since 2000 have had little effect (Klussmann, 2004).

In the long run reforms will not succeed unless broad segments of society recognize a stake in their success and are able to act on those interests – a development that requires the sort of sustained, committed political contention discussed in chapter 2. In that regard current trends of political reform are grounds for pessimism (McFaul, Petrov, and Ryabov, 2004). Recent anti-democratic moves by the Putin government, including those to control the mass media and the effective renationalization of key segments of Yukos, should not be confused with the solidification of effective government. No more promising are Putin's political debts to the Yeltsin "family" and to other oligarchs who helped finance his 2004 election campaign.

Corruption in Russia continues to evolve. Economic trends have been broadly positive since the 1998 Ruble collapse, which channeled domestic demand into locally produced goods, and rising oil prices have also benefited the economy and state budget. Capital flight has declined since 2000 and, by some estimates, is now exceeded for the first time by investment from abroad (Interfax, 2003). Business-related murders peaked in the mid-1990s, some official law enforcement agencies are gaining a measure of credibility, and a variety of private security firms now compete with organized crime; some *mafiya* figures have moved into legitimate business while others have shifted into more traditional criminal activities (Volkov, 2002: ch. 4 and p. 125). The key variables to watch will not be specific corrupt actions or reform initiatives, but rather the overall strength of institutions and of the political and economic participation that they do or do not protect and sustain. The flourishing of such participation could be a first step toward building political institutions, a civil society, and an accountable state capable of checking the oligarchs. But if top state officials get the upper hand on both oligarchs and society the result could well be something worse – perhaps the Official Moguls syndrome to be outlined in chapter 7.

The Philippines: oligarchs, the Marcoses, then ... oligarchs?

The late President Ferdinand Marcos, his powerful wife Imelda Romualdez Marcos, and her world-class collection of dress shoes may dominate popular images of corruption in the Philippines, but reality is more complex and deeply rooted. Geography, colonialism under Spain and the United States, and sixty years as a strategically important American client state have led to pervasive corruption. Entrenched oligarchs and their followings have inhibited the growth of democratizing movements while their dealings enriched the few at the expense of the many, distorting development in what ought to be – if only because of aid received – a far more affluent country.

Over 84 million people live on the more than 7,000 islands of the Philippine archipelago, but politics and the economy are dominated by only about eighty families (Riedinger, 1995: 209–210; Sidel, 1997, 2000; Moran, 1999: 577). Some are landholding provincial dynasties, while others have risen to prominence more recently through banking or industry; either way they have frequently plundered a weak and decentralized state (Girling, 1997; Montinola, 1999; Hutchcroft, 2002, 2003; on Philippine institutions generally see Hutchcroft and Rocamora, 2003). Some oligarchs and their followers have turned segments of the state into fiefdoms; others have used corrupt influence to keep the state out of their business dealings; and in other cases they have simply stolen from the nation. The Marcos era – especially the long period of martial law (1972–86) – complicated the picture: favored families thrived while others saw their property and privileges vanish. Such abuses helped mobilize the "People Power" revolution that brought Marcos down in 1986, and since that time anti-corruption activities have proliferated. Still, the Oligarch and Clan syndrome remains very much alive, and indeed some prominent families have done better than ever in recent years.

Oligarchs in the Philippines: who they are and what they do

Unlike Elite Cartel cases, where a relatively small network governs and profiteers through the state apparatus, Philippine oligarchs are more numerous, and much of their power and wealth are derived from *outside* the state – to the extent that the distinction makes much difference. Oligarchs exploit the state much more effectively than the state exploits them (Hutchcroft, 1991: 424). Guaranteeing corrupt deals and property rights in a setting of weak institutions is a chronic problem, however, and thus presidents are handy friends to have. Presidential cronies do very well indeed: as we shall see, Marcos associates bought out competitors' corporations at bargain prices and forced other oligarchs out of business altogether. Marcos himself, and Imelda, ended up as actual or *de facto* owners of many such firms.

Violence is part of the story too (Moran, 1999: 582), particularly in remote areas, but overall the Philippine case is not as wild as the Russian model. There are several possible reasons: many oligarchs have been in place in the Philippines for a century or more, producing a kind of bailiwick system geographically and within state institutions. The economic stakes in the Philippines – particularly those involving natural resources – are smaller than those in Russia. Property rights are more secure in the Philippines: after all, oligarchs dominate the banking system and, through their political and economic clans, the courts, bureaucracy, and at times the presidency as well. Many of the benefits sought by Philippine oligarchs come from without – from the United States, international aid agencies, or investors – and thus there is value in cultivating connections (and tolerable reputations) with those external sources rather than a scrambling for domestic advantages with international competitors barred.

Still, Oligarchs and Clans corruption has been immensely damaging in the Philippines. Both the power of the oligarchs and weak, faction-dominated official agencies work against the development of broad-based democratic movements, a strong and independent civil society, and (until 1986 at least) credible elections. Democratic alternatives to the oligarchs have little to offer voters, particularly in remote areas; political parties tend to be personal followings rather than broad-based groups rooted in lasting social interests. On the economic side, oligarchic privilege makes for a fragmented, unpredictable, and in key areas closed economy, regardless of official policies. International aid has been extensive, but too often has enriched presidential cronies.

Building family empires

Central authority has long been a shaky proposition in the Philippines. Spain ruled for three centuries, and yet its local authorities were so short of resources that they often had to rely on Catholic Church personnel in remote areas (Hutchcroft, 2000: 3–4). Those friars ruled with impunity at the day-to-day level, and allegations of abuses on their part were common (United States, 1901). Largely Islamic Mindanao was even more of a land unto itself in those years (Warren, 1985). Land was an obvious base for local power, but Sidel (1997) cautions against reducing the rise of the oligarchs to landholding alone. At times ownership was the *result* of power or force: vote-buying, fraud, and violence helped launch some provincial oligarchs and protected many more. Indeed, the American style of colonial rule did more to create the modern oligarchs than the old Spanish system ever had (Sidel, 1997; Sidel, 2000; Hutchcroft, 2003), because the US paid more attention to creating representative institutions than to building an effective central administration. Local elections beginning in 1901 allowed *caciques* (chieftains) in remote areas to control administrative posts; elected national legislative bodies followed in 1907 and 1916 (Hutchcroft, 2003: 6).

Opening up participation in the absence of a framework of strong institutions – a key aspect of the Oligarchs and Clans syndrome – had far-reaching implications. Oligarchs and their followers quickly established their political beachheads. Public resources, land, preferential access to markets and capital, and unfavorable treatment for competitors could all be had through the strategic uses of influence, cash, and (where needed) violence. The Philippine Commonwealth, a multi-branch, decentralized interim structure set up by the Americans in 1935 as a step toward independence, quickly fell under oligarchic domination (McCoy, 1989b; Hutchcroft, 2000: 294–299).

Independence, in 1946, left the pattern largely intact. The United States reduced its day-to-day administrative presence but remained an essential source of aid, investment, and political backing. Its strategic interests and immense military bases both maintained a flow of resources and bound US policy to the status quo: any democratic movement strong enough to oust the oligarchs might also be strong enough to end the leases on military bases. The oligarchs, by contrast, were stable and cooperative. Moreover, the post-war state was not much stronger than its Commonwealth predecessor. It vested considerable power in the President, but the presidents were typically heads of various political families and – unlike their counterparts in Korea – were more concerned with rewarding their cronies than with national development. Distinctions between public and private loyalties were (and remain) vague; bureaucrats have often been guided much more by loyalty to their patrons than by formal duties or agency mandates, with the result that the bureaucracy has long been large, factionalized, and ineffective (Hutchcroft, 1998: 53; but Kang, 2002a, dissents).

The Ferdinand and Imelda show

Ferdinand Marcos is a dominant figure in the Phillippine corruption story. He was the son of a locally powerful family in the Ilocos region of Luzon, but his father moved the family to Manila in the 1920s to pursue a national political career. In 1935 an Ilocos politician who had defeated the elder Marcos in a Congressional election was murdered; young Ferdinand was charged, convicted, and then freed in a sensational retrial. Marcos's next moves are unclear, and may have involved wartime collaboration with the Japanese; but his successful race for Congress in 1949 featured wholly fictitious tales of wartime heroism. In 1954 he married beauty queen Imelda Romualdez, merging two political clans in the process. By 1959 Marcos was a rising figure in the Senate; he became President of the Senate in 1963, and was President of the Republic from 1965 until the "People Power" revolution of 1986 (Hamilton-Paterson, 1998).

As President, Marcos enjoyed extensive US backing, particularly for his active support of the Vietnam War. Early on he was seen by some as a modernizer, but very quickly he moved to enrich himself and his cronies while making life more difficult for rival families. These trends accelerated in 1972 when, after a series of alleged communist provocations (many staged by government security forces), he declared martial law (McCoy, 1989a: 192). The legislature and political parties were abolished in favor of Marcos's own Kilusang Bagong Lipunan (KBL), or "New Society Movement." The US, apparently liking what it saw, rapidly increased assistance. The crackdown, Marcos claimed, would help him pursue land reform and fight corruption, but any such measures were aimed mostly at personal opponents. Meanwhile the President, the First Lady, and their cronies were hard at work building a large network of interlocking businesses (many of them monopolies), using state power to favor those enterprises and drive out competitors, and extracting bribes, commissions, and kickbacks wherever they could be found (Montinola, 1993; Wedeman, 1997a: 470). Toward the end of the Marcos years it was commonly said that corporations in the Philippines were like towels in a bathroom – labeled "His" and "Hers."

Marcos made some administrative changes during martial law, but they mostly aided and protected his own enrichment (Hutchcroft, 1991: 438, 440): state capacity increased in some respects but bureaucrats were no more independent of the President than before. Kang (2002a: 136–150) argues that martial law reversed a metaphoric pendulum of corruption: before, family oligarchs had plundered the state, but now the state controlled the oligarchs. It seems more accurate, however, to characterize martial law as a very difficult time for some oligarchs and clans (and for society at large), and as a very lucrative phase for others who enjoyed Marcos's personal favor.

Me and mine: crony capitalism in action

Many oligarchs consolidated both their local bailiwicks and their administrative networks early in the twentieth century, at a time when sugar producers operated with near impunity. Politically connected growers extracted so much capital from the Philippine National Bank between 1916 and 1920 that it nearly collapsed. After independence in 1946, local election fraud – backed up where necessary by violence – and self-enrichment by presidential cronies were common. Both the state and businesses depended on American capital, and the state was further weakened by persistent guerrilla warfare in some provinces. Political parties were weak, personalized, and all but indistinguishable on ideological grounds; the real competition was among factions seeking to elect friendly presidents who could grant access to credit, foreign aid, and tax and tariff favors (Stanley, 1974, as cited in Hutchcroft, 1991 at n. 19; Hutchcroft, 1991, 1998; Batalla, 2000; Kang, 2002a).

When Ferdinand and Imelda Marcos became President and First Lady in 1965 their joint net worth was only about US$7,000. By 1986 that figure had climbed to between US$5 and 10 billion. Martial law, beginning in 1972, made it easier for Marcos to enrich himself and his cronies. For example, he imposed a special tax on coconuts and copra to be collected by an agency run by Eduardo Conjuangco, a member of his inner circle. With the proceeds Conjuangco acquired a bank, using one of its subsidiaries to buy coconut processing facilities. Marcos then ordered that subsidies once available across the industry be restricted to that subsidiary, creating "a near monopoly over the export of coconuts and copra" (Wedeman, 1997a: 471). Similar maneuvers created a sugar exporting monopoly for crony Robert Benedicto; eventually his firm was reorganized into a quasi-regulatory body empowered to set domestic prices. Marcos backers Herminio Disini and Lucio Tan put competing cigarette companies out of business with the help of favorable import–export policies; kickbacks and equity interests in such dealings flowed to Marcos himself (Aquino, 1987; Hawes, 1987: chs. 2, 3; Wedeman, 1997a: 471; Chaikin, 2000).

Imelda Marcos not only became an international symbol of conspicuous consumption but also held a business empire of her own. She helped channel foreign aid, bribe income, and funds from organized crime into a series of bank accounts and asset funds. As Mayor of Metro Manila, Minister of Human Settlements, and head of a regional development authority she was in a position to award lucrative construction contracts in exchange for a percentage of the action. But the largest share of the wealth likely came from outright theft: during the Marcoses' reign an estimated US$5 billion disappeared from the national treasury. Ferdinand Marcos died in Hawaii in 1989, but in 1993 Imelda brought his body back for reburial and continued her attempts to re-enter politics. Imelda was convicted, but not imprisoned, as a result of a 1993 corruption trial; late in the 1990s she was charged with embezzling US$680 million. In 2003 the Philippine Supreme Court ruled that those funds, held in Swiss bank accounts, had been stolen, and that Imelda would have to stand trial. At the same time she was facing another ten counts of corruption, as well as over thirty charges of currency smuggling, but trial dates were repeatedly postponed in 2004 (Aquino, 1987, 1999; Seagrave, 1988; Chaikin, 2000; Hutchcroft, 2003; *Sun-Star*, 2003).

Revolution or restoration?

The Marcos era ended with surprising suddenness in 1986. A presidential election in February was apparently won by Corazon Aquino, widow of opposition leader Benigno Aquino who had been assassinated by Marcos operatives as he disembarked from an airplane in Manila in 1983. But Marcos declared himself the winner despite evidence of egregious fraud, touching off massive demonstrations in the heart of Manila. Military leaders chose not to fire on nuns and ordinary citizens, siding with the "people power" demonstrators; that, and the loss of US and Catholic Church backing, brought down the regime. President Aquino was a powerful unifying symbol and had a prominent lineage of her own. She dismantled martial law; Malacañang Palace, the presidential residence, was opened to the public, who flooded in to inspect the spoils of the Marcos era, including all those shoes. The Congress and genuinely competitive elections were restored, and the military returned to the barracks – in theory. But her regime was weak and unstable, facing nine military coup attempts in its first four years. In some respects the new era was as much a restoration of oligarchic power and corruption as it was a democratic revolution (McCoy, 1993: 517; Moran, 1999: 580).

Marcos may have rearranged the Oligarch and Clan system in favor of selected cronies but he had done little to change it fundamentally. Once he was gone, there was little to restrain powerful families from regaining or extending their influence. McCoy (1993) offers an epic account of the rise, fall, and restoration of the Lopez family, who began with large land-holdings in the Western Visayas sugar region and built a business empire in Manila. Relying less upon violence than presidential connections, the family moved into the sugar-exporting, mass media, transportation, and energy sectors as well as politics. During Martial Law Marcos moved against the Lopez empire and crushed its principal figures, one of whom had been his own Vice-President. After 1986, however, the Lopezes were back – at first through the help of President Aquino, who restored many of their industrial holdings, and later by building a new satellite-based media empire. By the time Fidel Ramos became President in 1992, Eugenio (Geny) Lopez, a fifth-generation family leader, was a close presidential associate. McCoy portrays the Lopezes' return as part of a post-1986 restoration of elite family power in a weak state (Mc Coy, 1993: 513–517; see also Hutchcroft, 1991; Wedeman, 1997a; Moran, 1999).

General Fidel Ramos, who had played a critical role in overthrowing Marcos, succeeded Aquino in 1992, although he won less than a quarter of the vote (Kang, 2002a: 155). His government attempted a number of anti-corruption reforms (Riedinger, 1995: 211–212; Batalla, 2000) with increasing backing from international agencies and domestic business organizations. Ramos's Presidential Commission Against Graft and Corruption (PCAGC), established in 1994, is the country's most sustained reform effort to date (Batalla, 2000: 6); it builds upon the 1987 Constitution, which among other changes created an anti-graft court (*Sandiganbayan*) and an Ombudsman's office with anti-corruption responsibilities (*Tanodbayan*) (Batalla, 2000: 6–7). But while the Ramos campaign generated major publicity, evidence of real progress was scant.

In 1998 Ramos was succeeded by Joseph "Erap" Estrada, whose 40 percent of the vote was the most solid mandate of the modern era (Kang, 2002a: 175) but owed much to his former film career. Within less than a year Estrada was surrounded by scandals: his connections to gambling interests were one major issue, but family members and political allies were also implicated in bribery cases involving government contracts for drug testing of law enforcement officers, school textbooks, and police and military radio equipment. Estrada and his wife concealed business holdings worth over US$600 million, along with directorships of a variety of businesses. Philippine law requires top officials to disclose financial information on themselves, their spouses, and children under eighteen, but was never designed to deal with someone like Estrada who had families with several women and used those ties to conceal even more wealth. Impeachment proceedings dragged on for two years, all but collapsing in 2001 as key figures refused to give evidence. Demonstrations reminiscent of 1986 demanded Estrada's removal, and with Supreme Court backing Gloria Macapagal Arroyo – leader of yet another prominent political family – assumed the presidency in January, 2001. Estrada, refusing to accept the handover, was placed under virtual house arrest at Malacañang and eventually resigned; he has since been charged with major offenses (Batalla, 2000; Coronel, 2000; PCIJ, 2000).

A tenacious syndrome

The damage produced by Philippine corruption is difficult to overstate. In 1999 the Ombudsman's office estimated losses due to corruption at about 100 million Philippine Pesos (about US$2.5 million) daily; World Bank estimates put the loss at around one-fifth of the national government budget, or at about 3.8 per cent of GDP (Batalla, 2000: 7,

8–10; appendices 1 and 2). Such figures are approximations at best, but if corruption did siphon off 3–4 percent of GDP that, in most years, would be the difference between stagnation and solid growth. Such losses help perpetuate a weak and ineffective state, inhibit the rise of challengers to the oligarchs, and reflect massive transfers of wealth into the hands of a few families – and then, most likely, out of the country.

Oligarch and Clan corruption in the Philippines is hardly a clone of the Russian model, but it is marked by a similar organization of power, and contention, among personalized followings that extends deep into an ineffective state. Formal moves to liberalize the economy have likely helped key families extend their empires – as did the end of the Marcos dictatorship – although as in Russia the real extent of liberalization in an economy so dominated by clans, connections, colonized public agencies, and occasional violence is open to question. Institution-building and anti-corruption efforts have had only indifferent success, and are unlikely to become much more effective as long as a few wealthy families and widespread poverty, rather than a truly open economy and an active civil society, dominate national life.

Mexico: oligarchs in the making?

Mexico's presence as our final case in this category may be a bit surprising. As recently as the late 1980s Mexican corruption coexisted with – indeed, was integral to – an impressive (if stultifying) political stability. Presidents dominated political life; they had large secret funds at their personal disposal and the power to hand-pick their successors. They had ruled since 1929 through the venerable Institutional Revolutionary Party (Partido Revolucionario Institucional, or PRI), a near-monopoly party that was part political machine, part repository of nationalist ideology, but first and foremost a means of control and the nation's strongest single institution. In many respects Mexico embodied the Elite Cartel syndrome.

But lately there has been change. In 2000 the PRI suffered its first-ever defeat in a presidential election; for years before that, drug gangs and corrupt police had been undermining central authority in some states. Liberalization opened up some segments of the economy and made it more difficult for the PRI to monopolize opportunities; international and domestic pressures for reform, particularly after the deeply suspect presidential election of 1988 (Preston and Dillon, 2004), attacked the PRI's dominance as well. The PRI's loss in 2000 hardly changed Mexico from an Elite Cartel to an Oligarchs and Clans case by itself: just how much that election really changed remains an open question. But the erosion of the PRI's power over two decades and a change in corruption toward a more open scramble might both reflect deeper trends toward significantly increasing participation in a setting of weak institutions – defining characteristics of the Oligarchs and Clans syndrome.

Government of the party, by the party, for the party

The PRI subjected both state and society to its own interests via a complex mix of incentives and force. Stephen Morris (1991) points out that a young person hoping to move up in life, a politician or bureaucrat seeking advancement, or a business person in need of a break had to deal with the PRI, and on the party's terms. In some federal agencies "employees of confidence" – workers appointed by and beholden to PRI patrons – numbered three-quarters of the workforce (Morris, 1991: 43). Petty benefits flowed downward and outward through the party and into society; personal and political loyalties flowed upward, and civil society and social pluralism were weak. Corruption helped hold politics and a broader social system together (Knight, 1996), with stability itself being one of the PRI's main appeals (Levy and Bruhn, 2001).

Political life in Mexico revolves around the six-year presidential term, or *sexenio*; presidents, like all other elected federal officials, are barred from succeeding themselves. Under the PRI each *sexenio* followed a typical rhythm, beginning with grand promises and initiatives, and often with politically useful revelations of past corruption. After Miguel de la Madrid left office in 1988, for example, successor Carlos Salinas de Gortari revealed some of the corruption–narcoviolence connections of the previous *sexenio* (Morris, 1995: ch. 3; Jordan, 1999: 152–154). But corruption-as-usual would return; the fifth or sixth year of a *sexenio* was often called *el año de Hidalgo* ("the year of Hidalgo"), referring to the face on the Peso (van Inwegen, 2000), although open venality sometimes receded as the party set about the business of winning another election.

PRI hegemony lasted from 1929 until 2000, and the party will be a force once again in 2006, but economic changes beginning in 1982 and political developments that date from 1988 both revealed the weakness of state institutions and created vulnerabilities in the dominant party (Fröhling, Gallaher, and Jones, 2001). In 1982 a global recession, the end of the oil boom, and a Peso crisis created a severe economic squeeze, derailing once again Mexico's hopes of joining the ranks of high-income nations. Recovery strategies, strongly influenced by the IMF and international business interests, emphasized liberalization of the economy and upgrading of state capacity. Both trends shifted considerable power to a growing class of technocrats (Levy and Bruhn, 2001: 165–177; Tornell, 2002).

De la Madrid, elected in 1982, began to roll back state ownership of enterprises, cut taxes while improving collections, reduced *reglamentismo* – the culture of rules, licenses, and political interference that had long marked PRI economic policy – and opened up the economy to foreign investors and enterprises. Privatization gathered pace during the 1980s; remaining state enterprises saw subsidies and favored market positions restricted or eliminated. Within a few years Mexico moved from a closed economy to one of the world's most open (Tornell, 2002: 127).

De la Madrid was in many ways a typical PRI president, and his *familia feliz* ("happy family") – a network of relatives, politicians, and business associates – fit the Elite Cartel pattern. Like some of his predecessors he promised a crusade against the corruption of past presidencies. He amended the important, but deeply flawed, Law of Responsibilities defining the obligations of public servants, and an anti-corruption campaign debuted to much fanfare and early optimism. But high-level abuses carried on as usual. The *familia* extended its empire on several levels, acquiring legitimate businesses and joining with drug traffickers. Particularly profitable was narcotics-related money laundering, for which legitimate real-estate and banana businesses provided useful cover. Electoral fraud, the murder of at least one critical journalist, official theft in the region of tens of millions of dollars, and police torture and corruption also marked the later years of de la Madrid's presidency (Morris, 1991: 98, ch. 3; Jordan, 1999: 152–154).

Economic liberalization was long overdue and won considerable international favor, but it deprived the PRI of carrots and sticks useful in controlling business and channeling benefits to its mass constituency. The changes cut off some sources of illicit revenues for the party and its top figures, or at least made such funds harder to collect and conceal. Technocrats increasingly displaced PRI operatives in important administrative posts, weakening both the party's hold on policy implementation and its control over jobs. By some accounts the technocrats were not much less corrupt than those they replaced; now, however, corruption was less tightly controlled from above (Morris, 1991: 125). Other problems were ideological: a party that had long manifested public hostility to business – an offshoot of nationalism dating from times when most major firms were foreign-owned (Morris, 1991: 52–53) – was recasting itself as business-friendly and open to the world economy. The most basic threat, however, was structural: a party that had maintained dominance by monopolizing channels of social mobility (Morris, 1991) was now committed to policies that would weaken its hold on existing opportunities and create new paths of advancement beyond its control.

As long as it controlled elections, however, the PRI would retain power, and for many years that was easy. Electoral fraud was frequent and effective, as noted, but the party had deeper sources of strength too. It was heir to the nation's nationalist-revolutionary tradition, commanding important symbolic and ideological appeal. It faced few countervailing forces: the revolutions that created the PRI also weakened the political clout of the Catholic Church, landholding classes, and business. The party's presence in everyday life preempted the growth of an independent civil society. One-party politics extended deep into the federal system; for many years opposition wins in state and local elections were unusual, and when the PRI lost the governorship of Baja California in 1989 it was big news. It was thus able to channel visible benefits to many parts of the country when doing so served party interests: in the run-up to an election it was not unusual for poor villages to find that a long-awaited electrical service was finally being installed – on poles painted in PRI colors. Dissident and indigenous movements, by contrast, could and did find themselves staring down the barrel of a gun.

1988: PRI outdoes itself

The 1988 presidential election, however, created a crisis (Levy and Bruhn, 2001: 88–89, 97–98; Preston and Dillon, 2004). Economic troubles and social fallout from liberalization left Carlos Salinas de Gortari, the PRI candidate, vulnerable. Many citizens believed corruption – particularly involving PEMEX – had become more rapacious, and there were protests against vote fraud in states such as Oaxaca, Zacatecas, and Durango (Morris, 1991). To make matters worse PRI elites had split over the issue of the social consequences of economic liberalization: Cuauhtémoc Cárdenas, son of a popular former President, and his faction ran against Salinas as the Partido de la Revolución Democrática (PRD). PRI pulled out all the stops to elect Salinas, arranging for vote-counting computers to break down, burning ballots, and forging ballot totals (Levy and Bruhn, 2001: 89). Salinas thus took office under intense suspicion and faced growing demands for reform.

The 1988 election was a strong indication that the PRI might be vulnerable, a trend reinforced by events during the 1990s. International investors became less tolerant of corruption, as did aid and lending agencies – views that could not be ignored. United States officials criticized Mexican political, human rights, and corruption abuses, after having paid little attention to them in decades past. Most ominous, however, were the continuing rise of the drug trade and the power of gangs involved in production and shipping (Andreas, 1998; Toro, 1998; Jordan, 1999: 84–88). Mexico is not Colombia, but as the last stop on many routes to the American market it had become a strategic battleground. Drug gangs collaborated with police forces and military officers and undermined PRI governments in several states (Jordan, 1999), and offered paths to wealth and power outside of the PRI's direct control. International responses made matters worse in some ways: interdiction of drug shipments may ironically aid major traffickers by driving out smaller competitors and lifting market prices (Toro, 1998), and can raise the ante in terms of violence. The "internationalization" of US drug law enforcement via interdiction actions in Mexico undermined the autonomy and credibility of Mexican police and drug policy, as both were effectively annexed by the US (Toro, 1998). By the end of the 1990s it was an open question whether the federal government, the military, or drug lords actually governed some areas of the country (Bailey and Godson, 2000).

Mexico in that era had many formal attributes of democracy: elections had been held since the late 1920s, opposition parties offered candidates, and there was some criticism of the government in the press (although often answered with official harassment). Repression could be violent – notably in the massacre of student protesters in 1968, and in the regime's dealings with some indigenous peoples and local opposition groups – but Mexican presidents hardly fit the stereotypical image of Latin American dictators, and the military generally stayed out of the politics. Mexico was, and is, a rapidly modernizing society in many ways: particularly after 1982 skilled technocrats became increasingly influential in government. The economic picture, too, has been hopeful at many points: a long economic expansion took place between the 1950s and 1970s, in the early 1980s after the oil boom a rapid takeoff seemed imminent, and such hopes arose again in the early 1990s.

Still, corruption and crime add to a pervasive sense of insecurity in society (Levy and Bruhn, 2001: 15–20); late in 2004 a mob in a poor district of Mexico City lynched two police officers and burned them alive, a scene shown live on television (McKinley, 2004). Elite Cartel-style abuses, while extensive, had generally stayed under PRI control for years. But beginning in the 1980s more disruptive, higher-stakes varieties and a sense of impunity spread through sections of the hierarchy and outward into the states, particularly as regards law enforcement. Those changes had a number of causes – notably, rapid economic liberalization and a significant if slower opening-up of politics in the context of weak state institutions and, later, decaying PRI hegemony. The result has been a shift toward a more disruptive Oligarchs and Clans pattern.

Mexico's corruption, old and new

PRI leaders used corruption both for self-enrichment and to sustain the party's dominance and internal hierarchy. Election fraud, extortion and kickbacks, and protection schemes were common. The PRI exploited not just private interests but public institutions too, such as NAFINSA, a national development bank; IMSS, the federal social security institute; the Secretariat of Land Reform; and the state coffee firm. Booming oil revenues during the late 1970s made Petroleos Mexicanos (PEMEX), the state-owned oil company, a ripe target for official theft and contracting abuses: 85 percent of PEMEX construction contracts were illegally issued. Leaders of the petroleum workers' union shared in the no-bid contracting process, sold jobs, and diverted union dues to their personal enterprises. During the 1980s the scale of abuses increased, and shifted toward higher levels; major allegations were made against former Presidents López Portillo and de la Madrid while PRI resisted inquiries and attempted to silence critics (Grayson, 1980; Morris, 1991: 48; Knight, 1996: 227).

When the PRI could not win elections it stole them, as noted. Vote-buying, intimidation, stuffing or "losing" ballot boxes, and false counts were common; procedures were primitive and, until the 1990s, were overseen by PRI operatives known as *mapaches*, or "raccoons." Polls might not open at all in some locations; in others they might be moved at the last minute, with voters left to scurry around like *ratones locos*, or "crazy mice," searching for a place to vote. Those lacking specific street addresses could vote by claiming to be known as a resident of a given area – a procedure easily abused. Those wanting to vote more than once might fold several ballot papers together into a *taco* and put them into the box. PRI appointees ran the national tally as well, and in a close election such as 1988 they would do whatever it took to win (Pastor, 2000; Fröhling, Gallaher, and Jones, 2001; Falken, 2005).

For many years Mexico's presidents used sizeable personal funds (officially, *erogaciones contingentes*) to solidify their positions within both party and state, as well as for personal benefit. Such funds were an open secret among top figures, but no accounting was made of their scale or use. Secret funds came under increasing attack after 1994, particularly by groups such as Civic Alliance, and by the end of the decade the Controller General's office claimed that the practice had all but ended. An important corrupting influence was brought under control, but increased political factionalism may also have been encouraged to the extent that presidential patronage may have been reduced (Morris, 1999: 631, 637; SHCP, 2000).

The shift toward Oligarch and Clan corruption did not start with any one case, but rather with the gradual unraveling of PRI and its ability to impose discipline on corruption and other activities. Beginning with the late-1970s oil boom and continuing into the 1990s corruption increased in scale, frequency, and disruptive potential (Morris, 1991: 123–127). Ballooning oil prices, for a time, drove a scramble for wealth (Grayson, 1980), while the subsequent "oil bust" intensified contention over a shrinking pool of revenues. The drug trade fueled violence (Toro, 1998: 138–142) and a more unstructured style of corruption. Benefits that might have been distributed within the PRI to keep the peace, or used to maintain its popular base, were siphoned out of the party. Political violence and corruption of law enforcement, at times connected to *los narcos* and their gangs, grew from the 1980s onwards. The 1994 kidnapping of a wealthy businessman yielded a huge ransom; when nearly $30 million in marked bills were discovered in the possession of PEMEX officials, a Deputy Attorney General made arrests and began an investigation, only to see his brother, PRI secretary-general José Francisco Ruíz Massieu, murdered a few days later. Other murders included those of Cardinal Juan Jesús Posadas of Guadalajara in 1993, and of PRI presidential candidate Luis Donaldo Colosio in 1994. Drug cartels and old-line ("dinosaur") factions of PRI were widely regarded as orchestrating the violence. Lower-level corruption and violence to protect drug shipments, neutralize law enforcement and military anti-drug activities, and intimidate or eliminate judges, witnesses, and competing gangs has been less organized, and in some areas has recently been increasing (Toro, 1998: 138–144; Jordan, 1999: 154–156; Elizondo, 2003).

The fragmented and contentious style of more recent corruption is reflected in a scandal surrounding Andrés Manuel López Obrador, Mayor of Mexico City, and the activities of his political "fixer" René Bejerano. Obrador is a leading PRD figure and a 2006 presidential front-runner; Bejerano has been Obrador's campaign manager and more recently served as majority leader in the city's legislative body. Bejerano was caught on a surreptitious videotape accepting large amounts of cash from a contract-seeking businessman whose face was obscured, but who was later identified as Carlos Ahumada Kurtz. Bejerano got to witness his own undoing: invited as a guest on the morning television program *El Mañanero* – a popular program of news, commentary, and scandal hosted by "Brozo the Clown" (in reality a comedian named Victor Trujillo) – Bejerano was welcomed with a screening of the video. Obrador's standing among his party followers has been little affected. But under the old order few if any non-PRI politicians would have had enough power to attract money on such a scale and few television presenters would have dared embarrass a powerful party figure on live television. The PRI, at one time, might well have stood by its man – had such damning evidence even come to light – but the PRD has announced that it will not aid in Bejerano's defense and did not object when his legislative immunity to prosecution was lifted by the Chamber of Deputies. A tantalizing question is just how the video "sting" came to pass: speculation continues as to which factions or competing parties' leaders might have helped lure Bejerano into the trap (*El Universal*, December 20, 2004; Guillermopietro, 2004).

Mexican corruption in transition

In 2000 the PRI lost the presidency to opposition candidate Vicente Fox in a closely monitored, well-organized election. It is tempting to see Fox's historic victory as the beginning of a new era in Mexico, but it might also be the culmination of multiple processes, including both corruption and reforms, that weakened once-dominant Elite Cartels. Mexico is not yet as clear a fit in the Oligarchs and Clans category as Russia and the Philippines, but its corruption has been tending toward that syndrome. International influences, ranging from pressures to liberalize the economy to the continuing demand for illegal drugs in the United States, and continuing institutional weaknesses are long-term causes. But as the PRI weakened (in 2004 it had to mortgage its headquarters building to fund campaigns), with it went networks and incentives that had imposed a kind of order on corruption. The key issue is not where Mexico falls on international corruption indices but rather the rise of a *kind* of corruption more disruptive to development, and more closely linked to violence, than that of decades past.

In the early 1980s Mexico, in some ways, was a one-party version of Italy, with an all-encompassing party controlling competition and serving as a guarantor for corrupt deals, or perhaps a Korean-style system with less regionalism and fewer powerful generals. But Mexico's Elite Cartels faced unique challenges. The PRI won elections for decades, unlike the short-lived parties of Korea before the late 1990s, and unlike Italian parties was in a position to win outright. Yet each *sexenio* was a political era all its own. Electing powerful presidents who could not succeed themselves kept the PRI in power but disrupted the continuity of elite networks, a fact reflected in repeated presidential revelations of their predecessors' abuses. PRI strength and the state's weakness reinforced each other, but contention among PRI elites became increasingly intense. To the extent that these changes reflect the growing competitiveness of politics and openness of the economy they suggest that where institutions are weak and elites are divided, further liberalization may encourage more disruptive types of corruption (on the risks of political reform see Morris, 1995).

Mexico is now one of the world's most exciting (and, given its size and potential, most important) laboratories for reform. The IFE's successes in cleaning up elections have inspired many other countries. Some state institutions have been strengthened in impressive ways, and the IFAI, a new agency, has launched an impressive effort to build transparency and public trust. The national Controller's office, recently renamed the Secretariat for Public Functions, has become a much more credible body over the past decade; many of its efforts to prevent corruption in procurement and contracting involve innovative use of the Internet. Tec de Monterrey, an innovative university with extensive online programs, and the Mexican chapter of Transparency International have conducted some of the world's best surveys of popular experience with corruption. A new initiative at the Autonomous University of Mexico, funded by the World Bank and conducted by a team of social scientists, will provide assessments of corruption of a sort available nowhere else.

But if the Russian and Philippine cases are indeed parallels, Mexico has difficult times ahead. The Fox administration seemed to lack both a clear agenda and a political base from which to pursue one. Economic liberalization and democratization have cut in two directions. They have encouraged foes of corruption, unleashing new manifestations of the reformist spirit that has always been a part of Mexico's self-image (Tulchin and Selee, 2003). But growing economic and political participation, weak state institutions, and the decline of the PRI – for generations, the nation's real political framework – have also spurred corruption in riskier and more disruptive forms. If this analysis is correct, institution-builders in Mexico are locked in an all-important race with corrupt interests over the kind of future the nation will experience.

Oligarchs and Clans: who, if anyone, governs?

Influence Markets deal in access to decisionmakers and processes within relatively strong public institutions. Elite Cartels are corrupt networks that allow top figures to manage a weaker state apparatus, and to govern for better or worse, in the face of rising political and economic competition. But in Oligarch and Clan cases key influence networks are personal in their incentive systems and agendas, and collude or conflict depending upon the short-term stakes at hand. It can be unclear, in severe cases, whether anyone governs at all. After a generation of liberalization and privatization as a dominant development agenda, this syndrome of corruption is a useful reminder of the value of an effective state.

Oligarch and Clan societies do not simply have "more corruption." While some of their corrupt practices will be recognizable anywhere – the United States and Italy have police corruption, for example, just as do Russia, the Philippines, and Mexico – these cases embody qualitatively different systemic corruption problems requiring different reform responses. Transparency, privatization, streamlining official operations, and upgraded law enforcement and public management are excellent reform ideas, but they assume the existence of a state strong enough to perform basic functions, and lasting political incentives to do so. Absent that, opening up public processes or rolling back the state will be irrelevant, as real decisionmaking may already have been "privatized" in particularly damaging ways: Goldman's (2003a) term "piratization" has relevance well beyond Russia. Similarly, urging "civil society" to move against corruption – in effect, urging the weak to confront the strong – makes little sense where trust is weak (often for good reasons) and insecurity is a prime fact of life.

This syndrome – or to be more precise, the corruption along with the deeper problems that shape its dynamics – has particularly negative implications for democratic and economic development. It is unpredictable, feeding on and perpetuating insecurity and a weak state, and is often linked to violence. It is hard to see any positive agenda being aided by this sort of corruption, even in derivative ways. Still worse is its tenacity and capacity to adapt: elites and clans can exploit portions of a society, economy, or state with little by way of competition or official countermeasures to stop them, and can respond quickly to new opportunities or threats.

A final point is that the Oligarchs and Clans syndrome can significantly broaden the working meaning of "corruption." At one level this is definitional: where boundaries and distinctions between the public and the private, state and society, and politics and markets are indistinct and fluid, and where legal and social norms are contested or in flux, a wider range of activities (many murders in Russia, drug transport in Mexico, corporate takeovers in the Philippines) become a part of the problem. That fluidity of boundaries, norms, and distinctions intensifies development problems: the uncertainty of property rights, for example, is a consequence of corruption and institutional weaknesses, a cause of further abuses, and a factor deterring investment and sustained broad-based growth. The Oligarchs and Clans syndrome makes it clearer why we must think of corruption not as a particular category of behavior but in terms of systemic problems: the behavior, whether or not it fits formal definitions, is shaped by deeper problems that impede the open and fair pursuit of wealth and power, and weaken the institutional frameworks needed to sustain and restrain those processes.

Are Oligarch and Clan cases lost causes, then? Not necessarily, although reforms will have little chance of sustained support and success until deeper causes are addressed in ways that reflect the realities of those societies. How that process might work is a topic for chapter 8. First, however, we need to consider a final set of cases. They are societies in which it is quite clear who governs, but in which official power is integral to corruption – not compromised by it – and in which corrupt figures act with near-complete impunity. These are the "Official Moguls" cases of chapter 7.

crupt w/ impunity

7 Official Moguls: reach out and squeeze someone

Introduction: power, impunity, and the risk of kleptocracy

In Influence Market societies powerful private interests threaten the integrity of public institutions, but may be checked by those institutions and by competing parties and groups. Elite Cartels stave off rising competition by building corrupt networks, but they are restrained by the need to balance off the interests of various elites and by the fundamental goal of maintaining the status quo. Oligarchs face few constraints but still must manage conflict among themselves and find ways to protect their gains. But where state elites operate in a setting of very weak institutions, little political competition, and expanding economic opportunities, the stage is set for corruption with impunity. There Official Moguls – powerful political figures and their favorites – hold all the cards.

In China, Kenya, Indonesia, and countries like them, corruption is often rapacious and involves the unilateral abuse of political power rather than *quid pro quo* exchanges between public and private interests. Official theft of public land and resources, businesses owned by politicians and military figures, or smuggling and tax-evasion schemes organized by bureaucrats and including favored business people are not frequent in Influence Market or Elite Cartel societies. In Oligarch and Clan cases deals on such a scale are difficult to sustain in an uncertain and contentious climate, and require protection from forces in the private realm. In Official Mogul cases, however, there is little to prevent ambitious political figures or their personal clients from plundering society and the economy.

"Official Moguls" thus has a double meaning: officials and politicians enrich themselves through corruption more or less at will, at times moving into the economy by converting whole state agencies into profit-seeking enterprises, and ambitious businesspeople with official protection and partners take on a quasi-official status as they build their empires. Either way the locus of power lies not within the state but with officials who use political leverage to extract wealth. Boundaries between public and

155

private domains are porous or, in effect, non-existent. Indeed, many Official Moguls operate in a realm between state and society, using power and resources that are neither clearly public nor private (Johnston and Hao, 1995). Top-level offices are useful mostly to create monopolies of various sorts that are then exploited with few restraints. Some monopolies may be small-scale affairs while others may allow Official Moguls and their business clients to dominate major segments of an economy.

The results are distinctive kinds of connections between wealth and power. Seeking bureaucratic influence through payments to political intermediaries, as in our Influence Market cases, is usually pointless. The official policy process often bears little resemblance to reality, and those with *political* power or backing are out for themselves. Top figures in Official Mogul countries need not form cartel-style networks because political opposition is weak at best; indeed in many cases there is no doubt who is in control. Their clients become specialists, exploiting fragments of state authority and opportunities opened up by their political backers. And unlike Oligarchs who must continually find ways to reward and discipline their Clans, and to protect their gains, Official Moguls' followers have few alternatives and their claims to wealth and property face little real challenge.

The costs of impunity

Official Mogul corruption is driven by the unconstrained abuse of political and, by extension, official power. There may be one clearly dominant figure, as in Suharto's Indonesia, or more numerous Moguls operating their own monopolies in a more uncoordinated fashion, as in China. They often have personal clienteles including relatives, business people, and local leaders, but there is little political reason to share spoils with mass constituencies in the manner of machine bosses. Economic opportunities are growing in these societies (see table 7.1), but these cases lack the political accountability and strong institutions required for an orderly market economy. Opposing corruption can thus be risky business, and even those citizens who bitterly resent it may leave the heavy lifting to others.

Corruption of this type is often large-scale and free-wheeling, crossing international borders as well as those between the state and economy. Indeed, liberalization of politics and economies has exacerbated corruption problems in this group, as we shall see in the cases of Kenya and Indonesia. Like corrupt figures elsewhere, Official Moguls build monopolies (Klitgaard, 1988): one politician or his client may claim an entire segment of industry while another may simply control the issuance of a valuable permit in a local office. But these figures have few competitors

Table 7.1: *Statistical indicators for "Official Moguls" countries*

Indicator (units/range) and source	China	Kenya	Indonesia	98-Nation median*
Polity Score 1992 (Hi = more dem./0 thru 10) **P**	−7	−5	−7	7.0
Polity Score 2001 **P**	−7	−2	7	7.0
Institutional / Social Capacity 2002 (0 thru 100) **WEF**	33.7	35.7	37.3	44.7
Property Rights 2002 (Low = secure/1 thru 5) **HF**	4.0	3.0	4.0	3.0
Econ Freedom 1990 (hi = more free/0 thru 10) **FI**	3.72	4.98	6.69	5.15
Econ Freedom 2001 **FI**	5.50	6.60	5.60	6.45
TI CPI , 2003 (0–10, inverted) **TI**	6.6	8.1	8.1	6.3*
UNDP Human Dev Score 2001 (0–1.00) **HDR 2003**	.721	.489	.682	.750
GDP per capita, 2001 **WB**	$4,020	$980	$2,940	$5,940
Corruption Control 2002 (−1.89 thru 2.39) **KKZ**	−.41	−1.05	−1.16	−.22
Gov't Effectiveness 2002 (−1.64 thru 2.26) **KKZ**	.18	−.85	−.56	.10
Government Intervention 2001 (1 thru 5) **HF**	3.0	4.0	3.0	3.0
Government Regulation 2001 (1 thru 5) **HF**	4.0	4.0	4.0	3.0
Regulatory Quality 2002 (−2.31 thru 1.93) **KKZ**	−.41	−.50	−.68	.06
Voice/Accountability (−2.12 thru 1.72) **KKZ**	−1.38	−.58	−.49	.05

* Medians for the 98 countries that could be classified in statistical clusters (ch. 3); for TI CPI, median is for the 89 countries included in the CPI and in clusters. Unless otherwise indicated, high scores indicate high levels of an attribute.

Sources:

FI = Fraser Institute **http://www.freetheworld.com/**
HDR = UNDP *Human Development Report 2003* **http://www.undp.org/**
HF = Heritage Foundation Index of Economic Freedom reports
http://www.heritage.org/research/features/index/
KKZ = Kaufmann, Kraay, and Zoido-Lobatón, "Governance Matters III" dataset, 2002
http://info.worldbank.org/governance/kkz2002/tables.asp
P = Polity IV dataset, 2002 update **http://www.cidcm.umd.edu/inscr/polity/polreg.htm**
TI = Transparency International Corruption Perceptions Indexes for 2001 and 2003
http://www.transparency.org/
WB = World Bank Data Query online data source (GDP and population used to calculate GDP per capita) **http://www.worldbank.org/data/dataquery.html**
WEF = World Economic Forum, Yale Center for Environmental Law and Policy, and CIESIN (Columbia University), 2002 *Environmental Sustainability Index*
http://www.ciesin.columbia.edu/

and face little legal or political constraint. Such uncoordinated mono-polies, with no restraints upon the prices they exact, can choke off whole streams of economic activity (Shleifer and Vishny, 1993); unpredictable corruption is likewise especially harmful to economic development (Campos, Lien, and Pradhan, 1999). Even where Official Mogul corrup-tion coexists with rapid growth, as in China, it is difficult to argue that it is somehow beneficial for development: other effects can include inhibiting the national integration of markets; weakening secondary economic institutions, such as bond and equity markets, and the reality-testing and international integration functions they perform in a developing economy (Karmel, 1996); stunting the growth of civil society by choking off its economic base and autonomy; and increased externalities such as environmental damage and social disruption.

A lack of electoral opposition and legal accountability does not mean an absence of challenges, however. In a setting of weak institutions and significant social change top figures may face separatist movements, communal contention, personal rivals, or other forms of unrest. Any such insecurity encourages rapacious "hand over fist" corruption (Scott, 1972); so too, ironically, might poorly institutionalized efforts at democratization, as we shall see. The personal agendas of top leaders can thus make an immense difference: some may perceive threats to their rule, while others do not; some may tolerate or encourage corruption while others impose working limits upon exploitation, or even fight it. Not surprisingly, this group is marked by wide variation in corruption and development situations.

Three cases

In this chapter I consider three cases – the People's Republic of China, Kenya under Daniel arap Moi, and Indonesia during and following the Suharto years – located in this category by the statistical analysis in chapter 3 and collectively illustrating the systemic corruption problems outlined above. All have experienced significant corruption; all have seen ambitious elites exploit economic opportunities while most citizens remain poor – at times, desperately so. None would qualify as a well-institutionalized democracy. All have relatively intrusive but ineffective states – arguably, a hallmark of Official Mogul abuses – and weak mechanisms of accountability. Consider the indicators presented in Table 7.1.

China and Kenya broadly fit the Official Moguls profile of weak institutions, expanding economic opportunities, and undemocratic politics. Indonesia's Polity ratings improved markedly following the fall of Suharto in 1998, but as we shall see it is hardly a sound democracy yet. China and Kenya have moved toward the market – China, dramatically – in terms of economic policy; Indonesia has been a market economy for some time but has become somewhat less open, to judge by the data, of late, perhaps because of disruptions following the fall of Suharto. All remain relatively poor countries overall, and all but China fall below the median on the UNDP Human Development Index. China has experienced dramatic economic growth for the past generation; Indonesia's generation of rapid but unequal economic expansion was halted for several years by the events of 1998. In all three countries official institutions are weak and governance is ineffective. Property rights are not very secure, and corruption-control ratings fall well below the 98-nation median. These states are more interventionist than the three Oligarch and Clan cases in the previous chapter, yet Government Effectiveness and Regulatory Quality ratings range from middling to very weak. Finally, the impunity that characterizes Official Mogul corruption is reflected in these countries' very low ratings for Voice and Accountability – scores that in the case of Indonesia put rising Polity scores into a sobering context.

China: riding the tiger – for now[1]

Corruption is nothing new in China: reports of bribery, sometimes involving ambitious young men seeking to evade the rigorous examinations for official appointments, date back many centuries (Liu, 1978, 1979; Kiser and Tong, 1992; Reed, 2000). Local bribery and extortion have been longstanding themes too, their seriousness varying with the ability of central government to exercise effective power. In the twentieth century demands for official payments were common under Nationalist rule, a factor intensifying opposition to that regime.

When the People's Republic was proclaimed in October, 1949, eradicating past corruption was an early priority. Still, in the years before the death of Mao Zedong in 1976 and the launch of market-oriented policies in 1978, corruption was a continuing problem (Liu, 1983, 1990; Baum, 1991; Kung and Gillette, 1993; Lo, 1993; Goodman, 1994; Gong, 1994, 2002; Kwong, 1997; Bo, 2000; Fabre, 2001; Li, Smyth, and Yao, 2002; Sun, 2004). Favoritism was common; production was often falsely reported (Kwong, 1997: 111), but that served less to enrich anyone than as a way to avoid punishments for failing to meet the plans. Corruption for monetary gain was frequent but generally controlled in

---

[1] Sections of this discussion draw upon Hao and Johnston, 2002. I gratefully acknowledge Yufan Hao's analytical contributions, translations, and wise advice.

terms of both scope and the size of stakes involved (Hao and Johnston, 1995). Also controlled were basic ideas about what corruption was and what caused it: in the official view it was a problem of surviving feudal traditions and bourgeois values, or of individual deviance. Anti-corruption strategy emphasized well-publicized trials and punishments, political and ideological discipline efforts, and periodic mass campaigns. Examples of the latter included the "Three Antis" (corruption, waste, and bureaucracy) and "Five Antis" movements (bribery, tax evasion, theft of state property, cheating on government contracts, and stealing economic information) of the early 1950s, and the "Four Cleans" campaign (work groups' management of collective property) a decade later (Hao and Johnston, 2002).

Strong economy, weak institutions

In 1978 Deng Xiaoping's government launched the market-oriented reforms that have touched off an economic boom and set the stage for rapid growth of corruption (Gong, 1994; Goldman and MacFarquhar, 1999; Sun, 2004; Wong, 2004). Centrally planned and controlled prices and decisions were partially replaced by arrangements allowing goods to be sold more or less freely once planned criteria had been met. Many collective work groups were replaced by a "household responsibility system" and small family-owned businesses were permitted as well. Some central government subsidies were recast as loans; regional and local officials acquired more autonomy, both official and otherwise. Managers could now make personnel and production decisions, and were free to retain a significant share of profits for their firms. Some functionaries resisted reform, fearing threats to their status and jobs. But most benefited from the increased discretion and economic opportunities it brought them. The national economy was opened to foreign trade and investment – although contract enforcement and transparency have yet to approach international standards – and exports became a top priority. More recently stock markets have been established, and a scheme was proposed under which citizens would in effect become shareholders in state enterprises.

But economic reform was also notable for what it did not do. Distinctions between public and private realms were never particularly meaningful in pre-reform China, and economic norms were bureaucratic, political, and therefore ill-suited to markets. Reform, when it came, fragmented the Leninist party-state but did not build the oversight and facilitating institutions open markets require. Official profiteering (*guandao*) became a major problem, taking on various forms such as moonlighting, speculation, taking gifts, and bribery. Judicial institutions were reconstructed, but became politicized and unaccountable (Gong, 1994), as did lending and credit. Autonomous business, trade, labor, and consumer organizations – which in other systems defend important values and impose sanctions of their own – still do not exist. Victims of shady deals, and political demands reflecting both the success and difficulties of economic transformation, lack legitimate political outlets. State bureaucratic capacity lags far behind the spread of markets, and the party has entered a phase of organizational deterioration. Market forces abound, but institutionalization and national integration of the economy – admittedly immense challenges – have lagged far behind. Officials were able to contrive corrupt monopolies in all manner of places and economic niches (Gong, 1997: 285; Wedeman, 1997b; Lü, 2000: 193; Cheng, 2004).

The early results were impressive, as annual growth approaching 10 percent became the norm, but not surprisingly they were uneven. Pei (1999: 95) points out that reform created winners early while deferring losses (layoffs, closure of unprofitable state-owned enterprises, and so forth), thus winning considerable support within the party and bureaucracy. But a two-track price system in place for the first fifteen years of reform created incentives to buy coal, steel, and other commodities at artificially low planned prices and resell them at market prices several times higher. Production under the plan was unprofitable while the market was lucrative; many managers overstated or simply skipped planned production and moved directly to the market. Such dealings could be covered up by cutting bureaucrats in on a share of the profits. Bureaucrats went into business, often at their desks in state offices. Teachers compelled students to buy books and supplies from them, railway workers traded in scarce freight and passenger space, and military officers sold fuel, supplies, and special license plates allowing purchasers to avoid inspections, tolls, and fees (Dryer, 1994: 268; Johnston and Hao, 1995; Hao and Johnston, 2002).

Decentralization created pockets of impunity, often in a growing gray area between state and markets (Johnston and Hao, 1995). Managers in the state-owned sectors could tap into the cash-generating activities of their enterprises and enrich themselves with little risk of punishment (Cheng, 2004). Party cadres and bureaucratic administrators raised their own salaries, spent public funds on housing and extravagant banquets, speculated in foreign exchange, and earned black-market fortunes. City officials might wink at local manufacturers' tax obligations while levying special fees upon goods from other areas (Wedeman, 1997b: 807). Calling former grants "loans" did not, in the absence of a capital market and banking reform, mean they would be allocated on sound economic criteria; instead, funds were advanced to politicos and their business protégés, often with no expectation of repayment. After about 1988 officials began to build informal coalitions with entrepreneurs based on shared interests and interpenetrating powers and assets, with political connections becoming more valuable to entrepreneurs of many sorts (Choi and Zhou, 2001). State and party power remain important, but ineffective oversight and weakened political discipline have turned scattered fragments of authority into valuable commodities for exploitation. Not only party and state officials, but also professionals such as reporters, lawyers, teachers, and doctors, solicit money and favors with little systematic restraint. International businesses found that officials at many levels expected payments, and while a contract might describe desirable outcomes it did not guarantee results or protect rights.

Assessing the full scope of corruption in China with precision is impossible. Official figures are unreliable, and reforms are changing both official rules and day-to-day norms. Wedeman (2004) argues that corruption accelerated beginning in the mid-1990s, but that China is still not exceptionally corrupt either in global terms or by historical standards. In 2001 alone the state's People's Procuratorates handled 36,477 corruption cases worth 4.1 billion *yuan* and involving 40,195 people. Some 1319 cases totaled at least one million yuan (roughly $120,000); those proceedings involved 9,452 participants – 2,700 of them county-level officials or higher, and six at provincial or ministry levels (*People's Daily*, 2002b). Party enforcement activities are even more sweeping: in 2001 Discipline Inspection committees investigated 174,633 cases, punishing over 175,000 civilian officials including 6,076 holding county posts and 497 in prefectural agencies (*People's Daily*, 2002a). The sums involved in corrupt deals have also grown: a generation ago, bribes and embezzlements usually amounted to a few thousand *yuan* or less, but now cases involving millions are common. Overall, Pei (1999: 96) estimates that corruption may cost China 4 percent of its GDP annually.

Changing norms and values

Not surprisingly, given economic changes and the party's problems, China is experiencing a crisis of values. Generations raised on egalitarian ideology have been urged "to get rich and to get rich fast" (Deng, 1983, quoted in Hao and Johnston, 2002: 589), and their children live in a country – and increasingly, a global society – Mao might have had difficulty imagining. Market reform began at, and may have been in part a response to, a time of widespread disillusionment during the decade following the catastrophe of the Cultural Revolution. Many young people turned to the pursuit of wealth, while an absence of strong overriding norms blurred boundaries of behavior. By now it can be difficult to say where corruption ends and reform begins: the question of what is an acceptable personal reciprocity or market transaction, and what is a corrupt payment, lacks clear answers. In some places those who pay or earn commissions are praised, while else-where they have been jailed (Su and Jia, 1993: 180).

Similarly, public office-centered conceptions of corruption have been supplemented by newer ones reflecting the rise of markets (this discussion is based on field research by Yufan Hao as reported in Hao and Johnston, 2002: 584–585; see also Sun, 2001) In the late 1970s "corruption" had three meanings: *tanwu*, *shouhui*, and *tequan*. *Tanwu* (malpractice) involved state officials who misappropriated public property by embezzlement, theft, or swindling. *Shouhui* meant using official positions to extort or to accept bribes. *Tequan* (privileges) covered widespread privilege-seeking by officials. Since the early 1990s, however, "corruption" has more often had connotations of *fubai* – decay and putrefaction – and now embraces a broad range of abuses of wealth as well as of power. Activities termed "corrupt" in the Chinese press now include economic illegalities such as profiteering, blackmail, and black-market currency dealings; establishing illegal busi-nesses, smuggling, and dealing in counterfeit or defective goods; tax evasion, excessive housing and extravagant banqueting (*dachi dahe*), ticket scalping, gambling, usury, and visiting prostitutes – to name just some examples. As this list suggests, notions of limited public roles, and of private interests and situations, that both help define corruption and restrain elites in other societies are not easily applied in China.

Meet the moguls

Official Mogul corruption is pervasive and diverse, involving thousands of decentralized monopolies small and large (Fabre, 2001: 461–462). Weakening party discipline enabled cadres at many levels, already enjoy-ing considerable privilege (Gong, 1994: xviii), to amass and exploit frag-ments of power, which in turn became the main path to wealth. The ability to exploit such power without constraint may, ironically, function as a kind of commitment mechanism – that is, that a corrupt functionary free to cut his own deals will deliver the goods – and that might reduce some investors' apprehensions about the costs of corruption.[2] Still, the absence of political alternatives means that those unwilling to play the

---

[2] I thank Yufan Hao for his comments on that point.

game are unable to take countervailing action (Gong, 1994: 151). Would-be entrepreneurs learned that finding a sponsor or partner in the party or bureaucracy was good business.

Some corruption is straightforward bribery: in Henan Province Zhang Kuntong was imprisoned on bribery charges relating to road-building contracts, as was Li Zhongshan in Sichuan Province. But city and provincial officials often operate under-the-table business ventures. The practice is sometimes called "sign-flipping," reflecting the intermingling of official authority and business. The rewards are large and, for those few caught, the price is even greater: Hu Changqing, a former Vice-Governor of Jiangxi Province, was sentenced to death in 2000 for bribery and unexplained wealth. In that same year Zheng Daofang, deputy head of transportation in Sichuan province, was sentenced to death on bribery charges while his wife and son were imprisoned for unexplained wealth. The issue in such cases is not just wealth but the balance of power, with corruption allegations becoming weapons in the struggle. In Beijing in the 1990s Mayor Chen Xitong's skill at amassing wealth touched off that sort of struggle. Chen, his family, and his political clients engaged in numerous illicit deals, but their real offense was to become a perceived political threat to the national party leadership – part of long-running political tensions between national politicians and Beijing city leaders. Chen was forced out; along with his wealthy and powerful son Chen Xiaotong and forty other local officials he was tried and imprisoned on corruption charges. A senior vice-mayor committed suicide, and the city's party secretary was later convicted of corruption (BBC, 1998; Lü, 1999; ABC News.com, 2000; Bo, 2000; Voice of America 2000; *People's Daily* Online, 2001a).

Tax fraud and embezzlement can also enrich officials and their allies (Sun, 2004: ch. 3). Two tax bureaucrats and a former prosecutor created fictitious corporations in the late 1990s, facilitating tax evasions totaling over $7 million. The scheme featured repeated shipment of empty containers between Guangdong and Hong Kong, backed by bogus paperwork claiming value-added-tax rebates on fictitious exports. The corporations did produce some goods, but they were sold locally, off the books. The three officials and four others received death sentences in early 2001. More recent export tax fraud cases may total 50 billion *yuan* (about $6 billion) according to the Shanghai Customs Office. Xu Jie and Du Jiansheng, two bureaucrats from Guizhou Province, were given death sentences in late 2000 for embezzlements totaling nearly $9 million. In 2001 several dozen provincial road-building officials were convicted of embezzlement (CNN.com, 2001; *People's Daily* Online, 2001a).

Increasingly Chinese corruption involves collusion among officials, and often includes their business favorites. An official embezzlement ring in Hebei province, fraudulent dealing in land leases by twenty bureau or department heads, and a corruption ring involving public security officials and a business leader in Quinghai Province are examples (Gong, 2002: 86). The largest schemes can be quite lucrative: a major smuggling ring in Xiamen, Fujian province, may have brought over $6 billion worth of oil, cars, and other goods into the country between 1996 and 1999, avoiding as much as $3.6 billion in taxes. The deal began in an international trading company but required systematic participation by nearly 600 local customs, tax, and harbor officials (ABC News.com, 2000; *People's Daily* Online, 2001b; Gong, 2002; Yao, 2002).

Official impunity extends into the smaller cities and countryside too, aided by economic reform (Sun, 2004: ch. 4). Local party cadres and bureaucrats have acquired wider powers while supervision has weakened, producing a range of abuses at the expense of peasants and villagers. Early in the reform process local functionaries administering grain production, harvests, and seed allocation learned how to pursue personal gains (Oi, 1991). In the 1992 "IOU Crisis" local governments and bankers (the latter very much a part of the official apparatus) in rapidly growing areas diverted funds into unauthorized loans, creating such a cash shortage that payments for crops came in the form of "white slips" (*baitiaozi*) while subsidy programs went into default (Wedeman, 1997b). One result of such abuses has been a loss of faith, in rural areas, in efforts to govern through laws, and renewed backing for Maoist-style mass anti-corruption campaigns (Li, 2001).

The death sentences noted above may seem contradictory to the notion of weak constraints on official behavior. But looked at another way they say more about the party-state's inability to control officials on a continuing basis. A state capable of maintaining economic fair play and administrative standards through the courts and bureaucracy would apply a variety of moderate penalties quickly and credibly, and would not need to resort to extreme measures. But China faces a complex dilemma: unable to enforce either party discipline or state policy effectively, it still devolves important powers and growing *de facto* discretion to individuals throughout the country. Control from above is weakening, and the opposition parties and civil society that help check official impunity elsewhere do not exist. In an economy that is liberalized but not institutionalized, skillful Moguls who do not overreach themselves politically have much to gain. Relatively few are caught: Pei (1999: 101) reports that in 1996 only around a fifth of township level corruption allegations, and even fewer at higher levels, were even investigated. Those who are punished often have engaged in egregious offenses – economic, political, or both. Such abuses might well attract extreme penalties in any event but the party-state, having relatively few opportunities to win credibility for anti-corruption decrees, often seeks the maximum demonstration effects possible.

The party: leaders in search of a following

It was the Communist Party that founded the People's Republic and provided such discipline and coherence as it possessed for its first thirty years. Ideological direction, political education, and thought-reform extended downward into work groups and neighborhoods. Since at least the 1980s, however, the party has been beset by organizational rot. Lü Xiaobo characterizes that process as "involution": the failure of the party either to transform itself into a rationalized administrative regime or to sustain its revolutionary strengths. Caught in that contradiction, cadres fall back upon traditional practices and norms (Lü, 2000: 22) or just go through the motions. Older and more personal modes of getting things done – notably kinship and the web of ties and reciprocities known as *guanxi* – resurface, at times in updated forms (Kipnis, 1997; Gold, Guthrie, and Wank, 2002; Ku, 2003; Peng, 2004). Party leaders have responded with periodic discipline campaigns, but they failed to re-energize cadre commitments or local organization. A recent self-evaluation concluded that half of the party's rural cells were "weak" or "paralyzed"; meanwhile, the party presence within new business organizations is nearly non-existent (Pei, 2002). Part of the problem is that the party attempts to perform irreconcilable roles: Gong argues that ideological purity conflicts with the practicalities of governing, particularly during an era of reform and rapid change; the party's need for discipline inhibits the development of an autonomous and effective bureaucracy; and political goals conflict with effective policy implementation. In the end party and state elites "become an elite group in itself and for itself" (Gong, 1994: xviii-xix, and ch. 8) – a good working definition of Official Mogul corruption.

Corruption is just one of China's problems, but it is a particularly critical one – not just because of its scope, which no one knows with any precision, but because it takes a particularly damaging form. Official Mogul corruption is symptomatic of deeper problems that raise real doubts about whether China, over the middle to long term, can be governed at all. Pei (2002) suggests China may be approaching a governability crisis in which the administrative shortcomings of a "feeble state" are compounded by a deteriorating party unable to deal with the changes it has unleashed. The party-state's response, so far, has been to avoid political liberalization. Over the short term that strategy maintains party hegemony, limits disorderly influences upon policy and development, and in the view of the leadership allows the country to build a material basis for eventual change. Some have also argued that liberalizing the economy but not politics has allowed China to avoid the sorts of disruptive and violent forms of corruption seen in Russia (Sun, 1999).

But the party's continued political hegemony may not so much answer the governability question as avoid it. It has deprived the party of competition that would encourage needed changes, and of the credibility it could earn by responding effectively to social problems. It has denied the state vital feedback on the social consequences of economic transformation. Citizens and businesses lack legitimate ways to air grievances and affect the implementation of policies, while the overall system has been deprived of legitimate flexibility. Looked at that way, Official Mogul corruption is not just a response to economic incentives but an unofficial political process too; but because China's politics do not adapt and bend as a matter of course, the fear is that at some point the whole system could break. Absent an outbreak of political activity from unexpected sources, any sustained push for accountability will have to come from the party and the state bureaucracy. Neither, however, seems equal to the task, and Pei (1999: 100) reminds us that Western notions of accountability have no direct Chinese equivalent.

Prospects for reform: rule by law, political reform, or . . .?

Influence Market and Elite Cartel societies often respond to serious outbreaks of corruption with new legislation or renewed enforcement of laws on the books. Even Oligarch and Clan societies, whose legal frameworks have much more serious credibility problems, seek to improve the quality and enforcement of legislation. In China, however, the most basic notions of the "rule of law" – that is, of the law as an impersonal set of standards applied to all in a fair, authoritative, and impartial manner – long played little role in government. For decades laws were just one part of the party's political repertoire, to be defined, applied, and controlled by the top leadership. The lack of an independent judiciary further politicized the legal system. Party considerations overrode legislation; laws were means of political discipline, not popular mandates and certainly not limits on official powers. Accusing anyone in power of breaking the law could be both risky and pointless. Enforcement, particularly as regards abuses by party figures, was spotty, and penalties were small compared to the gains offered even by middling corrupt deals. As economic reform gathered momentum, the weak and politicized state of the law made corruption easier, deepened normative confusion, contributed to the emergence of an active economic "gray area" between the state and society, and reinforced the sense of official impunity at many levels.

During the 1990s courts and prosecutors became more active in the corruption field; periodic announcements of large numbers of cases investigated and punishments meted out became an integral part of anti-corruption strategy. More important, however, has been a gradual change in the role of law itself – not the full development of the rule *of* law, but rather an increasing tendency for the leadership to rule *by* law (Hao, 1999; Feinerman, 2000). The National People's Congress has been a more active legislature in recent years, enacting laws on speculation and bribery, and party leaders have relied more heavily on written standards as political discipline has lost its edge. A 1995 law created a process through which victims of official abuse could claim compensation, and indeed several hundred cases pursued under that law have produced settlements in favor of citizens. Ironically, corruption may push the party-state toward greater reliance upon laws and formal regulations as it copes with the complexity, vigor, and adaptability (at times, even, nefariousness) of the economic system it has unleashed.

Too much should not be made of such developments. Manion (2004) points out that law-oriented reform efforts suffer from functional and jurisdictional tensions arising between the party's anti-corruption agency (the Central Discipline Inspection Commission) and that of the state (the Supreme People's Procuratorate), and from the leadership's own mixed messages and behavior with respect to the importance of laws. Still, to the extent that officials become bound by written standards instead of by ideology, if citizens acquire recognized rights and the ability to make claims upon the regime, and if new limits to self-interest take root, China might develop the institutions market economies need in order to thrive without devouring themselves. If standards governing the sources and uses of power emerge, and acquire credibility, distinct from the personal will of top leaders, stronger restraints upon Official Moguls are possible. If corruption comes to be seen as a threat to China's economic transformation, rather than just as a byproduct of it, the backing to sustain reform may be at hand. Those, of course, are systemic political changes, not just anti-corruption measures.

Corruption control may thus depend upon the one kind of reform China has yet to try: political reform. China's path of change will be very much its own. But involving citizens as an active force shaping reform, rather than as the audience for mass campaigns, is an essential first step. Proclaiming standards is one thing; addressing the grievances citizens have because of corruption is quite another. If impunity is a key characteristic of Official Mogul corruption, reform will require sustained and effective countervailing forces (on popular contention in China see Perry, 1999). Basic civil liberties and clear, secure property rights would be major steps; real political competition might give leadership the feedback and political signals they now suppress (but as we shall see in the cases of Kenya and Indonesia, too fast a growth in competition might encourage insecure elites to steal more than ever). Broad-based demands through a political process might compel party elites to escape the "involution" trap (Lü, 2000) and resolve the conflicting imperatives (Gong, 1994) that are so debilitating at present.

Such changes are both a utopian "wish list" and utter necessities. China's transformation has been based on economic reform, but its current dilemma is largely political. What is to be done about the hopes and resentments of hundreds of millions of people who see others profiteering at their expense, and who have nowhere to turn for redress? We cannot minimize the awesome challenges involved: for the party, "letting go" would in all likelihood mean the end, while the state would face huge institutional stress. But while such a system may shake and sway, if it is politically flexible it *might* not break. The same cannot be said of the Chinese pressure cooker today.

Kenya: the "big man" and his moguls

During the long rule of Kenya's President Daniel arap Moi (1978–2002) corrupt officials had a reach that their counterparts in established market democracies might only envy. Americans may worry about the future of their social security system; in Kenya, well-placed political figures simply stole the National Social Security Fund – twice (Human Rights Watch, 2002: 7–8). One of Moi's political backers stole the land on which a flourishing public market had operated for decades (Klopp, 2000). A citizen seeking redress of such abuses through the courts stood a strong chance of ending up before a corrupt judge. National commissions of inquiry compiled significant evidence on major corruption cases, but little or no action followed. Corruption in Kenya was a smash-and-grab operation with disastrous effects on development, all based on the power of a dominant national leader.

Kenya can point to a number of hopeful developments. Competitive elections have been held since 1992, and brought victory for the opposition, led by Mwai Kibaki, in December, 2002. International aid and scrutiny have been extensive, with assistance being withheld and restored at key junctures based on Kenya's implementation of political and administrative reforms. Civil society is active, the press publishes unfavorable news and critical commentary about the government, and non-governmental organizations – many of them advocating reform – have proliferated. Economic policymakers have responded to international pressures and incentives with significant liberalization. A proposed new Constitution is intended to build more accountable government and reduce presidential domination by creating a Prime Minister and cabinet; the draft document was adopted by a national conference early in 2004 but has drawn much opposition from segments of parliament and the executive. While poor, divided along ethnic and tribal lines, and burdened by a history of dictatorial rule, Kenyans may finally be moving toward an open, viable economy and accountable, effective government.

But Kenya's many problems were also reflected in the rapacious pattern of Official Mogul corruption during the Moi years. Monopoly political power in a setting of extremely weak state institutions created strong incentives to corruption for the President and his personal favorites while weakening legal checks and countervailing political forces. As in China (albeit on a far smaller economic scale), economic liberalization meant that political favorites could devise a wide range of dispersed monopolies, exploiting "squeeze points" of varying types with impunity – often with Moi's protection. Opposition groups and much of society as a whole were not only denied opportunities, but were victimized: farmers and small merchants saw their land and assets taken by Moi cronies, and had few opportunities for political or legal recourse. While international organizations took limited action against Kenyan corruption, they tended to conceive of it in terms of high-level bribery of state officials, as discussed in chapter 1. As a result, some of the worst abuses – notably, the illegal seizure of private and public lands by government insiders – drew relatively little international attention (Klopp, 2000). Meanwhile, legitimate as well as corrupt economic opportunities in many sectors were dominated by the President and his personal allies. Corruption in Kenya not only enriched the President and his backers; it helped keep the nation undemocratic, the government ineffective, and the people poor.

A legacy of corruption

As the Official Moguls notion suggests, corruption in Kenya has been shaped by chronically weak institutions, economic liberalization – which in a setting of pervasive poverty translated into compelling economic opportunities for a very few – and, most of all, unchecked and unaccountable political power. Since independence in 1963 politics and the quest for wealth have revolved around the presidency – an office strengthened considerably by the Constitution, drawn up under British tutelage (Ross, 1992: 424). The legendary Jomo Kenyatta provided powerful symbolic leadership, but behind him a broad nationalist coalition quickly deteriorated into a factional scramble to tap presidential power and prestige for enrichment and political advantage. By the time of Kenyatta's death in 1978 the nation was governed by a presidential but largely authoritarian regime (Nyong'o, 1989: 231).

Moi, Kenyatta's successor, initially released some political prisoners and presided over a degree of political decompression (for early optimism see Berg-Schlosser, 1982). But he began his move toward one-man rule and a pervasive national personality cult after a coup attempt in 1982. Moi's Kenya African National Union party (KANU) was unopposed from 1969 through 1992 (Ross, 1992: 425); in 1987 it did away with secret ballots in parliamentary elections. KANU and Moi's personal networks were sustained by a powerful and pervasive system of patronage distributing jobs, administrative decisions, and money (Human Rights Watch, 2002: 4), often in such a way as to intensify tribal and ethnic divisions. Where carrots failed there were always sticks at hand: persistent critics were subject to repression and violence. In 1990 Foreign Minister Robert Ouko, a vocal opponent of corruption in Moi's government, was murdered (Ross, 1992: 434). That crime was eventually traced to some of Moi's personal cronies, and had severe effects upon incoming aid, trade, and investment (East African Standard, 2003a). International pressure led Moi to agree in late 1991 to constitutional changes allowing the existence of other parties and competitive elections. But by then, a legacy of one-man rule, thinly veiled by democratic and nationalistic rhetoric, was firmly in place (Ross, 1992: 440).

The opposition that emerged in 1992 and again in 1997 was divided among forty or more parties and as many tribal groups (Human Rights Watch, 2002: 4). Its campaign and candidates were denied full press coverage, particularly outside the capital city of Nairobi. Election procedures, while reformed somewhat during the 1990s, were still marred by fraud, vote-buying, and a degree of violence, and produced shaky mandates: Moi's victory in 1992 for example, came with only 36 percent of the vote in a four-way race (Holmquist, Weaver, and Ford, 1994: 69). The judiciary was corrupt, intimidated, and demoralized; victims of human rights abuses, illegal land seizures, and corruption have had little success in seeking legal remedies or compensation.

Under the elections agreement reached in the early 1990s Moi was obliged to step down after two five-year elected terms, and in December, 2002, Kenya had its most competitive presidential election to date. The victory of Mwai Kibaki, candidate of the opposition National Rainbow Coalition (NARC), over Uhuru Kenyatta – Jomo Kenyatta's politically inexperienced son, and Moi's hand-picked choice as successor – was decisive, by a margin of 63 to 30 percent (World Factbook Online,

2004). But the new government faces severe problems and resource constraints, and both Kibaki and a major segment of his political backing only recently split from KANU itself. A decade of multiparty elections may actually have intensified corruption in significant ways, as we shall see.

Helping oneself: corruption with impunity

Monopoly-style corruption by the President and his cronies was not the only kind of corruption to occur in Kenya during the Moi era. So-called petty corruption took place in everyday encounters; foreign investors and multinational corporations were involved as well, at times through bribery and extortion at high levels, and also through preferential access to resources. But the ability of the President and his allies to plunder the economy was the most significant corruption problem from the standpoint of development and justice. Corruption had been common under Kenyatta, but the Moi years brought a change. Before, major corruption had generally consisted of padding budgets, or of percentages paid as kickbacks and bribes, in connection with legitimate development projects. As Moi's regime took hold, however, the projects themselves were more and more dubious, conceived and funded essentially to benefit the President and his clients (Ross, 1992: 433).

Both the power to extract corrupt gains and the weakness of political and legal constraints derived from Moi's dominant position. Numerous cases were investigated by special commissions but few punishments resulted, and the resulting reports were generally never published (Human Rights Watch, 2002: 3–4). In contrast to Influence Market cases, legitimate business was often the target of corrupt schemes, not the instigator. There was no doubt who was in charge in Kenya; unlike Elite Cartel cases, patronage and corrupt elite networks added to Moi's backing but his rule did not depend upon them. There were no powerful oligarchs outside Moi's circle to plunder the weak state or build economic bases of their own. Instead, Moi and top figures used monopoly power to enrich themselves, allowed lesser allies to create and exploit smaller corrupt advantages, and used patronage to keep society politically dependent and fragmented along tribal lines.

The President and his cronies exploited both politics and the economy. In the Goldenberg scandal of the early 1990s a politically favored businessman claimed tax breaks on fictitious exports of gold and jewels. State officials and KANU leaders allegedly shared the spoils. Thanks to their protection no official accounting of the losses, or of culpability, was made until late 2003, when a commission of inquiry held widely reported public hearings. Other cases of theft from the public sector, often involving both officials and their private-sector allies, included the looting of the National Social Security Fund, both in the early 1990s and again (to the tune of 256 million Kenya Shillings, or about $3.2 million) at the end of the Moi era in 2002. Smuggling involving officials was widespread; imported food was a particularly hot commodity given the high duties that applied until mid-decade. Once in the country contraband was sold at market prices, converting unpaid duties into large profits while depriving the government of much-needed revenues (Human Rights Watch, 2002: 7–8; *East African Standard* Online, 2003b, 2003d).

Elections were one-party affairs until 1992, and featured patronage and electoral abuses throughout the Moi years. A pervasive patronage system fed by misappropriated state assets and international aid reinforced tribal divisions, turning exploited groups against each other rather than against KANU. Money, jobs, land, and other rewards were given to supporters and systematically withheld from others, giving Moi a personally loyal and economically dependent political base. Moi's own tribe, the Kalenjin, were widely seen as major beneficiaries of political spoils, as were the Maasai and the Luo; their youths were mobilized to attack members of "opposition" tribes such as the Kikuyu, the Luhya, and the Kamba. Moi agents intimidated voters, stole ballots and election records, and seized non-KANU voters' identification cards. Such abuses were part of a broader link between corruption and human rights violations; they also helped maintain the dependency and poverty that made patronage effective to begin with (Ross, 1992: 430–431; Human Rights Watch, 2002).

Judicial corruption was extensive as well, with judges deciding cases along tribe-and-party lines, at times on demand from the President himself. The judiciary was severely compromised for most of the post-independence period, with expatriate British jurists often tolerating some of the most egregious violations of due process and human rights. Judges protected corrupt figures and helped preserve the culture of official impunity; many solicited bribes and participated in corrupt schemes with other officials and business figures. In the Fall of 2003 President Kibaki suspended twenty-three judges and appointed two high-level investigative tribunals; charges against up to eighty others were under consideration. Court of Appeal Judge Richard Otieno Kwach, one of the most prominent jurists implicated in the 2003 cases, had chaired a Judicial Reforms Committee a decade earlier that provided some of the first authoritative evidence on judicial corruption during one-party rule (Ross, 1992; Human Rights Watch, 2002: 7, 13–14; *East African Standard* Online 2003b, 2003c, 2003d; Lacey, 2003b).

Land thefts: using and defending personal power

Official impunity was clearest and most rapacious in the outright theft of land from private citizens and the public (Klopp, 2000, 2002). Ministers, political families, well-connected business people, and "local tycoons" with top-level protection seized valuable urban and rural land for themselves. In a one-party system with a corrupt judiciary and a President who could see that critics were "taken care of" there was little or no recourse. In 1994, for example, land under Nairobi's Westlands open-air market, officially granted to the city council for exclusive use as a market, was claimed in a private deal by developers headed by a Nairobi city politician with KANU backing. Efforts by stallholders to buy the land themselves encountered official resistance and ultimately failed. Most of the vendors were Kikuyu, and were thus seen as threats to the local KANU MP. In 1998 public lands in the Karura Forest just north of Nairobi were handed over to developers; public outcry was to no avail. The following year the Ministry of Lands, under pressure from opposition MPs and human rights groups, revealed that over half of the forest had been given to sixty-seven developers whom the Minister of Lands and the Attorney General could not or would not name. Information on almost a third of those firms had vanished from the Registrar General's office. MPs who sought to plant trees on some of the seized lands were beaten by security guards. In 1997 Operation Firimbi, a civil society protest against land grabs, documented over 250 such cases. Official Moguls and their protégés also carried out dubious "privatizations" of other public assets (Amnesty International, 2000; Klopp, 2000; Human Rights Watch, 2002).

The land thefts (Klopp, 2000) are notable both for what they tell us about the dynamics of Official Mogul corruption and for their effects upon society. In some respects land-grabbing under Moi was an extension of practices dating from the colonial era. In the short run, however, both the Westlands Market case and the seizure of Karura Forest lands reflected Moi's personal power and determination to reward important followers. Hope of access to such deals in the future would have been a strong motivating factor for other Moi clients. Land theft was facilitated by Kenya's compromised judiciary and weak bureaucracy; victims and critics seeking redress by political means had nowhere to turn. In both cases valuable resources were converted into patronage and exploited with few constraints.

The land-seizure cases also show how liberal reforms require a framework of political and state institutions and support from civil society. As Klopp (2000: 16–17) points out, the advent of competitive elections in

Kenya, in the early 1990s, came at a time when cuts in development aid and international scrutiny of political repression were depriving Moi and KANU of many of the traditional tactics and more modest benefits that had long sustained their patronage systems. While Moi faced only a weak and divided opposition, he took no chances; in the face of increased uncertainty created by competitive elections land and other major assets became extremely attractive political rewards. Klopp (2000) argues that through land seizures and other high-level theft Moi kept the patronage system going and, in effect, shifted some of the costs of aid cuts on to society at large. That international anti-corruption scrutiny tended to focus on high-level bribery and overlook this particular form of patronage only made it more useful. Human Rights Watch (2002: 7) concluded that multiparty elections and international pressure for reform made for more corruption, of more rapacious sorts, during the 1990s as Moi fought to defend his power by any means at hand.

Liberalized state, vulnerable society

Because economic and limited political liberalization had proceeded without necessary institution- and civil-society building, victims and opponents of land-grabbing had few choices. They could get little or no help from the courts or police. Voting for the opposition was likely to have little effect; indeed, to the extent that stronger opposition gave Moi a sense of insecurity it might intensify his abuses. Journalists and the press could report the stories, but civil society in general, and institutions of vertical and horizontal accountability, were too weak to take on the Moguls. Protests against land-grabbing did take place, and may have helped build some strength in civil society for the longer term: new organizations were formed, and demonstrations held. Students, already energized by corrupt dealings within their universities, mobilized against corruption. The issue was one reason why the fragmented opposition began to unify in advance of the 2002 presidential election (Human Rights Watch, 2002: 4–7). Once it became clear that Moi actually would relinquish the presidency fissures deepened within KANU, ultimately leading to the exit of the Kibaki faction which joined the opposition to form NARC. But the land grabs were done – testament to the risks of premature political liberalization, and to the difficulty of creating countervailing forces sufficient to restrain corruption.

Kenya's need was, and is, not just for elections, but for deeper demo-cratization and a sound, accountable state. That means more than just rolling back the state role in the economy, instituting a measure of electoral competition, and assuming that a healthy balance of forces will emerge on its own. It requires that people and groups perceive a strong, self-interested stake in politics and markets *and* a realistic chance of defending their interests. Strong public institutions (and, as China's case shows, a workable conception of what "public" does and does not mean) are essential to that sort of reform, but they cannot be created by fiat, legislation, or enhanced administrative procedures alone. Critical sustaining energy for reform, based on lasting identities and interests, must come from society itself (on the history of such efforts see Klopp, 2002). But organizing citizens for reform as a worthy social purpose will rarely be sufficient: reduced corruption is a public good, often won at considerable risk and sacrifice, and free-rider problems can be severe. Extensive contention among social forces with real roots in society is essential if broadly supported political and economic settlements are to be reached and sustained by lasting interests.

Power without accountability

Kenya's corruption reflects deeper and broader problems. The 31 million residents of this former British colony have a GDP per capita of only about $1,000 per year, and suffer from some of the world's highest mortality rates. Over two million suffer from HIV or AIDS, and the disease claims nearly 200,000 lives per year. Less than a tenth of the country's land is arable. Human rights abuses, police violence, and a weak court system for years made the rule of law a doubtful proposition for most citizens (Ross, 1992: 429; Amnesty International, 2000). For a generation the economy has been stagnant or contracting, while the population has grown at over 1 percent per year, enlarged also by a quarter-million refugees fleeing conflicts in nearby regions. Kenyans are poorer now than they were a generation ago, and the state's ability to deliver essential services has deteriorated (Human Rights Watch, 2002: 3).

As with other African societies those problems are not the whole story. Kenya is a vigorous society with widespread literacy and considerable grassroots activism. Corruption, human rights abuses, environmental issues, and violence against women have all been the focus of demonstrations and organizational activity. The Kibaki government has only been in office a short time and faces problems on a fearsome scale, but it has moved aggressively against judicial corruption. Early reports suggested a renewed social optimism, resistance to corruption and other abuses, and trends toward improved official behavior (Lacey, 2003a). There are poorer societies in Africa and elsewhere, and there are places plagued by more extensive violence. Tribal identities and loyalties, a source of conflict in some respects, also draw upon rich historic traditions. Still, it is clear that corruption has helped divide those social forces, pitting them against each other instead of fostering groups capable of checking official abuses, and has deprived Kenyans of basic rights and opportunities. Without corruption, Kenya would still face poverty, AIDS, rapid population growth, human rights abuses and other problems. But with significantly less of it the country would be better able to confront those challenges, and to use the resources at its disposal in effective, accountable ways.

Kenya, of course, is not alone in experiencing Official Mogul style corruption. The specifics of the syndrome will vary according to a variety of local factors – notably, just who is in charge and what he or she chooses to do with political power. To examine some of those variations, and to look further into the implications of democratization for serious corruption, we turn to one final case – that of Indonesia.

Indonesia: *korrupsi, kollusi, nepotisme*

Indonesia experienced forty-plus years of Official Mogul corruption under Presidents Sukarno and Suharto. Misappropriation of government funds and international aid, judicial and bureaucratic abuses, business ventures by politicians and military officers, and widespread patronage marked Sukarno's Guided Democracy (1955–65). Those practices reached even more pervasive and profitable levels under Suharto's New Order regime (1966–98). From the mid-1970s onwards, patronage and elite privilege were aspects of a broader political settlement under which citizens tolerated official abuses and personal rule in exchange for rapid economic growth and occasional political spoils. These were interlinked in complex ways: Suharto's personal power was cemented by his national patronage system, one-party dominance through his Golkar organization, and the loyalty of military leaders who shared in the spoils (Liddle, 1985; Cole, 2001; Makarim, 2001). He could give and withhold major rewards, enforce commitments both of the state to its policies and of individuals to specific deals both legitimate and otherwise, and impose working limits upon the exploits of his subordinates (MacIntyre, 2003: 11–13). International investors could thus factor corruption into their business plans as a somewhat predictable cost, and take advantage of an attractive mix of political order, labor docility, and lax regulation. Indonesia enjoyed a rapid economic rise between the 1970s and 1997.

Ambitious institutional reforms followed the fall of Suharto in 1998. A President, chosen before 2004 by the People's Consultative Assembly and now popularly elected, is both head of state and head of the government. The legislative branch was reconstituted in 2004 into a popularly elected House of Representatives and House of Regional Representatives. The economy, weaker than before the Asian crisis of 1997, has been growing at about 3 or 4 percent annually in recent years and produces a GDP per capita of around $3,100. Over a quarter of the population lives in poverty, however, and many more are underemployed or living near the poverty line (World Factbook Online 2004). Despite – or, perhaps, because of – democratization, the governments that followed Suharto, lacking his mechanisms of control, have been less effective at sustaining growth and have had even less success in restraining corruption.

New Order corruption

Indonesia would be difficult to govern under the best of circumstances. A Dutch colony until 1949, the country spans 3,500 miles or more of ocean and islands from Sumatra in the west to Irian Jaya in the east. Its 235 million people live in twenty-seven provinces encompassing about 6,000 of its over 17,000 total islands, with a total land area of approximately 750,000 square miles. Javanese (45 percent) are the dominant ethnic group, and Islam (88 percent) is by far the largest religion, but much of the nation is divided by ethnicity, language, and geography, which in areas such as Aceh and East Timor (the latter granted independence in 2002) have produced extensive conflict (World Factbook Online, 2004).

Suharto's New Order was presented to Indonesians as a form of national, social, and political redemption through strong presidential leadership. When then-General Suharto and his fellow military plotters took power after seeing off a 1965 coup attempt by communist forces they promised security – an end to contention between often-abusive local leaders and radicals – and development, aided by extensive international aid (Cole, 2001: 14). Corruption from the top down was not only a temptation, but also the essence of political strategy: the loyalties of local elites, bureaucrats, military leaders, and would-be politicians and businessmen could not be compelled in such a large and far-flung nation, but they could be bought. Suharto began the construction of an extensive patronage system that by the 1980s distributed benefits and bought support throughout the country (Makarim, 2001: 6). Spoils were obtained from dummy lines on (and off) the national budget, or from government and foreign aid funds that were simply stolen; from the proceeds of military-run businesses, at least until the economic liberalization of the 1980s; from kickbacks on construction and development contracts, and from international businesses receiving key concessions; and from a string of personal "foundations" operated by Suharto himself

(King, 2000; Cole, 2001: 15; Makarim, 2001: 6–7; MacIntyre, 2003: 12). Bureaucrats were kept on board through job-based patronage and compulsory membership in an official organization of civil servants (Robertson-Snape, 1999: 592; Cole, 2001, 15); military officers found it easy and lucrative to go into business. In the absence of an autonomous, effective state framework (never a Suharto goal in any event) this personal political network became the key institution of the New Order regime (Liddle, 1985: 70, 71).

Like Elite Cartel cases real power in Suharto's Indonesia was exercised through corrupt networks rather than official public institutions. But – critically – unlike Elite Cartel cases those networks were not coalitions of elites with diverse power bases pursuing a common interest in staving off increasing competition. They were the only game in town: hierarchical, tightly controlled, dispensing benefits available nowhere else, and centralizing power in the hands of one man. At the peak of the pyramid, the President, his family, and select associates took the largest share of the spoils. But for others seeking economic opportunity in Indonesia there was much to gain from falling in with this system, and everything to lose by opposing it. For those in more traditional and remote segments of society, patronage and the growth it helped sustain not only delivered at least fragmentary benefits; it also reinforced hierarchical and deferential traditions dating from the Dutch colonial era and also, perhaps, back to the days of Javanese kings (Robertson-Snape, 1999: 597–600).

Corruption, Suharto style

The New Order enabled Suharto to impose structure and order upon corruption. Bureaucrats, military leaders, and Golkar figures could divert public resources, go into business, or extract bribes and rents, but their dealings were not allowed to disrupt economic development or political order. A network of military officers or retirees reporting to Suharto served as Inspectors General in all public bureaucracies, enforcing that discipline (Liddle, 1985: 78; MacIntyre, 2003: 9). Those who stepped across the invisible line were fired, punished, or held up to public ridicule – the more so after 1973, when particularly egregious scandals touched off unrest. In 1985, for example, excessive corruption in the customs service resulted in its handover, for a time, to a private Swiss firm. Top cotton-importing officials were fired the following year when their take began to harm the broader textile industry; and in 1996 a transport minister who threatened to become a political problem was publicly shamed (MacIntyre, 2003: 11). Some of those moves – most prominently, the temporary privatization of customs – could usefully be advertised as evidence of reform, but they were equally important as warnings to other officials to keep their illicit dealing within limits.

The President amassed considerable wealth, but even more remarkable were the companies, import–export concessions, and whole industries held by "Suharto, Inc." – his six children, his grandchildren, nieces, nephews, and other relatives. Family members held significant equity in over 500 domestic corporations and many more overseas, and controlled lands that combined were larger than the area of Belgium (King, 2000: 613). Holdings included banks and manufacturers, the national lottery, and a monopoly over the marketing of cloves (lucrative in Indonesia, where tens of millions of smokers prefer tobacco laced with clove). Family members also struck alliances with top figures in Indonesia's economically powerful Chinese minority. After liberalization in the 1980s the only major industries that continued to enjoy protectionist policies were Suharto family holdings. A 1998 estimate of the family's wealth put it at over $15 billion, and by one reckoning over $70 billion passed through family members' pockets and businesses between the mid-1960s and 1998 (Liddle, 1996; Robertson-Snape, 1999; King, 2000; Cole, 2001; Hornick, 2001).

The military was a full partner in the New Order from the beginning, and in corrupt dealings too. Official military outlays were modest by regional standards, but other expenditures were hidden elsewhere in the budget, took place off-budget, or were laundered through agencies such as the state oil corporation. Funds from the President's personal foundations helped purchase advanced weapons, another factor that maintained the generals' political loyalties. The result was a continuing flow of unaccounted resources to top brass, many of whom were active in business or real-estate. Others took kickbacks on military procurement contracts or parlayed top military positions into lucrative consultancies or directorships, both before and after retirement. The military remains a significant economic as well as political force today (Liddle, 1985; King, 2000; Makarim, 2001; Malley, 2003).

Judges and bureaucrats shared in the wealth as well. A 1995 estimate by a retired Supreme Court jurist had it that half of the nation's judiciary would fix trials for a price (Hornick, 2001: 9). Low-level bureaucrats in Indonesia, in the 1990s, were paid the equivalent of just $25 per month plus a rice allowance; they thus had little choice but to partake of Suharto and Golkar patronage, available so long as they made friendly decisions, and were always on the lookout for bribes. Banks often made "command loans" to favored business people. A Canadian firm that discovered what appeared to be major sources of gold ore found its license applications held up while a family member put together a competing proposal; the two bidders ended up hiring competing family members to expedite their proposals, for fees and percentages that could have amounted to hundreds of millions of dollars. Similar deals involved oil and timber concessions and international bids to construct factories (Robertson-Snape, 1999; King, 2000; Hornick, 2001).

After Suharto – ?

Resentment of corruption – notably, but not limited to, Suharto's wealth and the fortunes amassed by his children and relatives – mounted during the 1990s, reinforced by resurgent regional, religious, and ethnic antagonisms. When the Asian economic crisis of 1997 hit Indonesia with full force it both disrupted the growth that had given many citizens a modest but real stake in the regime and dried up the funds supporting Suharto's patronage network (Robertson-Snape, 1999: 618). State institutions, including the bureaucracy and judiciary, had long been weak and compromised (and remain so today); thus, when Suharto's personal authority was undermined the political settlement collapsed. Students took to the streets demanding his ouster; one of their most frequent chants – *"Korrupsi, Kollusi, Nepotisme"* (KKN), or "corruption, collusion, nepotism" (Robertson-Snape, 1999: 589) voiced the grievances of millions.

After Suharto was replaced by President B.J. Habibie there was widespread hope that the New Order and its abuses had been swept aside. At least sixty new political parties were formed in the early months of the Habibie government (Seabrook, 1998). But KKN scarcely came to an end; indeed many practices continue, now lacking the structure provided by family ties, a dominant President, military monitoring, and Golkar discipline. The result is corruption that is if anything even more disruptive – both an unstable universe of fiefdoms and mini-monopolies like that seen in China *and* a scramble to meet the rising costs of multiparty politics and patronage resembling the experience of Kenya. Political turmoil produced three weak Presidents in a row and did nothing to strengthen state institutions. Elections turned into a scramble for political money; legislators, faced with the task of funding campaigns, became more adept at demanding payments for favors and support (Malley, 2003: 144–145). The new Indonesia has experienced significant liberalization of the economy from the mid-1980s onwards, and a sudden political decompression beginning in 1998, in the absence of a sound state framework and civil society; it now must contend with "hundreds of little Suhartos" (MacIntyre, 2003: 17).

What next for Indonesia?

New Order corruption began in an authoritarian system with very weak state institutions, reached well beyond elite circles to distribute various forms of patronage, and helped maintain the personal rule of the President. But it also fed upon, and embodied, a system of control that ended in 1998, and changes since that time may be driving the country in an Oligarch and Clan direction. President Megawati Soekarnoputri attempted to rebuild a portion of the old national political machine, but still lost the 2004 presidential runoff to former General Susilo Bambang Yudhoyono by a 60 to 37 percent margin. Yudhoyono is able, educated, and unlike Megawati is actively interested in governing (*New York Times*, September 22, 2004). But the fragmentation of politicized state mono-polies, frantic competition among dozens of parties desperate for cash, chronic violence, weak and corrupt courts and judiciary, and the major natural resources and economic opportunities at stake in Indonesia might well remind us of early-1990s Russia. Any such claim is of course speculative at best, and will require careful continuing study: some New Order figures, political habits, patterns of bureaucratic corruption, and military influence remain potent (Cole, 2001: 16–17; Malley, 2003: 143–145).

Conclusion: hopeless cases?

We have come quite some distance from the Influence Market cases that have done so much to shape international thinking about corruption and reform. From situations in which private interests seek relatively specific influence within strong institutions we have arrived at a syndrome in which powerful state and political officials plunder the economy and society more or less as they please. This sort of corruption – like the Oligarchs and Clans syndrome – has devastating implications for demo-cratic development. Its economic implications are more complex; indeed, some societies in the Official Moguls group have experienced long periods of sustained growth while corruption flourished, and in Indonesia and some of its neighbors growth was part of a national political settlement that helped corrupt officials stay on top. Perhaps these countries would have grown even faster with less corruption, but that is difficult to know. Moguls such as Suharto, development-minded and willing to use corrupt influence to create commitment mechanisms for the state and major entrepreneurs, are corrupt monopolists, but their regimes operate more like coordinated monopolies than the much more destructive uncoordinated kind (Shleifer and Vishny, 1993; MacIntyre, 2003). Still, such economies would seem less open and adaptive than suc-cessful markets – a possible contributor to the Asian crisis of the late 1990s.

Those sorts of ideas must await further exploration elsewhere. What is clear though is that simply to say China, Kenya, and Indonesia rank higher on a corruption scale than other societies does not capture the impunity, the weakness of institutions and vulnerability of society, or the far-reaching consequences of corruption there. Indeed, it is hard to know just what "more corruption" means: we can easily imagine a system (such as Kenya's, perhaps) in which, because of the weakness of countervailing forces, a small number of corrupt deals at high levels have as much societal effect as does widespread "money politics" in Japan. Further, China shows that within the Official Moguls syndrome basic notions of corruption can become very broad and diffuse. Using index numbers to compare such cases and changes seems pointless.

Another important contrast is that Official Mogul societies would seem to be the most vulnerable, among our four groups, to state capture (Hellman, Jones, and Kaufmann, 2000; Kaufmann, Hellman, Jones, and Schankerman, 2000). Elite Cartels may colonize parts of the state, but they are still coalitions of differing elite interests; and, judging by our statistical indicators, official institutions retain moderate levels of strength and capacity. In Oligarch and Clan societies the state is very weak but corrupt influences are fragmented and contentious. Moi's Kenya and Suharto's Indonesia, by contrast, were run by and in the interest of dominant leaders and their personal clients. China is far more complex; the role of the party in creating the state meant that it was captured in some respects from the very beginning, but the sheer size of the society, and of the economy that is emerging, resist control by anyone at the moment.

It is also clear that Official Mogul cases differ among themselves in ways we cannot ignore. Moguls' personal agendas matter a great deal. Strong institutions, in a bureaucratic and information-oriented age, tend to resemble each others in important ways, while weak ones come in many shapes and sizes and can pose a wide variety of problems. The same is true of liberalizing economies: China's example shows that such economies do not immediately become integrated capitalist systems, but rather can evolve a complex and contradictory mix of market, patri- monial, and bureaucratic mechanisms that may not be well integrated with each other and across a given society. Indonesia's post-Suharto political liberalization likewise shows that when a dictatorship collapses elite discipline can go with it. For these reasons the Official Mogul group is the most diverse of our four.

Still, societies in this group do share a common corruption problem – officials who can plunder economies and societies with impunity. Perhaps it is most accurate to say that the consequences of that sort of power can be very diverse indeed. That is not only an analytical point. If Official Mogul corruption does differ qualitatively from that found in Influence

Market societies, and among cases as well, reforms originating in affluent market democracies are likely to be irrelevant at best. Even though those advanced countries have had periods of more intense and disruptive corruption in their history, their reform ideas tend to emphasize the remedies that keep corruption moderate to low, not necessarily those that brought it under control in the first place. Their "best practices" seem more likely to be the results of sustained democratic and economic development than ways of launching it – particularly where Official Moguls (or, for that matter, Oligarchs) are strong. The move to multiparty elections in Kenya and Indonesia in the absence of necessary foundations seems to have intensified corruption. International aid can become just another revenue stream for entrenched political leaders. Businesses are more critical of corruption than in decades past, but many still choose to adapt to the realities of Official Mogul countries. Recommendations to build up civil society seem futile in places where ordinary citizens lead lives marked by deprivation, insecurity, oppression, and isolation. Calls for "political will" in countries whose leaders rule with impunity look increasingly like a bad joke.

At the same time we cannot simply write off the worst cases (nor has anyone proposed to do so). Many Official Mogul countries are large societies, strategically important in economic, democratic, and security terms. Corrupt regimes in some of these countries provide safe havens for terror groups, drug networks, and the illegal global traffic in arms, contraband – and human beings. Their futures will affect the emerging global system in profound ways. A bit of historical perspective is helpful too: few might have bet much on the prospects of controlling corruption in seventeenth- and nineteenth-century Britain or the nineteenth-century United States; similarly, as recently as the early 1980s Korea would not have seemed a likely candidate for democratization.

Change can come, at times from surprising directions, and it can unfold quickly. Positive trends may emerge in the form of halfway measures, or even come disguised as bad news. China has not attained rule *of* law, but rule *by* law may be a necessary if not sufficient step toward a system of specified, limited official powers. Building a new national political machine in Indonesia to take the place of Golkar would require some kinds of corruption but could impose enough order to avoid others far worse. Further, the limited effects of stepped-up investigations and prosecutions in China – particularly those culminating in capital punishment – suggests that thinking about corruption as a law-enforcement problem (a luxury appropriate in Influence Market societies, but not where Moguls make their own law) is too narrow a scope, either for analysis or reform. Similarly, institution-building should be thought of as a whole-society process, with grassroots and bottom-up efforts at least as important as reforms instituted from top-down (Carothers, 1999). Finally, change seems best when it is gradual and moderated by sound institutions. Politics too can be a positive part of the mix, particularly if we conceive of it less in terms of elections and more in terms of engaged and even contentious relationships among social groups. It may be no accident that Korea, long thought of as a tense and contentious society, was a surprise winner in the democratization processes of the 1980s and 1990s.

It is one thing to say that reform agendas will need to be tailored to the realities of differing syndromes of corruption, but quite another to say what the major contrasts and adaptations will have to be. Some initial thoughts on that issue, as well as questions for further research, are the focus of our final chapter.

8 From analysis to reform

Seeing corruption in new ways

It is unlikely that this book will persuade the world that corruption occurs in exactly four syndromes precisely as discussed in the preceding seven chapters. My goal is both more modest and more subversive: I hope the arguments offered here will help change the ways we think about corruption, development, and reform. It is time to rethink the current emphasis on corruption-index scores; the notion implicit in that approach that the problem is essentially the same everywhere; the view of corruption as a primary cause of developing countries' difficulties; and the notion that reform means eliminating corrupt behavior by emulating affluent market democracies. It is not that such ideas are utterly wrong: they have helped put corruption back on the international policy agenda and have strengthened pressures upon leaders around the world to improve the ways they govern. But understanding contrasting syndromes of corruption can open up a new and productive debate over democratic and economic development, reform, and justice. Even if that debate eventually supersedes much of what I have argued here – as will likely be the case – this book will have been a success.

This final chapter has two purposes. First I will briefly revisit some of the main points of the book in part to bring out analytical problems on which further work is needed. Then I will turn to reform. At many points I have suggested that differing systemic corruption problems require differing responses, and that understanding their deeper causes is essential. The question is not just of policy choices but also of expectations: what should we expect anti-corruption reforms to accomplish, and how will we know whether we are succeeding? The discussion will not produce any sort of anti-corruption "toolkit" – indeed, I argue against that approach – nor any "national action plans." Instead it will offer propositions about ways to choose among reform measures, many of which are familiar but need to be deployed in combinations and sequences appropriate to underlying contrasts in participation and institutions.

What have we learned?

We began with three questions: What are the links among political and economic liberalization, the strength or weakness of state, political, and social institutions, and the kinds of corruption societies experience? What syndromes of corruption result from various combinations of those influences and how do they differ? What kinds of reform are – and are not – appropriate for these contrasting corruption problems?

A definitive answer to the first question would require a comprehensive critique of globalization, both as a bundle of processes and as an influence upon international policymaking, and knowledge of the full extent of corruption that we are unlikely ever to have. Still, I have sought to demonstrate connections by comparing the ways people pursue, use, and exchange wealth and power within the context of institutions of varying strength and composition. Trends in political and economic liberalization are among the defining characteristics of our four syndromes, both conceptually and in the data analysis. "Institutions" are understood here in broad terms: not just constitutional or administrative, but also political and social. In some cases the national bureaucracy is the institutional focus, while in others the state of political parties or patterns of traditional authority in society are critical – a level of variation that consensus prescriptions about governance tend to overlook. Diverse combinations of participation and institutions guide the response to the second question, as seen in the categories and scenarios offered in chapter 3. The notion of syndromes is important: it emphasizes not only distinctive patterns of corruption but also complex webs of cause and effect.

Reform – the third issue – is a matter of strengthening and balancing both participation and institutions over the long term. Worthwhile schemes for improving public management and strengthening civil society abound, as do calls for "political will," but elites and society must have a stake in their success. Even then the criterion for success may not be whether aggregate levels of corruption are decreasing: often that is impossible to judge, and change may also be qualitative. At one level, successful reforms will help a society withstand corruption and may shift the problem itself toward less disruptive forms. But at a more basic level the issue is *justice* – enhancing citizens' ability to pursue and defend their own economic and political wellbeing free from abuse and exploitation by political and economic elites. The opportunity to participate in open, competitive, and fair political and economic processes, and the ability of institutions to sustain those processes and link them to each other while restraining their excesses, are both defining characteristics of our four syndromes and ultimate goals of reform.

The syndromes and cases

The core argument is for the existence of four qualitatively different major syndromes of corruption. There is no magic in the number four: many more combinations of participation and institutions can be imagined, and cluster analysis can isolate as many groups as we have cases. Statistical indicators, however, do point to an imperfect tendency for participation and institutions to strengthen or weaken in broad patterns. The four ideal types I propose are simply commonly observed variations. While it is not difficult to name exceptions, cluster analysis of data on almost 100 countries shows that they can be classified into four groups reflecting those variations. We do not have data on every country, and some cases do stretch the boundaries of their groups; I have included some such countries among the case studies for that reason. There is no suggestion that corruption within the groups is identical in every case. The approach is only a way of asking whether we can use evidence on participation and institutions to identify groups of countries coherent enough to guide the case studies that are the real test of the scheme.

Other questions might arise regarding my emphasis on the state. States do vary in strength, credibility, and day-to-day significance, both among and within countries, and in a global system even the most powerful are scarcely autonomous entities. But states remain significant – why else would people go to the expense and risk of corrupting them? Variations in the integrity (in its most basic sense) and autonomy of states are reflected, imperfectly, in our data on institutions. Still, treating whole countries as units of analysis assumes a significance for the nation-state, and a degree of uniformity within each one, that may be inappropriate particularly where corruption is most severe.

Do the cases differ in expected ways? For those countries I have tried to identify the most critical corruption issues, following the idea of systemic corruption problems laid out in chapter 2 – that is, emphasizing corruption issues most important for democratic and economic development. In most cases, the literature reflected general consensus as to the most important kinds of corruption to be considered. (At the same time there is considerable overlap at some levels: countries in all four groups have police corruption, for example.) The goal is to study qualitative variations: who abuses wealth and power, in search (or defense) of what, and with what consequences? The risk, of course, is that a strategy aimed at identifying contrasts will be disposed toward finding them. I have tried to avoid that temptation by looking at countries within each group that differ in important ways, and by specifying in advance the sorts of variations I expected to find.

In many ways expected contrasts did emerge. The Influence Market group has corruption issues that inhibit political competition and undermine the credibility and effectiveness of democratic processes, a fact that one-dimensional corruption indices underemphasize. Connections between wealth and power can be a systemic problem even when the giving and getting are legal and publicly disclosed. More important, however, is that Influence Market countries, while influential in shaping international reform agendas, differ qualitatively from others. Elite Cartel countries generally have institutions of only middling strength, and behind a façade of political competition elite hegemony is the rule. Parties colonize the bureaucracy, colluding to freeze out prospective competitors. Oligarch and Clan countries have weaker institutions still; much power resides in the hands of contending elites who are backed by personal networks spanning politics and the economy, state domains and private interests. So insecure is the situation that corruption is linked to violence in ways that have few parallels in Elite Cartel cases and virtually none in Influence Markets. Official Mogul cases, finally, stand influence markets on their heads: official power, not wealth, drives most corrupt activities, as officials reach out and plunder the economy; *quid pro quo* exchanges occur but the biggest cases are little more than theft. The tax and duty-avoidance schemes of China, the Philippine oligarchs whose personal networks extend deep into the state and economy, and the politician–*chaebol* alliances of Korea are not just "more corrupt" than the political contribution scandals of Influence Market countries; they embody different patterns of participation and institutions, and different sorts of connections between wealth and power.

A focus on syndromes changes our view of regional issues. Speculation abounds over contrasts between "Asian" and "African" corruption, particularly given the widely divergent economic records of those regions. African states do tend to cluster in the Official Moguls group, but there are intriguing variations: Benin, for example, is an Oligarch and Clan case while Botswana falls among the Elite Cartels. We should be cautious in generalizing about "African corruption," and at the very least must consider influences beyond the geographical and (often more assumed than demonstrated) cultural commonalities. Similarly, Asian states are included in all four groups, with Japan, Korea, the Philippines, and Indonesia illustrating major contrasts. It is difficult to claim that fast-growing Asian countries hit upon some variety of beneficial corruption for a thirty-year period when corruption problems differ as they do. We might better look at how their economies did or did not withstand its effects for a time – particularly, via policy and intra-elite political processes – and how those connections changed over time.

Other contrasts that did, and did not, emerge raise intriguing questions. Chapters 6 and 7 develop ideas about how and why the corruption problems of China and Russia differ. But many analysts of East Asia will be surprised (and perhaps less than persuaded!) that Japan and Korea are in different categories. Mexico's presence in a group with Russia and the Philippines may draw objections, particularly considering how recently we might have called it an Elite Cartel case. Patrimonialism and clientelism are sometimes treated as distinctive syndromes in their own right; in my schema the former is found in both the Oligarchs and Clans and the Official Moguls groups, while clientelism is found in various forms there and in Elite Cartel cases too. But a focus only on techniques of corruption might obscure important underlying factors: clientelism and patronage in Korea, the Philippines, and Kenya, for example, involve differing kinds of participants, and have contrasting consequences, reflecting (I argue) systemic contrasts.

Another issue is that of contrasts *within* groups. To put two countries into the same cluster is not to say that their corruption is identical in every respect, as the relatively loose distribution of the Official Moguls group in figure 3.4 suggests. Elite Cartel corruption preserved a political stalemate in Italy while, in Botswana, it helped a modernizing traditional elite make policy credible enough to launch sustained growth. Italy experienced widespread colonization of the economy and state apparatus by major parties, while Botswana's most important cases were focused upon specific bodies such as development banks and functions like housing construction (Frimpong, 1997). In both cases elites used corrupt incentives to defend their hegemonies, enrich themselves, and see off potential competition, but Botswana is a small society with an elite to match, had one dominant party, and did not have Italy's mature economy, large state sector, and overblown bureaucracy. Their Elite Cartel corruption reflects differences, therefore, but the comparison is still more informative than any blanket claim that either country is "more corrupt" than the other.

Contrasts within groups become greater as we move from Influence Markets toward Official Moguls. In one way that is not surprising: affluent market democracies resemble each other in many ways, and it would be surprising if their corruption problems did not have important commonalities too. As we move to the other groups, however, institutions become weaker, climates of political and economic opportunities become more diverse and changeable, and the risks involved in corrupt deals become more unpredictable. Like Tolstoy's happy and unhappy families, advanced political and economic systems tend to be advanced in similar ways, while weaker ones can have problems that are diverse and very much their own. In the former, impersonal laws and institutions are relatively strong. In the latter accountability is weak; the personal agendas and interrelationships of political and economic elites matter, and can vary, immensely.

Comparative corruption research

A basic concern throughout this book has been the need for broadly comparative research on corruption. Cross-sectional analysis and detailed case studies both make major contributions to our knowledge, but as suggested earlier the former approach imposes common models upon diverse cases while reducing contrasts to matters of degree, while the latter brings out important contrasts and details but too often does not systematically compare cases. The middle level of comparison sought here will not be wholly satisfying by the standards of either tradition: it does not assign relative explanatory weights to the factors defining our four groups, for example, nor can it account for the full complexity of any country's corruption issues. International influences are incorporated into the analysis via the emphasis on consensus worldviews and policies, and in our four groupings through the measures of economic (and to a lesser extent, political) liberalization, but because of the focus on corruption patterns within countries they are more a part of the background in the case studies than we might wish.

Many may argue that cultural factors have been overlooked, particularly with respect to a problem so closely linked to social values, and indeed I have not explicitly used culture to *define* the four syndromes. That is for several reasons. The most important is a strategic choice to focus on participation and institutions as key aspects of global change, and of the policies shaping it, in order to see whether they help differentiate among corruption syndromes. In addition there are a number of problems regarding the role of cultural factors in the study of corruption. Arguments from culture are often asymmetrical, emphasizing actions that might be tolerated or praised within a given culture but not those that are proscribed. Culture is frequently raised to justify exceptions – as a reason why comparisons cannot be made and parallels across societies cannot be drawn – while explicit claims as to what it *does* explain, with respect to corruption at least, are few. Three further problems have to do with explanation itself. First, culture-based explanations are often too "far-sighted": longstanding and sometimes diffuse traditions are used to explain specific contemporary activities, at times to the exclusion of more proximate and specific influences. Alternatively they are selective and circular: we say people do specific things because it is in their culture to do so, but we infer the elements of the culture from their behavior. Third, arguments from deep-rooted cultural factors are not well-suited to account for change (Bufacchi and Burgess, 1998: 90).

Still, my argument is emphatically not that culture is unimportant as regards corruption. Rather, it is that we must be specific about where and how it is important rather than making culture the explanation of first resort. Culture is particularly relevant to reform, a point to which I will return below. How people *respond* to corruption, to the changing opportunities and constraints that shape its forms, and to elites and institutions are questions with profound cultural dimensions (consider the role of family and region in Korea, or of tribal identity in Kenya), and those connections are noted in the case studies. The role of guarantors for corrupt deals will also be rooted in social trust and traditions of authority and exchange (recall the importance of organized crime as a key guarantor in southern Italy). So too is the significance, in the broadest sense of that term, that people see in corruption issues. As research proceeds many of the problems noted above will be minimized, and as that occurs an understanding of the varying syndromes of corruption will be essential to make the most of cultural insights.

The typology and data

Any typology of the sort employed here is at best a useful simplification. It reflects a range of assumptions and choices, as acknowledged above, and will lay out concepts and interrelationships in general terms. The four categories proposed in chapter 3 spring from the first of our three major questions about links among political and economic liberalization, the strength of institutions, and variations in corruption. They rest on several assumptions: first, that corruption is not something that "happens to" a society, but rather is embedded in deeper processes of economic and political change; second, that those changes are not only characteristics of countries but are also experienced as real opportunities and constraints; and third, that people will respond to those opportunities and constraints in understandable ways. The hypothesized corruption syndromes may best be regarded as ideal types (see Coser, 1977: 223–224) useful for guiding more detailed analysis of cases.

Operationalizing the typology raises more problems. Country-level political and economic indicators, some more valid and reliable than others, have proliferated in recent years. Nearly all are attempts to measure elusive aspects of state functions (accountability, security of property rights, and of course corruption). Many are based at least in part upon surveys of public or expert opinion; some are so recent in origin that we cannot yet track trends or assess reliability. While methodology is improving and underlying data bases are expanding, such indicators remain suggestive at best. The problems are particularly difficult with respect to changes in our cases: Mexico, I argue, has moved from Elite Cartel to Oligarch and Clan corruption, for example, while Italy, Japan, Korea, the Philippines, and Indonesia have undergone political changes of varying types and magnitudes, and in some cases it is not clear whether a given syndrome should be discussed in present or past tense. Other cases, such as Russia, might be said to be in continuing crisis, and generalizations about its politics, economy, and corruption show their age very quickly. Yet the data at hand cover only limited time spans and are gathered at intervals ranging from one to five years. I cannot yet say how the clusters have evolved, or what time lags might occur between crises and qualitative changes in corruption in specific cases. Better answers must await the publication of longer data series, the observation of more systemic changes, and continued refinement of this analysis.

In this book I have tried to deal with data problems in two ways. One is to emphasize construct validity – that is, the extent to which various measures are related to each other in theoretically expected ways, and in particular to data in which we have high levels of confidence (Adcock and Collier, 2001; Babbie, 2001: 143–144). In chapter 3 the four groups are defined using a cluster analysis of six indicators and then compared in terms of a range of other statistical data (Tables A–C in the Appendix). Then, in chapters 4 through 7 they are compared again using qualitative accounts of corruption issues. The results are generally consistent with the basic typology and hypotheses. Second, the statistics are used to frame questions rather than answers: the cluster analysis is primarily a way to define groups for study while reducing the likelihood of pre-selecting for expected results. Those cases do suggest that an understanding of trends and contrasts in participation and institutions helps identify contrasting syndromes of corruption. The challenge now is to improve the statistical evidence, to develop models giving a clearer indication of the relationships and priority among variables, and to continue to develop richer case studies, particularly in less frequently analyzed countries. Such research might yield more or fewer categories, and will certainly change our understanding of the corruption found within each, but it would fuel the comparative debate this book is intended to encourage.

Relationships among the groups

A final question is both methodological and substantive. We have arrived at categories that, broadly speaking, illustrate important contrasts both qualitative and quantitative. But might we merely have rediscovered the effects of increasing amounts of corruption? The question is a serious one, but for several reasons I argue that the answer is no. For one thing, the corruption indices used in the plots in chapter 3 – which, it is worth repeating, were not used in defining the four groups – are open to considerable doubt on grounds of validity and, to a lesser extent, reliability (Johnston, 2001a). Perception-based indices emphasizing high-level bribery likely exaggerate overall differences between affluent market democracies and societies like Russia, Kenya, and Indonesia. Even if not, "more corruption" can mean many different things – frequent cases, high-level involvement, major political or economic costs, links to violence – involving a range of possible stakes and participants, as our case studies have shown.

Moreover, to suggest that amounts of corruption account for the sorts of contrasts on view in our case studies is to put an immense explanatory burden on one factor. Those contrasts are multidimensional and exist on several levels, ranging from attitudes to politics and social trust to behavior such as theft and violence to factors such as the security of property and strength of civil society; it seems unlikely that they are explained by more or less of any one thing. Further, it is not obvious that corruption *by itself* explains as many development problems as we are sometimes told it does. It is embedded in, and interacts with, complex processes of change – indeed, it is more likely symptomatic of such factors than their cause. Corruption is an attractive *ex post* explanation for poverty (Sindzingre, 2005) and political pathologies, particularly from the consensus view of corruption as both cause and effect of difficulties in economic liberalization. But can we really say, with respect to any of the cases discussed here, that reducing corruption by X would yield Y amount of additional growth or Z improvement in democracy? Making the systemic changes required to check corruption would likely pay major economic and democratic dividends, but that just brings us back to the question of what contrasting societies' corruption problems, and their underlying causes, might be.

The activities we see in the four groups – "money politics," complex exchanges of corrupt incentives networking diverse elites, economic and political empire-building by oligarchs, and outright exploitation by powerful political figures and their protégés – differ from each other in important respects. Further, the scatter plots in chapter 3 suggest a discontinuous pattern: most Influence Market and Elite Cartel cases have high development scores, despite widely varying apparent amounts of corruption, while Oligarch and Clan and Official Mogul cases exhibit widely divergent levels of development despite comparably high corruption scores. That discontinuity makes it difficult to account for contrasts in our four groups via the cumulative effects of more corruption, to the extent that the latter can even be known. At some point in the corruption-and-development relationship *something changes*. That "something," I suggest, is best understood in terms of societies' differing kinds of corruption and differing abilities to withstand it – issues that bring us to our discussion of reform.

Reform: widening the worldview

Anti-corruption reform has become a staple of development policy and a goal for many businesses too. The old view of bribes and extortion as "grease" for bureaucratic gears, or as a tolerable overhead cost of doing business in some parts of the world, has given way to a more systemic understanding of corruption as a drag on development, a threat to property and legitimate gains, and a surreptitious tax upon honest effort, as noted in chapters 1 and 2.

Solid results, however, have been difficult to show. The problems are deep-rooted while the current reform movement is recent in origin. Transparency International is little more than a decade old; frank discussions of corruption were rare at the World Bank until 1995, and the path-breaking OECD Convention on Combating Bribery – the first inter-governmental effort to address corruption on a global scale and attack its origins in wealthy as well as poor countries – did not enter into force until 1999 (OECD, 2003). The risks of reform are significant: corruption benefits well-connected people who will not surrender their advantages easily. Reform is often most urgent where institutions and oppositions are weakest, and as noted we cannot measure corruption with precision.

Other problems are more fundamental. Some have to do with the liberalization-driven agenda that has shaped development policy: few should quarrel with the idea of wider political and economic choices, and some corruption does indeed grow out of actual or contrived "squeeze points" in public processes. But it does not follow that markets – or market-like political processes such as elections – by themselves can substitute for strong state, political, and social institutions. Reducing the state's role to "governance" – a kind of societal referee function – makes it difficult to mobilize participants in public life and to make reform less risky for ordinary citizens. Not only has the hoped-for synergy between economic and political liberalization (Przeworski, 1995) proven difficult to develop; liberalization in either sphere without strong, accountable institutions quickly turns into choices for a powerful few, insecurity and deprivation for the many, and illicit connections between wealth and power.

Tactics without strategy?

This approach to reform often judges high-corruption countries mostly in terms of what they appear to lack when compared to affluent market democracies, rather than in terms of what forces actually are shaping their corruption problems. Reforms imported from those advanced societies often follow crime-prevention models in which punishments and (less frequently) positive incentives are aimed at specific kinds of individual behavior, or a transparency paradigm that relies upon news media, and citizens as voters or consumers, to avoid or penalize corruption through their own choices, regardless of whether people and the press are up to those tasks. There is nothing wrong with most such ideas, but much less attention is given to the systemic factors shaping and sustaining corruption or to the institutional and social foundations any reform model requires. The increasingly important role of civil society in most reform models is likewise shaped by the experiences of affluent market democracies, but in many other countries society is impoverished, fragmented, intimidated, and anything but civil.

For those reasons anti-corruption measures effective in one context may be irrelevant or harmful in another. Launching competitive elections in Kenya and Indonesia before legitimate resources and an effective judiciary and party system were in place arguably made corruption worse. Privatizing the Russian economy in the absence of a supporting institutional framework, and in a political system of dubious capacity, not only led to more corruption but to particularly devastating forms of it. Even where the state has some credibility more extensive laws and larger penalties may merely drive "amateurs" out of the process and leave it to formidable "professionals," and may create new corruption opportunities for those charged with enforcement. At worst, a public push for reform can be a smokescreen for continued abuses. Indeed, when we look at corruption as a problem embedded in long-term development difficulties and imbalances the wonder is not that there is so much of it but rather that it has ever been brought under control. But that view may also hold important clues to success if we think of reform not as specific measures but as a basic development process in its own right.

Systemic responses to systemic problems

The understandable temptation is to bombard corruption with every good idea that comes to hand. "Toolkits" offer a variety of "best practices", but how do those reforms succeed, or fail, in a given context, and when is a society prepared to implement them effectively? Reform emphasizing punishment and prevention too often treats corrupt deals as discrete problems, and their perpetrators as deviants. But if the problem is systemic – deeply embedded in society and its development – reform must also mobilize the interests and energies of society itself.

The forces keeping corruption within bounds in an advanced society are not necessarily those that brought it under control to begin with. Effective laws, punishments, and anti-corruption attitudes are as much the *results* of long-term democratic and economic development as their causes. Reform thus has critical social dimensions: laws and procedures must be *seen to be* consistent with cultural values and conceptions of fairness and legitimate authority. So must the responses expected of citizens. In some societies, urging citizens to report corruption draws a flow of useful responses; in others people refuse, for reasons ranging from distrust of government and the police to the after-effects of times when citizens were coerced into denouncing each other (post-war France is an example of the latter sort). Efforts to mobilize civil society will need to take patterns of identity and social divisions, levels of trust, citizens' and leaders' expectations about venality (Manion, 2004), traditions of reciprocity, and complex status systems into account. Thirty years of effort by Hong Kong's ICAC, for example, have produced a situation in which seven in ten citizens say they are willing to report corruption, but getting to that point required a long process of linking reform to language, social relationships, and traditional values (Chan, 2005). While behavior must come into line with the law, laws must be fitted to societies in realistic ways, as Influence Market societies have done (perhaps, at times, to excess). Detection and punishment will be most effective when backed by social consensus, and when people have real political and economic alternatives to corrupt practices and rulers. And reform is never finished: as we have seen, affluent market democracies need institutional renewal and infusions of participation and competition from time to time.

Influence Market and Elite Cartel societies have systemic corruption problems with important costs, yet in the long term they seem able to withstand the corruption they experience. Our syndromes and case studies suggest that they accomplish that in different ways – in the first instance, through a legitimate and effective framework of institutions, and in the second through political settlements among major elites.[1] The first governing strategy forms the core of consensus reform agendas, but the second might be more attainable for many societies in the short to middle term. Neither is a solution for all time: consider, for the former,

---

[1] I thank an anonymous referee for very useful comments on this particular comparison.

the political malaise of the United States and economic inflexibility of Japan, and for the latter, Italy's political crisis of 1993 or Mexico's apparent slide toward more disruptive corruption. As noted, Elite Cartels can become inflexible and, over time, fragile (Nelken, 1996). Elite Cartel corruption in Korea may have aided early growth but left the country less able to avoid the meltdown of 1997. Still, elite political settlements might help account for the contrast between rapid economic growth in several Asian countries versus the devastating problems of many African societies which, at independence, had economic prospects comparable to those of their then-poor Asian competitors. In the Asian cases a political-economic elite not only enriched but solidified by webs of corrupt deals was able to pursue coherent economic development policies and keep corruption predictable. The difficulties of many African states, by contrast, were compounded by weak states, fragmented societies, and insecure elites practicing unpredictable "hand over fist corruption" (Scott, 1972: 80–84).

Such speculation suggests that Influence Market and Elite Cartel societies might embody two quite different strategies of reform – the former a bureaucratic-technical-managerial strategy aimed at the reduction and, as far as possible, eradication of corruption, and the latter a political strategy containing its effects. Oligarch and Clan and Official Mogul countries lack the institutional foundations of Influence Market societies and their corruption problems make it difficult to build them; the result too often is a high-corruption/low-development trap (Johnston, 1998). Building a sound framework of social, political, and state institutions is the work of generations; Elite Cartel settlements might provide a workable basis for democratic and economic development in the middle term while being less threatening to elites who might otherwise resist reform. It is by no means inevitable that Elite Cartel societies will go on to build those national institutional frameworks (though I will suggest below that the "consensus package" of transparency and administrative reforms might be more appropriate to this syndrome than to any other), and as noted Italy and Mexico provide sobering reminders of the risks of this strategy. But the track records of bureaucratic reform efforts in the Philippines, or of competitive elections in Kenya and Indonesia, are not much more hopeful. A society that over time builds its economy and lays the foundation for civil society under Elite Cartel leadership would seem a better bet for eventual success.

The discussion of reform that follows is aimed at such questions of middle- to long-term strategy. I will offer no new institutional or public-management remedies. Rather, the emphasis is on strengthening, and striking a new balance between, participation and institutions, choosing countermeasures (most of them familiar) appropriate to particular societies and implementing them in the proper sequence, and avoiding changes that do more harm than good. Implementing "best practices" where institutions are weak and corrupt interests dominate may accomplish little. Lifting expectations but failing at reform wastes scarce opportunities and increases the difficulty of subsequent efforts. Long-term strategy requires careful thought about what is possible, often as intermediate steps. Building the institutional foundations and political constituencies reform measures require, enabling societies to withstand the corruption they experience, and shifting it over time toward less disruptive varieties are more appropriate goals, and more sustainable in the long run, than aiming directly at sizeable reductions in corruption.

A developmental ideal

If high-corruption societies should not simply emulate affluent market democracies or shoot for better scores on indices, what should they aim for? In chapter 2 I laid out a very general developmental ideal: a system in which political and economic participation are open, vigorous, and broadly in balance – in the sense that political actors do not dominate the economy, and *vice versa* – and where activity in both spheres is sustained and restrained by strong state, political, and social institutions. That ideal helped define our four corruption syndromes, but it may also be a kind of pole star for reform. Strong institutions and balanced participation enable societies to respond to corrupt activities more effectively. They provide non-corrupt economic and political alternatives for citizens and firms and enable them to defend their interests. Corruption would scarcely vanish in such a system, but if our analysis is correct it would occur in less disruptive forms. Further, to the extent that corruption actually is a consequence and cause of incomplete liberalization, well-institutionalized, competitive politics and economies are less likely to be dominated by corrupt elites or those offering cash to make things happen.

At first glance that ideal may seem just another way of saying developing societies should emulate affluent market democracies, but it is not: advanced societies themselves fall short of the ideal, as witness their own corruption problems. Further, the ideal has several dimensions – institutions of several sorts and two diverse arenas of participation – making reform strongly path-dependent. Problems can arise in a number of different combinations; the journey toward the goal will not run along a single dimension of less to more development, but will depend greatly upon a country's particular array of difficulties. Official Mogul societies, for example, do not have to pass through an Oligarch and Clan "stage" as they pursue reform.

Comparing the four corruption syndromes to the development ideal can suggest a number of strategic steps for dealing with each, along with some initiatives to be avoided.

Influence Markets

In Influence Market countries institutions are strong, legitimate, and in the case of the bureaucracy, relatively autonomous – enough so that political elites find their own access attracts rents from economic interests. Reformers enjoy a number of advantages: liberalization of politics and markets is more or less a *fait accompli*, minimizing both the sorts of systemic changes and imbalances experienced in many other societies and lucrative squeeze points defended by powerful entrenched corrupt interests. Prescriptions for improving state functions, law enforcement, and transparency are generally workable and enjoy broad support.

But corruption remains in these systems. Specific activities – the "pay to play" system of petty payoffs in several American states and many localities, the most scandalous political finance practices of Germany and Japan, or at another level the police corruption that occurs in many advanced democracies – do not fundamentally undermine prosperity. But popular suspicion of politics and political finance processes in the United States, and the incumbent advantages and lack of competition among parties apparent at many levels in our Influence Market cases, are not just minor problems but rather connections between wealth and power that erode the quality of democracy. In many democracies, particularly the presidential and federal systems, points of access abound; but as access becomes a tradable commodity those who cannot buy into the game become suspicious, as the poll data cited in chapter 4 suggest. Accountability weakens, and government's role as social referee and defender of fair play – the role envisioned by consensus development policy – loses credibility. Recent corporate scandals in the United States and elsewhere, executive compensation that is excessive by any common-sense standard yet bears little relation to company performance, and cavalier treatment of rank-and-file employees are examples of such developments. Many of these problems do not even involve illegality – a sign of indiscriminate liberalization? – but to the extent that they are linked to systemic corruption issues in the public's eyes they impair the public credibility of institutions and the efficacy of citizen participation.

Influence Markets diverge from our developmental ideal primarily on the participation side. Electoral turnout levels in many established democracies are only middling at best, and in some instances seem to be in significant decline. Inter-personal trust and perceptions of leaders and institutions are matters of considerable concern too (Pharr and Putnam, 2000; Putnam, 2000). Perceived corruption is often a factor depressing levels of trust in Japan (Pharr, 2000), and Americans' views on the influence of money (chapter 4) do little to increase participation in politics there. The connection runs the other way too: can citizens respond effectively by electing legislators through a political system in which the flow of funds underwrites the status quo, and in which electoral competition – as opposed to partisan contention – is weak? Germany's *Proporz* arrangements and the disinclination of voters and prosecutors to punish top figures involved in scandals mean that even major corruption rarely produces significant political change. Save for an interlude in the mid-1990s, political competition in Japan continues to take place as much within the LDP as among parties, and its dealings with business profoundly shape policy. As a consequence, many Influence Market societies are not as open as they may claim to be as they recommend their own reform approaches to other parts of the world, and they avoid key questions of justice by legalizing what some might see as abuses. Still, these are not Elite Cartel arrangements: national elites are not using corrupt incentives to shore up their collective position in the face of growing competition, nor does corruption underwrite elite networks embracing business leaders, bureaucrats, and military officials, as dis-cussed in chapter 5. Relationships among party elites are marked more by stalemate than collusion (though the latter is not unheard of) and tend not to produce partisan colonization of the bureaucracy.

Ironically, Influence Market societies – widely regarded as successful democracies, for the most part – must attend to their political weaknesses. There is nothing inherently wrong with having parties and candidates appeal to private citizens for financial backing, and allowing people to express their political views with reasonable contributions. Such practices could be one source of democratic vitality. Similarly, strong elected officials and a measure of continuity are essential to electoral politics, and parties and elected officials will always seek to make their positions more secure. But where competition is more apparent than real, and where citizens believe – rightly or wrongly – that monied interests dom-inate politics and policy, participation suffers. Influence Market countries should re-examine electoral and party laws, and pay particular attention to their political finance systems. In the former category, Japan's party-list ballot system helped fuel corruption for many years. In the latter, the American federal political finance system sets out to control outright bribery rather than to encourage open, competitive politics yet, judging by public opinion, ends up doing neither. Further, it does relatively little to curb the risk of extortion by secure multiterm incumbents. Refocusing political finance laws toward encouraging competition among distinct and separate parties – creating more single-member parliamentary constituencies to reduce party collusion, or encouraging varieties of proportional representation that avoid the Japanese pattern of competition within a dominant party – and creating ways and incentives to finance their activities in broad-based ways, would be positive changes. Making individual races more competitive, perhaps through subsidies to new parties and making it easier to challenge incumbents, could help check corruption indirectly through increased competition and mass participation. That there would be substantial resistance among the incumbents themselves who, after all, write the laws, is precisely the sort of issue that encourages public cynicism, and is a reflection of the competitive malaise found in the United States and other Influence Market systems.

No single set of measures guarantees revived political competition and renewed public credibility, but fresh thinking is in order, and a number of possibilities are available for experimentation. In two quite different American states – Maine and Arizona – "Clean Politics" initiatives providing the option of full public funding to candidates who first demonstrate reasonable levels of voter support have proven popular in their first few election cycles. Candidates wishing to run under the old rules of private donations and disclosure are free to do so, but indications are that "Clean Politics" candidates enjoy some advantages in terms of public opinion (Common Cause, 1999). A different approach is a "blind trust" system under which private contributions are made through a central clearinghouse and forwarded on to candidates and parties without indications of their sources. Records of contributions would be retained by that agency for legal purposes but not be made public; all contributors would have a cooling-off period during which they could retract a contribution. The key idea of blind trusts – implemented in limited ways in South Korea and the United Kingdom, and receiving close examination in Chile – is not that the sources of funds are kept secret, but rather that they be unverifiable, thus weakening the leverage of contributors and unscrupulous candidates alike.

Alternatively, matching-funds formulae could reward parties for registering voters and for increases in turnouts, or might generously augment small contributions while not matching larger ones. Setting incumbent opposition aside for one moment, we could even imagine a "tax" on very large contributions that would divert a percentage into a public-financing fund. The point is that there are many conceivable approaches to enhancing the public credibility of electoral politics, and even now-secure incumbents might benefit from a system in which they enjoy more public credibility. Whatever our choices the public must be educated in realistic terms as to what reforms can and cannot accomplish, and about citizens' own responsibilities in making the system work. Campaign finance legislation in the United States has often been accompanied by ringing promises of a new era of clean politics, raising expectations that give way to deeper cynicism when it becomes clear that fundamentally not much has changed.

That, in turn, points to a deeper problem. Influence Market societies have checked corruption in part by legalizing the political role of wealth; their liberalized economies generally function well too, due in no small part to strong state institutional frameworks. But not surprisingly, the policies issuing from the political process favor monied interests in many ways. Whether or not such policies are sound, they may well be seen by many citizens as the results of unfair or corrupt influence: in democracies as elsewhere corruption issues are a tempting way to criticize a regime without directly challenging its power or claims to rule. Thus affluent market democracies, for all their accomplishments, may be disposed toward policies that will continually undermine the public credibility of, and participation in, politics.

Influence Market countries need to look to their own problems in another sense too. Many of their most prominent businesses have historically been deeply involved in corruption elsewhere. Indeed, before the recent OECD treaty several affluent countries allowed firms not only to pay bribes abroad but to deduct them from their tax bills at home. The OECD treaty is a welcome change, as is a similar convention among the members of the Organization of American States, but global economic integration continues, as does contention among economic powers for export markets, while the push for liberalization may further weaken states *vis-à-vis* private wealth. As affluent countries and international organizations pursue reform they must look beyond trends in GDP per capita as measures of human wellbeing, and take care not to eviscerate the institutions of developing countries. They must also recognize the importance of open, competitive politics, not just as the means toward various development ends but as something immensely valuable in itself.

Elite Cartels

Elite Cartel cases have market economies and increasingly open politics, for the most part, but top figures often collude behind a façade of political competition and colonize both the state apparatus and sections of the economy. This corruption syndrome is not without its risks and costs, as noted earlier; its implications are complex and depend upon what elites choose to do with the influence corruption offers them. Elite Cartels in Korea and Botswana, for example, have been able to pursue their development agendas effectively; on the other hand, in pre-democratic Korea governing was at times a brutal and violent process. Italy too experienced steady growth during several phases of its pre-1993 era but the state, while pervasive, was ineffective. The *partitocrazia* regime and its component parties steadily lost political vitality – suggesting that even if Elite Cartel settlements have their early uses they can become stagnant after a time. Again, much depends upon who is in charge. Other elites may use corrupt connections to maintain hegemony for its own sake: Paraguay, also in this group, exemplified that political style during the later stages of the thirty-five-year rule of Alfredo Stroessner.

To move Elite Cartel countries toward the developmental ideal outlined earlier state, political, and social institutions need to be strengthened and existing trends toward increasingly open competition must continue. Multiparty elections and market economies (the latter sometimes extensively politicized) are already in place in most of these societies, but parties are weak, sometimes collusive, and serve the personal agendas of leaders rather than lasting interests in society. Political competition can be made more decisive by changing electoral systems: Italy's move, in the wake of *tangentopoli* and *mani pulite*, to a parliament including more single-member, winner-take-all constituencies was intended to inhibit collusion. That by itself will not end party colonization of the bureaucracy and the state sector of the economy; indeed, parties in organizational and financial disarray will exploit such connections more aggressively as competition grows. For that reason meaningful, well-enforced financial disclosure and caps on overall spending may be more critical here than in Influence Market cases. It will take a series of genuinely competitive elections, and of alternations of power, to change elite political habits and voter perceptions in Elite Cartel societies. But if citizens can reward effective government and punish the most corrupt over time, strong disincentives to collusion will have been created.

Those ideas in turn underline the value of an independent judiciary, free press, and long-term efforts to shore up administrative autonomy and professionalism. Bureaucracies in most Elite Cartel countries are of middling quality, improving significantly in some countries while in decline elsewhere. Enhancing transparency will be a worthy goal but its practical value will depend upon the rise of real political competition, and upon the emergence of a civil society and press able and willing to put transparency to use. Civil societies in Elite Cartel countries tend to be only moderately strong and independent. In many cases civil society too has been colonized by elite factions and their political parties, or riven by regional, ethnic, or other divisions that not only have deep roots but definite political uses for elites seeking to divide potential opposition groups and keep them under control.

The behind-the-scenes collusion, favoritism, and the colonization of bureaucracies and economic sectors that mark Elite Cartel corruption suggest that the "consensus package" of liberalization, improved public management, and enhanced transparency may be more productive in Elite Cartel cases than elsewhere. These countries' institutional frameworks can sustain enhanced political and economic competition; those trends, after all, are what the Elite Cartels are trying to contain. Such competition and its decisiveness should increase gradually but steadily, as Korea has done: competition that rises too abruptly may encourage insecure elites to engage in hand-over-fist corruption (Scott, 1972: 80–84) or can, by fragmenting elite networks, produce the shift toward Oligarch and Clan abuses we may be seeing in the case of Mexico. Enhanced funding, from sources less open to manipulation by specific elite factions, for bureaucracies and political parties will be needed if they are to gain functional independence and, in the case of bureaucracies, check those elites. Legal independence and greater professionalism for agencies controlling major social benefit and public investment funds must be guaranteed in meaningful ways, perhaps backed up by scrutiny from independent commissions or the judiciary, to avoid episodes such as the Development Bank scandals in Botswana. A stronger civil society with a stake in effective, accountable government rather than in particular elites will take a long time to emerge and must be sustained by a wide range of incentives (Johnston and Kpundeh, 2002); anti-corruption or good-government appeals by themselves are unlikely to be credible and will encounter serious free-rider problems. Emerging civil society groups will be better sustained by advocating their own interests, and even by contending among themselves, than by organizing for public goods.

Institution-building can take many forms. Steps should include more effective controls upon *pantouflage* (elite employment transitions back and forth between public and private sectors), and upon lobbying, particularly by former public or party officials. Legislation requiring open and participative party governance and finance, and checks upon conflicts of interest, may also reduce opportunities for collusion. The military must be professionalized and clearly under civilian (as opposed to politicians' personal) control. Effective, transparent, and fairer regulatory processes, tax collection, and restraints upon black markets will also be worthwhile investments. Enhanced transparency as regards banking, securities markets, property rights, and elites' business interests will also be useful; steps can range from disclosure schemes to enhanced regulatory scrutiny of companies' capital and indebtedness to avoid Korean-style interlocking structures of debt. Simply being able to figure out who owns what, and which debts are owed to (and guaranteed by) whom, is critical both for economic reform and for policing the political colonization of the economy. Korea's "real names" reforms of the 1993 thus potentially have far-reaching implications. Those changes, in turn, will be more effective where there is a free and competitive press.

These are all familiar measures. But their strategic purpose is to bring political and policy processes out from behind their façades, and giving both state and society more autonomy from inroads by networks of elites. The goals are not only to improve the quality of government operations, but also to deter collusion; foster a gradual increase in real and decisive political competition; define clearer working boundaries among the state, political processes, and the economy; give citizens more of an opportunity to reward effective government and to oust the corrupt; and discourage the interpenetration of political processes, the economy, elite networks, and bureaucracy. These countries are in a position to benefit from "consensus" reforms because of the political and economic foundations built by interlinked elites. That does not mean that the Elite Cartel syndrome is some special kind of beneficial corruption; nor, as the case of Mexico suggests, does it mean that a developing society basically has it made once it arrives in this group. Rather, as suggested earlier, many Elite Cartel countries have not so much controlled corruption as found a way to withstand its effects for a time. Making the most of that finite opportunity is a matter involving a gradual political transition in which elites' abuses and networks are curtailed and countervailing forces in society gather strength, but not so rapidly that elites break up into warring clans or engage in hand-over-fist corruption on their way out the door. That is a delicate process indeed, one that will require a political process in which elites who lose power at one point know they have not been sent out into the wilderness, but rather can win another day through credible commitments to govern well.

Oligarchs and Clans

The primary fact of Oligarch and Clan corruption is that economically and politically ambitious elites are insecure. In a climate of rapidly expanding but poorly institutionalized opportunities and contention they build bases of personal support from which they exploit both state and the economy, and protect their gains and interests by any means necessary. In post-Soviet Russia that state of affairs led to a toxic mix of corrupt influence and violence. In the Philippines extensive colonization of the state, economy, and politics by a small number of powerful families has distorted development and, at times, inhibited democratization. Mexico has engaged in extensive institution-building, and well-run competitive elections are a welcome development, but those changes together with a generation of economic liberalization have fragmented the country's single strongest institution – the PRI – and shifted corruption in some dangerous directions. Oligarch and Clan corruption is not only rapacious and highly visible; it is also unpredictable, threatening to democracy advocates and investors, and a powerful source of injustice.

The existence of oligarchs is not surprising in rapidly changing societies. Newly open economies and political processes, particularly where institutions are weak, confer advantages upon the few who are quick enough, and who possess the connections and backing, to take advantage of new opportunities (Khan, 2002). But pervasive insecurity means that violence will be all too tempting, while building a secure political or economic foundation by more conventional means can be a risky process of mobilizing the weak against the strong. Advocates of broader interests in society, and in particular those opposed to corruption, will find it difficult to locate the real processes of influence and even harder to change them.

Influence Market and Elite Cartel countries' corruption problems are worth serious concern; but both have bases for governing – relatively strong and autonomous state institutions in the first group and in the second, the elite political settlement underwritten by Elite Cartel corruption itself. Oligarch and Clan societies, however, lack such foundations, and they depart from our developmental ideal in several ways. State, political, and social institutions are very weak and ineffective, and are easily manipulated by oligarchs. Economic and political participation, while burgeoning, is risky, disorderly, strongly influenced by oligarchs, and (even more than in Elite Cartel cases) not confined to official arenas. Corrupt deals proliferate but lack guarantors, making them disruptive, unpredictable, and prone to violence.

Rapid liberalization of economies and politics in the absence of essential institutional foundations has fueled corruption in Oligarch and Clan directions; further liberalization in the name of reform may well make things worse, erasing the feeble boundaries between wealth and power, state and society, and adding to insecurity at all levels of society. Institution-building and improvements to public management are urgent needs but lack political backing. Nascent civil societies in these countries are divided, intimidated, and impoverished; parties and political followings are weak, personalized, and too narrow and numerous to produce anything like broad-based mandates. We may call for political will, but reform will be risky for reformers and society as a whole, and there is no guarantee that such willful politicians would pursue democratic goals. As a result political competitors and international investors stay home; development is uneven and discontinuous, benefiting the few at the expense of the many; and elections and periodic reform campaigns give citizens little real recourse against corruption. The "consensus package" of reforms is unlikely to work in such a setting, and indeed may well make corruption worse and development even more imbalanced. What, if anything, can be done?

Rather than aiming directly at eliminating corruption and firing up market and political competition, the initial strategy might be to reduce insecurity while creating legitimate alternatives to corrupt ways of pursuing and defending self-interest. In the short to middle term that means strengthening institutions that serve as guarantors for legitimate economic deals and political rights. In the economy emphasis can be placed on property rights, sound banks and currency, market-oversight bodies, bond and equity markets, reliable and fair tax collection, and on building business and trade associations capable of developing codes of practice backed up by rewards and sanctions. Basic improvements to the judiciary and law enforcement are top priorities. On the political and social side civil liberties, a free and independent press, protection for citizens and whistle-blowers who report corruption, and ombudsmen and citizen advice programs may increase the sense of security. These initiatives will not make the oligarchs go away, but they might reduce incentives to violence, stem capital flight, and bring more economic and political activity back within official arenas. For ordinary citizens they can gradually open up legitimate alternatives to corrupt treatment and influence. By contrast, attacking the opportunities that have given rise to oligarchs, or confiscating their gains – the "strong hand" option – would defeat the purpose of political and market transitions and might create more disorder.

In the longer run the goal is to shift corruption toward less disruptive forms while building political settlements capable of withstanding its effects. That sort of transition can ease insecurities not only for citizens and reformers but also for national leaders and oligarchs themselves. From the standpoint of the latter it would become possible to govern in a more predictable and credible fashion – perhaps as an Elite Cartel. Oligarchs, able to deal with officials who are better able to "deliver" in legitimate as well as illegitimate ways, need spend less time building and rewarding personal followings and cultivating linkages with political families or drug gangs; many will find incentives to shift their activities in legitimate directions. More effective markets, courts, and guarantees of property rights would discourage raiding of other oligarchs' holdings.

Bureaucratic improvements could be backed by amnesties with respect to back taxes, repatriated wealth, and the proceeds of privatization. Such moves, particularly if coupled with simplified and more predictable taxation, will eventually bring capital back into the legitimate economy, help finance higher and more regularly paid bureaucratic salaries, reduce incentives to administrative harassment, and help bring black markets in from the cold. Simple and credible property titling for ordinary citizens – for many, an amnesty of their own – would reduce vulnerability to exploitation and, over the longer term, stimulate the growth of legitimate economic competitors who could enter markets without needing personal clans for protection. Similar opportunities – to confess to corrupt deals and still keep a portion of the gains – could also be offered, with a time limit, to officials; those giving particularly sensitive evidence would need protection afterwards. Some public-sector improvements should be aimed at reducing risks within markets – simplified and credible regulatory and customs functions are examples – and can be matched by private institutional development: independent and efficient stock and bond markets, for example, subject private-sector deals to continuing scrutiny, reduce economic uncertainties, and can develop sources of capital less connected to political manipulation and violence. Improving the flow of information within and between state and economy will make legitimate economic initiative more beneficial and official harassment more difficult.

These recommendations too include familiar institutional reforms, but the key is that instead of confronting corruption directly in a crime-prevention mode in a setting of weak state and political foundations, these proposals aim first at reducing its most threatening forms indirectly by easing insecurity. Then the recommendation is to build a framework of institutions by political means, perhaps by tolerating elite cartels for a time; next, to work over time on strengthening state and social institutions; and only then to resume aggressive political and economic liberalization. Such a strategy must be sustained: more than the other syndromes, the dynamics of Oligarch and Clan corruption are rooted in history, as the role of longstanding family networks in the Philippines and the continuing influence of Soviet-era trends and developments in Russia make clear. Further, any "secure oligarchs" approach is a second-best option even by an optimistic reading; the latter phases of the strategy will by no means fall into place automatically. Still it is a more promising strategy than liberalization without institutional and political foundation, or attacking corruption in a crime-prevention mode when official powers are feeble and fundamentally compromised. It is a scenario consistent with some of the interests of the oligarchs – not one that begins by attacking them directly – but also with those of officials and citizen groups lacking the support, security, and at times the muscle needed to confront corrupt interests directly.

All of the above requires a political leadership that is itself secure. Political and electoral competition are obviously good things in the long run, but too much too soon will heighten insecurity. A political foundation for governing over the longer term, given the personalized nature of major political forces and weak state of civil society in these countries, may have to be constructed at the elite level first. Political finance systems and electoral laws that encourage coalitions and power-sharing among parties – perhaps even drawing competing factions in under a common organizational structure, as in the LDP model – are worth consideration. This is the opposite of our recommendations for Elite Cartel and Influence Market cases, but here the goal is to help someone get a foothold sufficient to govern through state and political institutions, and through political means rather than via bribery and intimidation.

Where institutions and internal anti-corruption forces are weak, outside influence and assistance – private as well as public – can be crucial. Businesses making large investments have an interest in training domestic employees on corruption and business transparency issues, as well as in learning as much as possible about particular kinds of corruption risks to be faced. Those businesses themselves must refrain from adding to the corruption. Enforcement of the OECD anti-bribery treaty within and among its wealthy signatory countries will be critical to reform in both Oligarch and Clan and Official Mogul cases. Over the longer term the more successful countries in the latter categories may ratify the treaty too, which would involve them in extremely useful peer-review processes regarding anti-corruption policies and enforcement. "Conditionality" – withholding aid from countries that do not take action against corruption and related problems – is another option. That idea has many attractions, particularly if it forces lenders and donors to examine what they have been funding. But conditionality must be judicious: setting standards too high may persuade would-be reformers that there is little they can do, and aid cuts that are massive or too abrupt may only add to insecurity. Better would be to reward progress toward specific, attainable, institution-building goals. Conditionality of that sort raises the question of measuring the progress of reform, an issue to be touched upon below; but for example, donors might reward demonstrable improvements in tax or customs procedures, increased speed or a reduced number of steps in the awarding of routine licenses and permits, or important judicial reforms.

These measures are aimed at building informal elite foundations for governing; in effect they defer strongly competitive politics, the resumption of aggressive marketization, and reforms that directly confront corrupt interests until the situations of both oligarchs and networks of governing elites have become more secure – in the latter case, capable of withstanding the stress of such initiatives. A political settlement can be built relatively quickly and then become a foundation for comprehensive institutional reform and building social support. Reformers aiming directly for those goals without the intermediate steps may perpetually be dealing from weakness. Corruption will not vanish during these early stages; indeed, the main change may be in its form. The most difficult part of the strategy, from a reform vantage-point, is that it requires a temporary tolerance of corrupt dealings that help link governing elites together across party, sectoral, and other lines.

Equally difficult will be turning elites toward reform once they have become more secure. At that point external influence and conditionality may become crucial. There is no guarantee that networked elites will be enlightened nor that, once in place, they will eventually give way to a more democratic order. The Korean regime before 1988 was highly corrupt in an Elite Cartel fashion and brutally repressive when threatened; democratization was never an inevitable "next stage." But histories of some of today's affluent market democracies include stages or episodes during which interlocking networks of political and economic elites arose, pursued important developmental objectives, and were eventually pushed aside by new competitors and fundamental democratization: consider, for example, nineteenth-century joint ventures and elite cartels that built the canals and railways of the United States (Trent, 1981; Bain, 1999: 675–710; Hauptman, 1999; Ambrose, 2000).

Official Moguls

The connections between reform and justice are posed most clearly by our final syndrome, where the core dilemma is official impunity. Official Mogul cases diverge from our developmental ideal in many ways: institutions are very weak, popular participation in politics is feeble or orchestrated from above, and in the worst cases corrupt leaders and their personal favorites exploit society and the economy, including aid and investment, rather than developing it. But it is also a diverse category of countries because, as noted, the implications of unchallenged power depend upon the agendas of those who hold it. Singapore's Lee Kwan Yew, for example, pursued highly successful anti-corruption and development agendas from the time he assumed power in 1959, and that city-state falls into our first group of cases, not our last. But where power serves the personal interests of a dominant leader, administrative reforms may be window dressing at best – or may be weapons against potential opposition leaders.

Corruption as such may fall rather far down the list of priorities in some of these societies: that is not to say it is unimportant, but rather that it is a symptom of problems so fundamental and systemic that specific reforms will accomplish little. In less desperate situations reform requires that impunity be checked. Full democratization will usually be impossible in the near term, and premature moves in that direction may produce abuses such as land-grabbing in Kenya. But Isham *et al.* (1995) have shown that the presence of basic civil liberties is linked to more effective use of external assistance – more so, in fact, than is full democracy. Civil liberties enable critics and those affected by misuse of aid to air their grievances – carefully, to be sure – and to enlist the backing of outside interests. Over time, clearer boundaries and distinctions between state and society (more secure property rights, for example) and giving groups in society even a small measure of autonomy from political figures (through micro-credit schemes and similar initiatives not controlled from above, enhanced communications, and press freedom) can open up "civic space" in which social activities and interests can gather strength.

Building a strong and active civil society will be a gradual process requiring basic political change, so here too indirect strategies are worth considering. Civil society groups need not have explicit anti-corruption or good-government agendas; indeed, if they do their activities will be more risky. Worse yet, they will encounter classic "free-rider" problems, as noted above, for reduced corruption and good government are public goods. As a consequence – and as the demise of many anti-corruption organizations in developing countries, once their external funding runs out, makes clear – overtly reform-oriented efforts may serve mostly to persuade citizens that little can be done. Groups animated by self-interest, however, will be more sustainable: Russia's Army Mothers, for example, organized to locate and protect their own sons – a compelling personal goal – and in the process became a voice for official accountability (Shelley, 2005). In an earlier chapter I noted that historically, many of today's affluent market democracies reduced corruption in the course of extended contention over other issues people cared about. Mobilizing farmers, entrepreneurs, and ordinary citizens in a setting of official impunity is a challenge, but groups employing diverse incentives and appeals – ranging from social activities to awards and recognition to mutual-assistance schemes (Johnston and Kpundeh, 2002) – can build strength.

Even more than in the previous group external pressure and resources will be critical. Here conditionality may need to take strong and direct forms: leaders who have been practicing corruption with impunity may have to face credible threats to end the flow of funds. Donor countries contemplating such steps must prepare themselves for resistance from domestic business interests accustomed to profitable deals with the Moguls, particularly since many countries in this group are dependent upon the extraction and export of natural resources. To the extent that Moguls have been siphoning off aid and loan funds some early reductions in corruption may result from restricting or cutting off the flow, but the longer-term benefits of conditionality may be preceded by social and economic difficulties in the target countries. Carrots, as well as sticks, may still be effective in Official Mogul cases: aid and loans can reward meaningful guarantees of civil liberties and encourage the development of "civic space" as noted above.

Aid and loans involve the movement of funds into countries, but the reverse flow is important too. Official Moguls and their clients (like Oligarchs in the preceding group) frequently send their corrupt gains abroad, where institutions are stronger and returns are greater. Measures to make it difficult to hide such funds – real names on bank accounts, rather than just numbers – the ability to freeze such funds quickly on credible evidence of corrupt origins or uses, and the willingness to seize and repatriate them when appropriate – may not prevent corruption but will make it more difficult to conceal and use the gains. Anti-money-laundering initiatives in 2000 and 2001 by the inter-governmental Financial Action Task Force (FATF, 2004) and "Know Your Customer" programs (Financial Services Authority, 2003) requiring banks and investment brokers to document the sources of large deposits are important first steps, but have also drawn significant criticism from business and libertarian groups (McCullagh, 1998; Singleton, 1999). Like the OECD treaty they reflect a growing recognition of the global scope of both corruption and the reform efforts it requires, and like that treaty effective action will require Influence Market and other advanced societies to examine the role of their own financial institutions in the international dirty money market.

Here again suggested reforms are familiar ones. But equally important are those that are not recommended, such as rapid political liberalization or privatization. Official Mogul societies have furthest to go in reform terms; indeed, many anti-corruption measures will have to await basic developments in institutions and the growth of at least some free countervailing forces in politics and the economy. Still, countries in this group are not condemned to pass through a stage of Oligarch and Clan corruption on their way to something better. We can imagine a more enlightened regime building institutions that are public rather than personal in their agendas and basis of authority. Indeed, the very lack of constraints that aids unscrupulous leaders and their protégés opens up an intriguing possibility not available in Elite Cartel or Oligarch and Clan societies. Could new leaders with an anti-corruption agenda use *their* unchecked power, along with a sharp tightening of law enforcement and monitoring of business excesses, to "flip" an Official Mogul society into a new, low-corruption situation? Imagine such a leadership refusing to get involved in corruption, cracking down on former protégés, and using its power and resources to support legitimate economic alternatives. Such efforts could make Moguls more secure by reducing international pressure for change, and through the social benefits of additional economic growth and reduced political exploitation. They could even make power more profitable to the extent that the pool of perquisites, while smaller after reform, would not have to be shared with clients. Such incentives make this scenario less fanciful than it might seem.

In the longer term that regime would need to embark on more conventional forms, increasing the pay of honest officials, judges, customs officers, and police (perhaps using repatriated proceeds of past corruption?), enhance transparency and guarantee that citizens and journalists could take advantage of it without fear, and strengthen the institutions protecting economic opportunities and gains. It would also have to deal with the grievances of would-be clients now cut out of their expected rewards and the resentments by citizens and emergent civil society groups of mistreatment under the old regime. Still, some such changes – notably, higher pay for honest service, and a crackdown on corruption as part of a dash to growth – were implemented in Singapore in a relatively short time (Quah, 2003), with dramatic results. Rapid, guided change of this order will be more difficult in large-scale societies; further, getting such leaders to yield eventually to open and competitive politics is something that despite its successes Singapore has yet to do. But few gave Korean democratization much of a chance at the time Ferdinand Marcos was ousted in the Philippines in 1986, and yet within two years a breakthrough had occurred. Admittedly, the elements of this scenario range from the possible to the fanciful to the pathologically optimistic. But the point is that if we see countries as moving toward a reform ideal from several different directions rather than along a single path, many different processes of change can be seen.

Processes of change: ends and means

Two questions remain. How can we assess the effects of anti-corruption strategies? How can citizens be brought into the process, lest reforms simply create a few new winners and millions of losers?

Are we there yet?

How do we know whether reform works? The question has no simple answer. I suggest, however, that we should avoid using opinion-based corruption indices to track change. How closely such figures correspond to actual corruption is open to considerable dispute, and the accuracy with which they reflect change is even more unproven (Johnston, 2001a). Moreover, such indices are oriented toward bribery, often at high levels and involving international trade, and thus tell us less about some kinds of corruption than others. Indeed, a country that mounts a serious offensive against corruption may well find that its perception ratings *suffer* as legal proceedings, long-suppressed evidence, and public reaction begin to make headlines. Surveys of the corruption experiences of households, businesses, and officials are a better strategy in many respects, but they are expensive and must be repeated frequently. The societies that need such data most may be least able to afford them.

A more feasible approach is to focus on aspects of government that create incentives to corruption and reflect its effects (Klitgaard *et al.*, 2000; Johnston, 2005b). A licensing process that takes seven weeks and involves thirty-two steps is an indirect indicator of problems: the delay itself (often contrived) creates incentives to pay up while each step is a potential squeeze point for extortion. A government that pays twice as much for petrol or concrete as its neighbor or charges suspiciously low prices for its crude oil is either experiencing or inviting corrupt dealings. If a tax returns only half the revenue it is projected to yield, or if calculations and collections involve wide discretion, the same suspicions hold. Indicators of this sort point out areas of vulnerability and can help gauge the effects of reforms. If the licensing process is cut back to five steps and four days, institutions have been improved because reasons to give and opportunities to get have been curtailed. If prices a government pays for asphalt fall toward the norm, incentives and opportunities for kickbacks are being reduced. Routinely gathering and publishing such indicators is itself an institution-building process. Inviting citizens to rate the quality of services they receive, as in the "citizen report card" system for the local government of Bangalore, India (Wagle and Shah, 2003), builds popular participation not just in reform but in government gene-rally. Officials who produce better services can take political credit for doing so – the real source of political will – and synergy between partici-pation and institutions may begin to build.

A further hint about assessing progress can be found in the basic notion of syndromes of corruption. A shift from a more- to a less-disruptive form of corruption – which, as noted, need not necessarily move through all four types in order – may take a long time to emerge, but is a sign of stronger, better-balanced participation and institutions. Judging such trends need not require elaborate data analysis. Instead, it is a matter of standing the analytical strategy of this book on its head: a country whose corruption is shifting from Official Mogul corruption toward Elite Cartels is likely increasing political competition and building a useful political settlement. An Elite Cartels case that begins to look more like an Influence Market society is very likely increasing its bureaucratic autonomy and capacity in useful ways, and may be experiencing a welcome increase in decisive, well-ordered political competition; it may, on the other hand, need to carefully monitor the vitality of that competition in the long run. A country moving from a less to a more disruptive syndrome may be letting opportunities for participation outpace institutional development (a move toward Oligarchs and Clans) or allowing participation to be squelched by dominant political power (Official Moguls). Either way, an understanding of corruption syndromes and of the underlying problems that shape them can help us extract the essential good or bad news from a welter of corruption stories and allegations. By contrast, simply tracking such changes using a corruption index – to the extent that they would affect scores at all, which is uncertain – would provide little diagnostic insight as to what is going wrong in a particular case.

"Deep democratization" and reform

The "consensus package" of reforms aimed at liberalizing politics and markets, and at a small but efficient "referee state," offers major benefits to well-organized economic interests but puts immense burdens upon poor and democratizing societies. Weak states and civil societies are urged to confront powerful entrenched interests – some of the latter originating in the very societies urging reform. Affluent market democracies are offered as reform models but much less is said about how developing societies get to that goal – what must be done first, what should be deferred or avoided – or about advanced societies' own corruption problems.

I have suggested that an Elite Cartel settlement may be attractive in some surprising ways. Elite Cartels are only an interim governance strategy – second-best at most, transitional, and perhaps appropriate only for some societies. But they are also a halfway situation similar to those experienced by many affluent market democracies during their own histories. They may enable high-corruption countries to pursue positive change on a foundation of elite political alliances before they possess the official institutions, participation, and legitimacy found in affluent market democracies – attributes that, as noted, are more the outcomes than the causes of long-term development. But a time will come when a country needs to adapt to new challenges and open up to more diverse political expectations – including those born of its own successes. At that point tight elite networks may prove too rigid.

In the end both reform and systemic adaptation require vigorous political contention among groups strong enough to demand that others respect their interests, rights, and property – not just stability or administrative improvements. Too often we think of reform as a process of asking people to back off from their own interests and "be good," or of trying to restrain political influence to as narrow a range of functions as possible. But in fact reform will be most sustainable and effective when driven by self-interest, and when distinctions between state and society, public and private, are not just abstractions but accepted boundaries drawn, redrawn, and defended by actively contending groups.

At several points I have noted Rustow's (1970) argument that the forces sustaining democracy where it is strong are not necessarily the ones that brought it into being. Affluence, literacy, a middle class, a free press and independent judiciary, and a strong civil society (to name but a few such elements) undoubtedly contribute to the vitality of democracy systems. But where did those elements come from, and how did democratic values take root? For Rustow, the answers lie in continuing political contention among groups embodying real social interests, over issues that are important to them (Rustow, 1970: 352). Democracy and good government are not necessarily the point of such struggles; more often they revolve around much more specific and immediate issues, with views on the ways government ought to operate serving more as weapons in the struggle than as ultimate goals (Rustow, 1970: 353). Much the same can be said with respect to controlling corruption: many of today's low-corruption societies brought the problem under control in the course of fighting over other issues. The matter at hand might have been land, taxes, religion, or language, but the deeper issue was who had power, how they got it, and what could *and could not* be done with it. The inconclusive nature of those conflicts, too, was essential to their significance: no group got all it wanted, but the resulting settlements defined acceptable domains of official power and private interest, and set workable limits as to how wealth and power could be sought and used. Such settlements are rarely precise and never permanent: boundaries between public and private dealings, for example, are often redrawn. But they survive and adapt not because they are "good ideas" but because people have a stake in them.

Magna Carta, for example, was not a ringing declaration of the rights of humanity or a scheme for good government, but rather a set of limits laid down by members of the aristocracy weary of royal abuses. Critical notions of accountable government in England emerged out of a blood feud between crown and parliament over taxation, religion, and the accountability of royal ministers (Roberts, 1966: 91; Johnston, 1993) – not as reforms but as clubs to swing in a political brawl. Similarly, election reform in nineteenth-century Britain – the secret ballot, limits on expenditures, and the long struggle over rotten boroughs – was in part aimed at checking the "old corruption," but also helped party leaders impose order on, and control the costs of, the growing nationwide competition for votes (O'Leary, 1962; Finer, 1975; Rubinstein, 1983; Cox, 1986). Botswana by most measures ought to have more corruption, in more disruptive forms, than it seems to experience. Its working political framework was no one's design for reform or good government, but rather an elite settlement, rooted in society itself, that reconciled important groups and values and provided a coherent basis for effective rule. In Korea it is more difficult to say whether the glass is half full or half empty in corruption terms, but there is little doubt that the country is better off than it was thirty years ago. Its transitions followed no overall plan but rather were arrangements in which important leaders and factions of a contentious society had their stakes.

Ultimately corruption and reform are questions of justice. Can government protect the rights and opportunities of the many against the interests of a few, and can it be held accountable? Are boundaries between public and private power sufficient to prevent either from overrunning the other? A generation of liberalization sought to protect private interests from an encroaching state, but in many places has weakened key public institutions and political constraints, inviting abuses of private power. Too often we have pretended that giving free rein to private interests will quickly create self-regulating substitutes for government. But who then protects the weak? Shifting that burden to civil society, perversely, can be a way of blaming the victims.

For that reason reform must ultimately involve deep democratization. By that I mean not just competitive elections or transparency schemes, valuable as they are, but rather enabling citizens to pursue and defend their values and interests freely, and to settle upon acceptable institutions and ways of using wealth and power. Citizens, of course, are not automatically endowed with collective wisdom. They must want to build and sustain those settlements, and to endure the effort and risk that are involved. But they are more likely to do so in defense of their own well-being than in the name of "being good." It is incumbent upon anyone concerned with government, development, and democracy to make sure such opportunities are accessible, credible, and safe. There is a wide gap between the GDP-and-elections development agendas of the past generation, on the one hand, and the full scope of change needed to control corruption, and reasons for doing so, on the other. A society actively pursuing deep democratization and justice will still have corruption, and may have to live with upheavals, at least for a time. But over time it can develop a capacity for avoiding the worst dilemmas seen in our case studies – a capacity rooted not just in punishments and administrative procedures but in the vitality of society itself.

Conclusion

We have come a long way from a discussion of corruption and development in an era of liberalization and globalization to a consideration of strategies for reform. All of these issues, however, have common dimensions of democracy, accountability, and justice, and unlike many other critics I believe most advocates of "consensus" policy are genuinely motivated by their understandings of those same issues. Still, those issues frame an urgent debate over the ways wealth and power can be pursued, used, and exchanged – a debate most notable by its absence in contemporary policymaking. And they are the reasons why corruption is worth our concern in the first place: all revolve around the fundamental right of human beings to a good life and to participate in decisions affecting their lives. I have tried to show that those concerns are not only the ends, but also essential means, of reform.

As noted at the outset the revival of interest in corruption has reflected interests and organizations central to globalization, and has been driven by a sense that corruption not only impedes economic growth and integration but is also on the rise. Those connections have been made in a narrow and technical way, for the most part: at the level of observed behavior, corruption was seen primarily as bribery, part and parcel of imperfect or politically blocked processes of exchange. Politics and the state have been envisioned, at best, as technical facilitators of markets, and at worst as the essence of the corruption problem. Not surprisingly public institutions were for many years secondary concerns in most discussions of reform.

Therein lies a less-recognized risk of the consensus liberalization agenda: we could conceivably minimize corruption – in a definitional sense at least – by doing away with public power and roles. But would we have reduced corruption in a real sense, or just have privatized it (Johnston, 2001a)? And would we like the world that would result? In my view the economic liberalization of the past generation has, paradoxically, made clearer than ever the need for strong and accountable institutions that are public in the best sense of that word. Building them is no simple business, and will encounter stiff resistance. The need to do so, however, and the diversity of challenges involved, can be seen in the range of corruption problems outlined in this book. Politics and strong public institutions are not the problem, when it comes to corruption, nor are they error terms in a larger economic design. They are the only ways to build states and a global system that are vigorous, yet honest and humane.

Appendix A: Countries in each cluster and distances from statistical cluster centers

Group 1: *Influence Markets (N = 18)*

Country	Abbrev.	Distance
Australia	AUL	7.28073
Austria	AUS	3.60012
Canada	CAN	2.78126
Costa Rica	COS	3.83813
Denmark	DEN	3.64826
Finland	FIN	8.24365
France	FRN	9.23645
Germany	GER	2.31558
Ireland	IRE	8.29991
Japan	JPN	2.91684
Netherlands	NTH	3.86855
New Zealand	NEW	0.91241
Norway	NOR	7.65654
Sweden	SWD	8.76099
Switzerland	SWZ	13.65410
UK	UK	1.28457
Uruguay	URU	9.89902
USA	USA	3.86244

Group 2: *Elite Cartels (N = 21)*

Country	Abbrev.	Distance
Argentina	ARG	5.71114
Belgium	BEL	9.06837
Bolivia	BOL	8.02854
Botswana	BOT	3.64404
Brazil	BRA	5.53851
Chile	CHL	2.34284
Czech Rep.	CZR	2.48849
Greece	GRC	9.00947
Hungary	HUN	5.74995
Israel	ISR	6.87926
Italy	ITA	2.97926
Korea South	ROK	3.21965
Namibia	NAM	4.57171
Panama	PAN	5.72047
Paraguay	PAR	4.64561
Poland	POL	3.74996
Portugal	POR	2.63078
Slovak Rep.	SLO	2.30728
South Africa	SAF	5.51737
Spain	SPN	7.38652
Zambia	ZAM	10.62383

Group 3: *Oligarchs and Clans (N = 30)*

Country	Abbrev.	Distance
Albania	ALB	8.67352
Bangladesh	BNG	9.40557
Benin	BEN	1.63571
Bulgaria	BUL	3.69379
Colombia	COL	4.81347
Ecuador	ECU	3.99340
El Salvador	SAL	2.30953
Ghana	GHA	6.99291
Guatemala	GUA	3.62980
Honduras	HON	2.98866
India	IND	3.72422
Jamaica	JAM	9.03862
Madagascar	MDG	6.78694
Malaysia	MAL	7.20240
Mali	MLI	2.47827
Mexico	MEX	7.09493
Nepal	NPL	3.08030
Nicaragua	NIC	2.86318
Niger	NER	9.06853
Pakistan	PAK	14.73081
Peru	PER	11.62208
Philippines	PHI	4.14257
Romania	ROM	4.25395
Russia	RUS	12.68638
Senegal	SEN	7.89667
Sri Lanka	SLK	9.48985
Thailand	THI	7.53286
Trinidad & Tobago	TRT	8.89195
Turkey	TUR	3.23513
Venezuela	VEN	8.28116

Group 4: *Official Moguls (N = 29)*

Country	Abbrev.	Distance
Algeria	ALG	5.86685
Cameroon	CAO	2.81497
Central Africa	CAF	10.59637
Chad	CHD	2.94259
China	CHN	6.12066
Congo, Rep. of	CRP	11.17139
Egypt	EGY	5.57582
Gabon	GAB	5.50351
Guinea-Bissau	GNB	7.92945
Haiti	HTI	2.54349
Indonesia	INS	9.59441
Iran	IRN	11.65739
Ivory Coast	IVO	7.19949
Jordan	JOR	13.76616
Kenya	KEN	2.10563
Kuwait	KWT	5.55828
Malawi	MAW	13.84777
Morocco	MOR	7.78743
Myanmar	MMR	11.53267
Nigeria	NIG	10.03197
Oman	OMN	8.63007
Rwanda	RWA	2.93964
Syria	SYR	12.32687
Tanzania	TAZ	5.66171
Togo	TGO	3.96091
Tunisia	TUN	2.36309
Uganda	UGA	13.63157
United Arab Emirates	UAE	7.43969
Zimbabwe	ZIM	8.38316

Appendix B: Statistical indicators for country clusters

Table A: *Governance indicators*

Corruption type: Indicator (units or range) (source):	1. Influence Markets (18)	2. Elite Cartels (21)	3. Oligarchs and Clans (30)	4. Official Moguls (29)	ANOVA p =
Regime durability, 2001 (years) (P)	79.6	20.5	15.3	13.1	.000
Civil liberties 2001 (1 thru 7; Low = extensive) (FH)	1.28	2.38	3.57	5.14	.000
Political rights 2001 (1 thru 7; Low = extensive) (FH)	1.00	1.71	2.87	5.52	.000
Black markets 2001 (1 thru 5) (HF)	1.47	3.10	3.88	3.93	.000
Government effectiveness 2002 (−1.64 thru 2.26) (KKZ)	1.68	.46	−.33	−.55	.000
Government intervention 2001 (1 thru 5) (HF)	2.50	2.60	3.02	3.78	.000
Government regulation 2001 (1 thru 5) (HF)	2.56	3.10	3.70	3.90	.000
Regulatory quality, 2002 (−2.31 thru 1.93) (KKZ)	1.50	.67	−.14	−.58	.000
Rule of law, 2002 (−1.79 thru 2.03) (KKZ)	1.74	.45	−.37	−.59	.000
Political stability, 2002 (−2.42 thru 1.63) (KKZ)	1.17	.39	−.31	−.70	.000
Voice/accountability, 2002 (−2.12 thru 1.72) KKZ)	1.44	.68	−.05	−.92	.000
Political constraints on leaders 2001 (0 thru 1) (PL)	.77	.70	.47	.17	.000
Political competition 2001 (1-10) (P)	10.0	9.2	7.9	4.6	.000

Table B: *Social indicators*

Corruption type: Indicator (unit) (source):	Influence Markets (18)	Elite Cartels (21)	Oligarchs and Clans (30)	Official Moguls (29)	ANOVA p =
Adult literacy 2001 (%) (HDR)	98.7	93.0	73.9	69.2	.000
GDP/capita 2001 (US$) (HDR)	$24,674	$12,258	$4,107	$4,031	.000
Gini index (most recent years, HDR)	31.6	42.8	44.3	42.1	.001
Life expectancy 2001 (years) (HDR)	78.2	68.6	65.5	56.2	.000

Unless otherwise indicated, higher scores indicate higher levels of attributes

Sources for tables A and B:

PL = PolCon V dataset **http://www-management.wharton.upenn.edu/henisz/POLCON/ContactInfo.html**

FH = Freedom House *Freedom in the World* cumulative dataset, 1972–2003 **http://www.freedomhouse.org/ratings/allscore04.xls**

HDR = UNDP *Human Development Report 2003* **http://www.undp.org/**

HF = Heritage Foundation Index of Economic Freedom reports **http://www.heritage.org/research/features/index/**

KKZ = Kaufmann, Kraay, and Zoido-Lobatón, "Governance Matters III" dataset, 2002 **http://info.worldbank.org/governance/kkz2002/tables.asp** "Range" for KKZ variables refers only to those cases included in this analysis

P = Polity IV dataset, 2002 update **http://www.cidcm.umd.edu/inscr/polity/polreg.htm**

Table C: *Groups in relation to world economy*

Corruption type: Indicator (unit) (source):	Influence Markets (18)	Elite Cartels (21)	Oligarchs and Clans (30)	Official Moguls (29)	ANOVA p =
Net FDI per capita, US$, 2001 (WB)	$907	$253	$68	$18	.000
High-tech exports 2001 % of mdse exp (HDR)	21.7	9.7	10.5	5.7	.002
Mfd. exports 2001 % of mdse exp (HDR)	68.6	59.6	50.1	30.5	.001
Primary exports 2001 % all exp (HDR)	28.0	38.7	48.4	70.5	.000

FDI = Foreign Direct Investment

Sources:

WB = World Bank Data Query online data source **http://www.worldbank.org/data/dataquery.html**
HDR = UNDP *Human Development Report 2003* **http://www.undp.org**

References

Note: "JRL," where listed, refers to Johnson's Russia List, an online collection of news reports on Russia assembled and distributed by email at least once a day. JRL is archived online at http://www.cdi.org/russia/johnson/default.cfm.

ABC News.com. 2000. "A Big Start: Trials Open in China's Biggest Corruption Scandal," September 13, online at http://abcnews.go.com/sections/world/DailyNews/china000913.html (viewed October 9, 2003).

Adcock, Robert, and David Collier. 2001. "Measurement Validity: A Shared Standard for Qualitative and Quantitative Research," *American Political Science Review* 95: 529–546.

Ades, Alberto, and Rafael di Tella. 1994. "Competition and Corruption," working paper: Oxford University Institute of Economics and Statistics, Oxford, United Kingdom.

— 1999. "Rents, Competition, and Corruption," *American Economic Review* 89, 982–993.

Agence France-Presse. 2003. "Torture, Crime Riddles Moscow Police: Study," August 6. Reprinted in JRL 7280, August 7.

Alam, M. S. 1995. "A Theory of Limits on Corruption and Some Applications," *Kyklos* 48: 419–435.

Albats, Yevgenia. 2003. "Abetting Russia's Oligarch," *Washington Post*, January 25.

Alemann, Ulrich von. 2002. "Party Finance, Party Donations and Corruption: The German Case," in Donatella Della Porta and Susan Rose-Ackerman, eds., *Corrupt Exchanges: Empirical Themes in the Politics and Political Economy of Corruption*, Baden-Baden: Nomos, pp. 102–117.

Alyoshina, Irina. 2004. "Bureaucrats to Tackle Their Own Corruption," *Gazetaru*, January 13. Reprinted in JRL 8012, January 13.

Ambrose, Stephen E. 2000. *Nothing Like It in the World: The Men Who Built the Transcontinental Railroad, 1863–1869*, New York: Simon and Schuster.

Amnesty International. 2000. "Kenya," in *Amnesty International Report 2000*, online at http://web.amnesty.org/web/ar2000web.nsf/0/1b92dd02fe9302ff802568f20055293a?OpenDocument (viewed July 22, 2004).

Anderson, Christopher J., and Yuliya V. Tverdova. 2003. "Corruption, Political Allegiances, and Attitudes toward Government in Contemporary Democracies," *American Journal of Political Science* 47: 91–109.

Anderson, Lisa. 1999. *Transitions to Democracy*, New York: Columbia University Press.

Andreas, Peter. 1998. "The Political Economy of Narco-Corruption in Mexico," *Current History* 97: 160–165.

Andreski, Stanislav. 1968. "Kleptocracy: or, Corruption as a System of Government," in Stanislav Andreski, ed., *The African Predicament: A Study in the Pathology of Modernization*, London: Michael Joseph, pp. 92–109.

Andrusenko, Lidiya. 2003. "The Khodorkovsky Effect," *Smysl*, May 16–31. English translation reprinted in JRL, May 27.

Appel, Hilary. 1997. "Voucher Privatization in Russia: Structural Consequences and Mass Response in the Second Period of Reform," *Europe-Asia Studies* 49: 1433–1449.

Aquino, Belinda. 1987. *Politics of Plunder: The Philippines under Marcos*, Quezon City, Philippines: Great Books Trading; U.P. College of Public Administration.

1999. *The Transnational Dynamics of the Marcos Plunder*, Quezon City: National College of Public Administration and Governance, University of the Philippines.

Arvedlund, Erin E. 2003. "Money, if Not Power," *New York Times*, November 11.

Babbie, Earl R. 2001. *The Practice of Social Research*, Belmont, CA: Wadsworth.

Bailey, John, and Roy Godson, eds. 2000. *Organized Crime and Democratic Governability: Mexico and the U.S.–Mexico Borderlands*, Pittsburgh: University of Pittsburgh Press.

Bain, David Haward. 1999. *Empire Express: Building the First Transcontinental Railroad*, New York: Penguin.

Baltimore Sun. 2003. "Poor Russia's Wealthiest Dozen," November 9.

Barro, Robert J. 1999. "Determinants of Democracy," *Journal of Political Economy* 107: 158–183.

Batalla, Eric C. 2000. "De-Institutionalizing Corruption in the Philippines: Identifying Strategic Requirements for Reinventing Institutions," Philippines: Transparent Accountable Governance. Online at http://www.tag.org.ph/references/PDFfiles/batalla.pdf (viewed June 1, 2003).

Baum, Richard. 1991. *Reform and Reaction in Post-Mao China: The Road to Tiananmen*, New York: Routledge.

Bayley, David. 1966. "The Effects of Corruption in a Developing Nation," *The Western Political Quarterly* 19: 719–732.

BBC News Online. 1998. "The Corrupt Comrade," July 31. Online at http://news.bbc.co.uk/1/hi/world/asia-pacific/143163.stm (viewed January 4, 2005).

Beck, Peter M. 1998. "Revitalizing Korea's Chaebol," *Asian Survey* 38: 1018–1035.

Berg-Schlosser, Dirk. 1982. "Modes and Meaning of Political Participation in Kenya," *Comparative Politics* 14: 397–415.

Berkofsky, Axel. 2002. "Corruption and Bribery in Japan's Ministry of Foreign Affairs," Cardiff, CA: Japan Policy Research Institute, Working Paper No. 86, June. Online at http://www.jpri.org/WPapers/wp86.htm (viewed January 15, 2003).

Bernstein, Jonas. 2002. "Corridors of Power: The 'Family' Is Dead – Long Live the 'Family,'" *RFE/RL Russian Political Weekly* 2: 42, December 11. Reprinted in JRL 6597, December 12, 2002.

Besley, Timothy, and John McLaren. 1993. "Taxes and Bribery: The Role of Wage Incentives," *The Economic Journal* 103: 119–141.

Birch, Douglas. 2002. "Russians Numb to Killing of Government Officials." *Baltimore Sun*, October 19. Reprinted in JRL 6500, October 19.

Blake, Charles H., and Christopher G. Martin. 2002. "Combating Corruption: Reexamining the Role of Democracy," presented at the 2002 Annual Meeting of the Midwest Political Science Association, Chicago, April 25–28.

Blechinger, Verena. 1999. "Changes in the Handling of Corruption Scandals in Japan since 1994," *Asian-Pacific Review* 6: 42–64.

———. 2000. "Corruption through Political Contributions in Japan: Report on Recent Bribery Scandals, 1996–2000," paper presented at a conference on Bribery and Party Finance, sponsored by Transparency International, Villa La Pietra, Florence, Italy, October.

Bo Zhiyue. 2000. "Economic Development and Corruption: Beijing beyond 'Beijing,'" *Journal of Contemporary China* 9: 467–487.

Boisseau, Jean-Marie. 1997. "Gifts, Networks and Clienteles: Corruption in Japan as a Redistributive System," in Donatella Della Porta and Yves Mény, eds., *Democracy and Corruption in Europe*, London: Pinter, pp. 132–147.

Boone, Catherine. 2003. *Political Topographies of the African State: Rural Authority and Institutional Choice*, Cambridge and New York: Cambridge University Press.

Brooke, James. 2004. "South Korea's Impeached President Gains Support in Vote," *New York Times*, April 16.

Bufacchi, Vittorio, and Simon Burgess. 1998. *Italy since 1989: Events and Interpretations*, New York: St. Martin's Press.

Burger, Ethan. 2004. "Corruption in the Russian *Arbitrazh* Court System," *International Lawyer* 38: 15–34.

Burnett, Stanton H., and Luca Mantovani. 1998. *The Italian Guillotine: Operation Clean Hands and the Overthrow of Italy's First Republic*, Lanham: Rowman & Littlefield Publishers.

Calise, Mauro. 1994. "The Italian Particracy: Beyond President and Parliament," *Political Science Quarterly* 109: 441–460.

Campaign Finance Institute. 2004. "House Winners Average $1 million for the First Time," 5 November, online at http://www.cfinst.org/pr/110504a.html (viewed 21 April 2005).

Campos, J. Edgardo, Donald Lien, and Sanjay Pradhan. 1999. "The Impact of Corruption on Investment: Predictability Matters," *World Development* 27: 1059–1067.

Carothers, Thomas. 1999. *Aiding Democracy Abroad: The Learning Curve*, Washington, DC: Carnegie Endowment for International Peace.

Castberg, Anthony Didrick. 1997. "Prosecutorial Independence in Japan," *UCLA Pacific Basin Law Review* 16: 38–87.

———. 2000. "Corruption in Japan and the US," United Nations Asia and Far East Institute, *Resource Material Series* 56.

Chaikin, David. 2000. "Tracking the Proceeds of Organized Crime: The Marcos Case," presented at the Transnational Crime Conference, Australian Institute of Criminology, Canberra, March 9, online at http://www.aic.gov.au/conferences 2005).

Chan, Jenny C. Y. 2005. "Language, Culture, and Reform in Hong Kong," in Michael Johnston, ed., *Civil Society and Corruption: Mobilizing for Reform*, Lanham, MD: University Press of America, pp. 95–113.

Chang, Eric C. C., and Miriam A. Golden. 2004. "Does Corruption Pay? The Survival of Politicians Charged with Malfeasance in the Postwar Italian Chamber of Deputies," presented at the Annual Meeting of the American Political Science Association, Chicago, September 2–5.

Chang, S. J. 2002. "Cultural Heritage and Financial Ethics in Korea," presented at the Korea Finance Association Meetings, November 2002, Chunchon, Korea, online at http://www.dure.net/~kfa/data/papers/announce/2002_autumm/ S.J.%20Jang.pdf (viewed April 14, 2004).

Cheng Tun-Jen and Chu Yun-Han. 2002. "State–Business Relations in South Korea and Taiwan," in Laurence Whitehead, ed., *Emerging Market Democracies: East Asia and Latin America*, Baltimore: Johns Hopkins University Press, pp. 31–62.

Cheng Wenhao. 2004. "An Empirical Study of Corruption within China's State-owned Enterprises," *The China Review* 4: 55–80.

Cho Juyeong. 2004. "The Interaction of Exogenous Forces and Domestic Political Institutions in Bank Reform: Korea and Japan," presented at 45th Annual Convention of the International Studies Association, Montreal, March 20. Online at http://www.isanet.org/archive.html (viewed December 28, 2004).

Cho Myeong-Hyeon. 2003. "Reform of corporate governance," in Stephan Haggard, Wonhyuk Lim, and Euysung Kim (eds.), *Economic Crisis and Corporate Restructuring in Korea*, Cambridge, Cambridge University Press, pp. 286–306.

Choi, Eun Kyong, and Kate Xiao Zhou. 2001. "Entrepreneurs and Politics in the Chinese Transitional Economy: Political Connections and Rent-Seeking," *The China Review* 1: 111–135.

Christensen, Raymond V. 1996. "Strategic Imperatives of Japan's SNTV Electoral System," *Comparative Political Studies* 29: 312–334.

1998. "Putting New Wine into Old Bottles: The Effect of Electoral Reforms on Campaign Practices in Japan," *Asian Survey* 38: 986–1004.

Chubb, Judith. 1981. "The Social Bases of an Urban Political Machine: The Christian Democrat Party in Palermo," *Political Science Quarterly* 96: 107–126.

Citizens Research Foundation. 2002. "Poll Data," online at http://www.igs.berkeley.edu/research_programs/CRF/Basics/opinion.html (viewed February 6, 2003).

Clifford, Mark L. 1994. *Troubled Tiger: Businessmen, Bureaucrats, and Generals in South Korea*, Armonk, NY: M. E. Sharpe.

CNN.com. 2001. "Seven Sentenced to Die in China Corruption Case," March 2, online at http://www.cnn.com/2001/WORLD/asiapcf/east/03/02/ China.execute/ (viewed October 9, 2003).

2004. "U.S. Warns Russia over Yukos Sale," December 23, online at http://www.cnn.com/2004/BUSINESS/12/22/russia.yukos.rosneft/ (viewed December 27, 2004).

Coalson, Robert. 2003. "Can the Kremlin Really Fight Corruption?" *RFE/RL Russian Political Weekly* 3: 28, 16. Reprinted in JRL 7253, July 17.

Colazingari, Silvia, and Susan Rose-Ackerman. 1998. "Corruption in a Paternalistic Democracy: Lessons from Italy for Latin America," *Political Science Quarterly* 113: 447–470.

Cole, William S. 2001. "Roots of Corruption in the Indonesian System of Governance," in Wilson International Center for Scholars, "Old Game or New? Corruption in Today's Indonesia," *Asia Program Special Report* 100: 13–18.

Collinson, Patrick, and Tony Levene. 2003. "Mob Cash Oils Wheels of Russian Economy," *The Guardian*, May 17.

Common Cause. 1999. "Campaign Finance Reform: Public Financing in the States," online at http://www.commoncause.org/states/CFR-financing.htm (viewed October 4, 2004).

2002. "Election 2002: – Incumbent Advantage: 98 Percent in House, 24 of 29 in Senate Win Reelection," online at http://www.commoncause.org/news/default.cfm?ArtID=38 (viewed April 5, 2004).

Coronel, Sheila S., ed. 2000. *Investigating Estrada: Millions, Mansions and Mistresses*. Metro Manila: Philippine Center for Investigative Journalism.

Coronel, Sheila S., and Cecile C. A. Balgos. 1998. *Pork and Other Perks: Corruption and Governance in the Philippines*, Pasig, Metro Manila: Philippine Center for Investigative Journalism, Evelio B. Javier Foundation, Institute for Popular Democracy.

Coser, Lewis A. 1977. *Masters of Sociological Thought: Ideas in Historical and Social Context*, 2nd edn, New York: Harcourt Brace Jovanovich College Publishers.

Cottrell, Robert. 2001. "Russia: Was There a Better Way?" *New York Review of Books*, October 4. Review of Reddaway and Glinski, *The Tragedy of Russia's Reforms*.

Cox, Gary W. 1986. "The Development of a Party-Orientated Electorate in England, 1832–1918," *British Journal of Political Science* 16: 187–216.

Cox, Gary W., Frances McCall Rosenbluth, and Michael F. Thies. 1999. "Electoral Reform and the Fate of Factions: The Case of Japan's Liberal Democratic Party," *British Journal of Political Science* 29: 33–56.

Dahl, Robert A. 1971. *Polyarchy: Participation and Opposition*, New Haven: Yale University Press.

Danevad, Andreas. 1995. "Responsiveness in Botswana Politics: Do Elections Matter?" *Journal of Modern African Studies* 33: 381–402.

Della Porta, Donatella. 2000. "Social Capital, Beliefs in Government, and Political Corruption," in Susan J. Pharr and Robert D. Putnam, eds., *Disaffected Democracies: What's Troubling the Trilateral Countries?* Princeton, NJ: Princeton University Press, pp. 202–229.

2004. "Parties and Corruption," *Crime, Law, and Social Change* 66: 35–60.

Della Porta, Donatella, and Susan Rose-Ackerman, eds. 2002. *Corrupt Exchanges: Empirical Themes in the Politics and Political Economy of Corruption*, Baden-Baden: Nomos.

Della Porta, Donatella, and Alberto Vannucci. 1999. *Corrupt Exchanges: Actors, Resources, and Mechanisms of Political Corruption*, New York: Aldine de Gruyter.

2002. "Corrupt Exchanges and the Implosion of the Italian Party System," in Arnold J. Heidenheimer and Michael Johnston, eds., *Political Corruption: Concepts and Contexts*, New Brunswick, NJ: Transaction Publishers, pp. 717–737.

Deng Xiaoping. 1983. *Select Works of Deng Xiaoping*, Beijing: People's Press.

Denzau, Arthur T., and Michael C. Munger. 1986. "Legislators and Interest Groups: How Unorganized Interests Get Represented," *American Political Science Review* 80: 89–106.

Dettmer, Jamie. 2003. "Putin Puts the Pride Back in Russia," *Insight*, February 4. Reprinted in JRL 7026, February 4.

Dietz, Simon, Eric Neumayer, and Indra de Soysa. 2004. "Corruption, the Resource Curse and Genuine Saving," London: working paper, Department of Geography and Centre for Economic Policy and Governance, London School of Economics and Political Science, online at http://econwpa.wustl.edu:8089/eps/dev/papers/0405/0405010.pdf (viewed November 30, 2004).

DiFranceisco, Wayne, and Zvi Gitelman. 1984. "Soviet Political Culture and 'Covert Participation' in Policy Implementation," *American Political Science Review* 78: 603–21.

Dobel, J. P. 1978. "The Corruption of a State," *American Political Science Review* 72: 958–973.

Doig, Alan. 1984. *Corruption and Misconduct in Contemporary British Politics*, Harmondsworth: Penguin.

Doig, Alan, and Robin Theobald, eds., 2000. *Corruption and Democratisation*, London: Frank Cass.

Dryer, June Teufel. 1994. "The People's Army: Serving Whose Interests?" *Current History* 5.

East African Standard Online. 2003a. "Ouko Murder Factor for Economy Slump," online at http://www.eastandard.net/headlines/news16102003011.htm (viewed October 16, 2003).

2003b. "Bosire Tells Muite off Over Nasser," online at http://www.eastandard.net/ (viewed October 16, 2003).

2003c. "Graft: Kibaki Names Judges, Sets up Tribunals," online at http://www.eastandard.net/ (viewed October 16, 2003).

2003d. "Judges Mentioned in Corrupt Dealings Named," online at http://www.eastandard.net/ (viewed October 16, 2003).

Economist, The. 1999. "Germany: Corrupt?" December 9.

Elizondo, Carlos. 2003. "After the Second of July: Challenges and Opportunities for the Fox Administration," in Joseph S. Tulchin and Andrew D. Selee, eds., *Mexico's Politics and Society in Transition*, Boulder, CO: Lynne Rienner, pp. 29–53.

Elliott, Kimberly Ann, ed. 1997a. *Corruption and the Global Economy*, Washington: Institute for International Economics.

1997b. "Corruption as a Global Policy Problem: Overview and Recommendations," in Elliott, *Corruption and the Global Economy*, Washington: Institute for International Economics, pp. 175–233.

Elster, Jon. 1989. "Social Norms and Economic Theory," *Journal of Economic Perspectives* 3: 99–117.

El Universal. 2004. "Making Sense of the Bejerano Case," December 20, by F. Rosen, online at http://www.mexiconews.com.mx/pls/impreso/web_columnas_sup.detalle?var=17672 (viewed December 28, 2004).

Esty, Daniel, and Michael Porter. 2002. "National Environmental Performance Measurements and Determinants," in Daniel Esty and Peter K. Cornelius, eds., *Environmental Performance Measurement: The Global Report 2001–2002*, New York and Oxford: Oxford University Press.

Etzioni, Amitai. 1984. *Money Rules: Financing Elections in America*, Boulder, CO: Westview.

Euben, J. P. 1978. "On Political Corruption," *The Antioch Review* 36: 103–118.

Fabre, Guilhem. 2001. "State, Corruption, and Criminalisation in China," *International Social Science Journal* 53: 459–466.

Falken, Andrea Suarez. 2005. "Seventy-One Years of PRI Come to an End? Electoral Reform in Mexico," in Michael Johnston, ed., *People, Corruption, and Reform: Mobilizing Civil Society*, Lanham, MD: University Press of America, pp. 131–148.

Farquharson, Marjorie. 2003. "After One Year, New Russian Criminal Procedure Code is Showing Results," RFE/*RL Newsline*, July 31. Reprinted in JRL 7272, July 31.

FATF, 2004. "Financial Action Task Force" (policy descriptions and annual reports), online at http://www1.oecd.org/fatf/FATDocs_en.htm (viewed October 1, 2004).

Feinerman, James. 2000. *The Limits of the Rule of Law in China*, Seattle: University of Washington Press.

Filipov, David. 2004. "In Russia, Police on Wrong Side of the Law," *Boston Globe*, May 31.

Financial Services Authority. 2003. "Reducing Money Laundering Risk: Know Your Customer and Anti-Money Laundering Monitoring," London: Financial Services Authority, online at http://www.fsa.gov.uk/pubs/discussion/dp22.pdf (viewed October 1, 2004).

Finer, S. E., ed. 1975. *Adversary Politics and Electoral Reform*, London: Anthony Wigram.

Fisman, Raymond, and Jakob Svensson. 2000. "Are Corruption and Taxation Really Harmful to Growth? Firm-Level Evidence," Policy Research Working Paper 2485, Washington, DC: World Bank.

Fjelsted, Odd-Helge. 2002. *Decentralisation and Corruption: A Review of the Literature*, Bergen, Norway: Chr. Michelsen Institute Report U4.

Freeland, Chrystia. 2000. *Sale of the Century: Russia's Wild Ride from Communism to Capitalism*, New York: Crown Business; London: Little, Brown.

French, Howard W. 2003. "Former Leader Is Caught Up in South Korean Maelstrom," *New York Times*, April 6.

Friedman, Eric, Simon Johnson, Daniel Kaufmann, and Pablo Zoido-Lobatón. 2000. "Dodging the Grabbing Hand: The Determinants of Unofficial Activity in 69 Countries," *Journal of Public Economics* 77: 459–493.

Frimpong, Kwame. 1997. "An Analysis of Corruption in Botswana," paper presented at the seminar, "Corruption and Integrity Improvement," OECD/UNDP, Paris, October 24–25.

Frisby, Tanya. 1998. "The Rise of Organised Crime in Russia: Its Roots and Social Significance," *Europe-Asia Studies* 50: 27–49.

Fröhling, Oliver, Carolyn Gallaher, and John Paul Jones III. 2001. "Imagining the Mexican Election," *Antipode* 33: 1.

Fukui, Haruhiko, and Shigeko N. Fukai. 1996. "Pork Barrel Politics, Networks, and Local Economic Development in Contemporary Japan," *Asian Survey* 36: 3.

Gallup Poll Archives. 1997. "Americans Not Holding Their Breath on Campaign Finance Reform," online at http://www.gallup.com/POLL_ARCHIVES/971011.htm. (viewed February 6, 2003).

Gaviria, Alejandro. 2002. "Assessing the Effects of Corruption and Crime on Firm Performance: Evidence from Latin America," *Emerging Markets Review* 3: 245–268.

Gerring, John, and Strom C. Thacker. 2004. "Political Institutions and Corruption: The Role of Unitarism and Parliamentarism," *British Journal of Political Science* 34: 295–330.

Gibbons, K. M. 1989. "Toward an Attitudinal Definition of Corruption," in A. Heidenheimer, M. Johnston, M., and V. LeVine, eds., *Political Corruption: A Handbook*. New Brunswick, NJ: Transaction Publishers, pp. 165–171.

Gierzynski, Anthony. 2000. *Money Rules: Financing Elections in America*, Boulder, CO: Westview.

Girling, J. L. S. 1997. *Corruption, Capitalism and Democracy*, London and New York: Routledge.

Glees, Anthony. 1987. "The Flick Affair: A Hint of Corruption in the Bonn Republic," *Corruption and Reform* 2: 111–126.

1988. "Political Scandals in West Germany," *Corruption and Reform* 3: 262–276.

Glynn, Patrick, Stephen J. Kobrin, and Moisés Naím. 1997. "The Globalization of Corruption," in Elliott, ed., *Corruption and the Global Economy*, pp. 7–27.

Gold, Thomas, Doug Guthrie, and David Wank., eds., 2002. *Social Connections in China: Institutions, Culture, and the Changing Nature of Guanxi*, Cambridge: Cambridge University Press.

Golden, Miriam A. 2002. "Does Globalization Reduce Corruption? Some Political Consequences of Economic Integration," paper presented at a Conference on Globalization and Equalitarian Redistribution, Santa Fe Institute, May 17–19.

2003. "Electoral Connections: The Effects of the Personal Vote on Political Patronage, Bureaucracy and Legislation in Postwar Italy," *British Journal of Political Science* 33: 189–212.

Golden, Miriam, and Chang, Eric C. C. 2001. "Competitive Corruption: Factional Conflict and Political Malfeasance in Postwar Italian Christian Democracy," *World Politics* 53: 588–622.

Goldman, Marshall I. 2003a. *The Piratization of Russia: Russian Reform Goes Awry*, New York: Routledge.

2003b. "Russia Will Pay Twice for the Fortunes of Its Oligarchs," *Financial Times*, July 26.

Goldman, Merle, and Roderick MacFarquhar, eds. 1999. *The Paradox of China's Post-Mao Reforms*, Cambridge, MA: Harvard University Press.

Gong, Ting (Kung T`ing). 1994. *The Politics of Corruption in Contemporary China: An Analysis of Policy Outcomes*, Westport, CT: Praeger.

1997. "Forms and Characteristics of China's Corruption in the 1990s: Change With Continuity," *Communist and Post-Communist Studies* 30: 277–288.

2002. "Dangerous Collusion: Corruption as a Collective Venture in Contemporary China," *Communist and Post-Communist Studies* 35: 85–103.

Good, Kenneth. 1992. "Interpreting the Exceptionality of Botswana," *Journal of Modern African Studies* 30: 69–95.

1994. "Corruption and Mismanagement in Botswana: A Best-Case Example?" *Journal of Modern African Studies* 32: 499–521.

1996. "Towards Popular Participation in Botswana," *Journal of Modern African Studies* 34: 53–77.

Goodman, David S. G. 1994. *Corruption in the People's Liberation Army*, Murdoch, WA: Asia Research Center, Murdoch University,

Grayson, George W. 1980. *The Politics of Mexican Oil*, Pittsburgh: University of Pittsburgh Press.

GRECO (Council of Europe, Group of States against Corruption). 2004. *First Evaluation Round: Compliance Report on Germany* (May 14, 2004). Online at http://www.greco.coe.int/evaluations/cycle1/GrecoRC-I(2004) 1E-Germany.pdf (viewed January 5, 2005).

Green, John *et al.* 1998. *Individual Congressional Campaign Contributors: Wealthy, Conservative – and Reform-Minded*, Chicago: The Joyce Foundation.

Greene, Robert W. 1981. *The Sting Man: Inside Abscam*, New York: Dutton.

Grigorian, Marina. 2003. "A Portrait of Corruption in Russia: A Disheartening Conclusion – Everyone Takes Bribes," *Vremya MN*, July 11. English translation by Arina Yevtikhova in JRL 7246, July 14.

Guillermopietro, Alma. 2004. "The Morning Quickie," *The New York Review of Books*, 51: 40–43.

Gupta, Sanjeev, Hamid R. Davoodi, and Rosa Alonso-Terme. 2002. "Does Corruption Affect Income Inequality and Poverty?" *Economics of Governance* 3: 23–45.

Gupta, Sanjeev, Hamid R. Davoodi, and Erwin R. Tiongson. 2001. "Corruption and the Provision of Health Care and Educational Services," in Arvind K. Jain, ed., *The Political Economy of Corruption*, London: Routledge.

Guzzini, Stefano. 1995. "The 'Long Night of the First Republic': Years of Clientelistic Implosion in Italy," *Review of International Political Economy* 2: 27–61.

Ha Yong-Chool. 2001. "South Korea in 2000: A Summit and the Search for New Institutional Identity," *Asian Survey* 41: 30–39.

Hall, Thomas, and Glenn Yago. 2000. "Estimating the Cost of Opacity Using Sovereign Bond Spreads," working paper, Capital Studies Group, The Milken Insitute, Santa Monica, CA.

Hamilton-Paterson, James. 1998. *America's Boy*, London: Granta Books.

Handelman, Stephen. 2003. "Oligarchs Cry Uncle as Putin Cracks Down," *Toronto Star*, August 5. Reprinted in JRL 7277, August 5.

Hao, Yufan. 1999. "From Rule of Man to Rule of Law: An Unintended Consequence of Corruption in China in the 1990s," *Journal of Contemporary China* 8: 405–423.

Hao, Yufan, and Michael Johnston, 1995. "Reform at the Crossroads: An Analysis of Chinese Corruption," *Asian Perspective* 19: 117–149.

2002. "Corruption and the Future of Economic Reform in China," in Arnold J. Heidenheimer and Michael Johnston, eds., *Political Corruption: Concepts and Contexts*, 3rd edn, New Brunswick, NJ: Transaction Publishers, pp. 583–604.

Harper, Timothy. 1999. *Moscow Madness: Crime, Corruption, and One Man's Pursuit of Profit in the New Russia*, New York: McGraw-Hill.

Hauptman, Laurence. 1999. *Conspiracy of Interests: Iroquois Dispossession and the Rise of New York State*, Syracuse, NY: Syracuse University Press.

Hawes, Gary. 1987. *The Philippine State and the Marcos Regime: The Politics of Export*, Ithaca, NY: Cornell University Press.

Heidenheimer, Arnold J. 1970. "The Context of Analysis", in Arnold J. Heidenheimer, ed., *Political Corruption: Readings in Comparative Analysis*, New Brunswick, NJ: Transaction Books, pp. 3–28.

Hellman, Joel S., and Daniel Kaufmann. 2004. "The Inequality of Influence," in Janos Kornai and Susan Rose-Ackerman, eds., *Building a Trustworthy State in Post-Socialist Transition*, New York: Palgrave, pp. 100–118.

Hellman, Joel S., Geraint Jones, and Daniel Kaufmann. 2000. "Seize the State, Seize the Day: State Capture, Corruption, and Influence in Transition," Policy Research Working Paper 2444, Washington, DC: World Bank.

Hine, David. 1995. "Party, Personality and the Law: The Political Culture of Corruption in Italy", in P. N. Jones, ed., *Party, Parliament, and Personality*, New York: Routledge.

1996. "Political Corruption in Italy," in Walter Little and Eduardo Posada Carbó, *Political Corruption in Europe and Latin America*, Basingstoke: Macmillan, p. 6.

Hoffman, David E. 2002. *The Oligarchs: Wealth and Power in the New Russia*, New York: Public Affairs.

Holm, John D. 2000. "Curbing Corruption through Democratic Accountability: Lessons from Botswana," in K. R. Hope and B. Chikulo, eds., *Corruption and Development in Africa: Lessons from Case Studies*, Basingstoke: Macmillan, pp. 288–304.

Holm, John D., Patrick P. Molutsi, and Gloria Somolekae. 1996. "The Development of Civil Society in a Democratic State: The Botswana Model," *African Studies Review* 39: 43–69.

Holmquist, Frank W., Frederick S. Weaver, and Michael D. Ford. 1994. "The Structural Development of Kenya's Political Economy," *African Studies Review* 37: 69–105.

Hornick, Robert N. 2001. "A Foreign Lawyer's Perspective on Corruption in Indonesia," in Wilson International Center for Scholars, "Old Game or New? Corruption in Today's Indonesia," *Asia Program Special Report* No. 100, pp. 9–12.

Hudson, Michael. 2004. "Reply to Schleifer (*sic*) and Treisman," JRL 8080, February 23.

Human Rights Watch. 2002. "Kenya's Unfinished Democracy: A Human Rights Agenda for the New Government," online at http://www.hrw.org/reports/2002/kenya2/kenya1202.pdf (viewed July 17, 2003).

Humphrey, Caroline. 2002. *The Unmaking of Soviet Life: Everyday Economies After Socialism*, Ithaca, NY: Cornell University Press.

Huntington, Samuel P. 1968. *Political Order in Changing Societies*, New Haven: Yale University Press.

Hutchcroft, Paul D. 1991. "Oligarchs and Cronies in the Philippine State: The Politics of Patrimonial Plunder," *World Politics* 43: 414–450.

1998. *Booty Capitalism: The Politics of Banking in the Philippines*, Ithaca, NY: Cornell University Press.

2000. "Colonial Masters, National Politicos, and Provincial Lords: Central Authority and Local Autonomy in the American Philippines, 1900–1913," *Journal of Asian Studies* 59: 277–306.

2002. "The Politics of Privilege: Rents and Corruption in Asia," in Arnold J. Heidenheimer and Michael Johnston, eds., *Political Corruption: Concepts and Contexts*, 3rd edn, New Brunswick, NJ: Transaction Publishers, pp. 489–512.

2003. "Reflections on a Reverse Image: South Korea Under Park Chung Hee and the Philippines Under Ferdinand Marcos," paper presented at the East Asia Institute, Korea University, and the Asia Center, Harvard University, 2000; revised 2003.

Hutchcroft, Paul D., and Joel Rocamora. 2003. "Strong Demands and Weak Institutions: The Origins and Evolution of the Democratic Deficit in the Philippines," *Journal of East Asian Studies* 3: 259–292.

Hwang Jon-Sung. 1997. "Analysis of the Structure of the Korean Political Elite," *Korea Journal* 37: 98–117.

Hwang, Kelley K. 1996. "South Korea's Bureaucracy and the Informal Politics of Economic Development," *Asian Survey* 36: 306–319.

Iga Mamoru, and Morton Auerbach. 1977. "Political Corruption and Social Structure in Japan," *Asian Survey* 17: 556–564.

IMF (International Monetary Fund). 1995. *Unproductive Public Expenditures: A Pragmatic Approach to Policy Analysis*, Washington, DC: IMF, Pamphlet Series 48.

Inflation Calculator, The. 2005, online at http://www.westegg.com/inflation/ infl.cgi (viewed June 28, 2005).

Interfax, 2003. "Kudrin Expects Capital Transfers to Russia to Exceed Flight in 2003," reprinted in JRL 7268, July 27.

Isham, Jonathan, Daniel Kaufmann, and Lant Pritchett. 1995. "Civil Liberties, Democracy, and the Performance of Government Projects," World Bank, Policy Research Department, Poverty and Human Resources Division, Washington, DC.

Ivanidze, Vladimir. 2002. "Conglomerates are the Product of an Alliance Between the Yeltsin 'Family' and the Bandit Clan, Says Jalol Khaydarov," *Le Monde*, November 28. Translated in JRL 6583, December 3.

Jack, Andrew. 2002. "Slavneft Auction Sends Out the Right Signals," *Financial Times*, December 6. Reprinted in JRL 6591, December 6.

Jarvis, Christopher. 2000. "The Rise and Fall of Albania's Pyramid Schemes," *Finance and Development* 37: 46–49, online at http://www.imf.org/external/ pubs/ft/fandd/2000/03/pdf/jarvis.pdf (viewed January 5, 2005).

Johnson, Chalmers A. 1982. *MITI and the Japanese Miracle*, Stanford: Stanford University Press.

1987. "Political Institutions and Economic Performance: The Government–Business Relationship in Japan, South Korea, and Taiwan," in F. Deyo, ed., *The Political Economy of the New Asian Industrialism*, Ithaca: Cornell University Press, pp. 136–164.

1995. *Japan: Who Governs? The Rise of the Developmental State*, New York: Norton.

Johnson, David T. 2000. "Why the Wicked Sleep: The Prosecution of Political Corruption in Postwar Japan," *Asian Perspective* 24: 59–77. Online as a 1997 working paper, Japan Policy Research Institute, at http://www.jpri.org/publications/workingpapers/wp34.html (viewed January 5, 2005).

Johnson, David Ted. 2001. "Bureaucratic Corruption in Japan," Cardiff, CA: Japan Policy Research Institute, Working Paper 76, online at http://www.jpri.org/WPapers/wp76.html (viewed January 5, 2005).

Johnson, Simon, Daniel Kaufmann, and Pablo Zoido-Lobaton. 1998. "Regulatory Discretion and the Unofficial Economy," *American Economic Review* 88: 387–392.

Johnston, Michael. 1979. "Patrons and Clients, Jobs and Machines: A Case Study of the Uses of Patronage," *American Political Science Review* 73: 385–398.

1982. *Political Corruption and Public Policy in America*, Monterey, CA: Brooks-Cole.

1986a. "The Political Consequences of Corruption: A Reassessment," *Comparative Politics* 18: 459–477.

1986b. "Right and Wrong in American Politics: Popular Conceptions of Corruption," *Polity* 18: 367–391.

1991. "Right and Wrong in British Politics: 'Fits of Morality' in Comparative Perspective," *Polity* 24: 1–25.

1993. "Political Corruption: Historical Conflict and the Rise of Standards," in Larry Diamond and Marc F. Plattner, eds., *The Global Resurgence of Democracy*, Baltimore: Johns Hopkins University Press, pp. 193–205.

1996. "The Search for Definitions: The Vitality of Politics and the Issue of Corruption," *International Social Science Journal* (English language version) 149: 321–335.

1998. "What Can Be Done About Entrenched Corruption?" in Boris Pleskovic, ed., *Annual World Bank Conference on Development Economics 1997*, Washington, DC: World Bank, pp. 149–180.

2001a. "Measuring Corruption: Numbers versus Knowledge versus Understanding," in Arvind K. Jain, ed., *The Political Economy of Corruption*, London and New York: Routledge, pp. 157–179.

2001b. "The Definitions Debate: Old Conflicts in New Guises," in Arvind K. Jain, ed., *The Political Economy of Corruption*, London and New York: Routledge, pp. 11–31.

2002. "Party Systems, Competition, and Political Checks against Corruption," in Arnold J. Heidenheimer and Michael Johnston, eds., *Political Corruption: Concepts and Contexts*, 3rd edn, New Brunswick, NJ: Transaction Publishers, pp. 777–794.

ed. 2005a. *Civil Society and Corruption: Mobilizing for Reform*, Lanham, MD: University Press of America.

2005b. "Measuring Corruption or Measuring *Reform?*" *Revista Mexicana de Sociologia* 2: 229–269.

Johnston, Michael, and Yufan Hao. 1995. "China's Surge of Corruption," *Journal of Democracy* 6: 80–94.

Johnston, M., and Sahr J. Kpundeh. 2002. "Building a Clean Machine: Anti-Corruption Coalitions and Sustainable Reform," Washington, DC: World Bank Institute Working Paper number 37208.

Jordan, David C. 1999. *Drug Politics: Dirty Money and Democracies*, Norman, OK: University of Oklahoma Press.

Jowitt, Ken. 1983. "Soviet Neotraditionalism: The Political Corruption of a Leninist Regime," *Soviet Studies* 35: 275–297.

JRL: Johnson, David. 1996–2005. Johnson's Russia List. Online collection of news reports on Russia assembled and distributed by email; archived at http://www.cdi.org/russia/johnson/default.cfm (viewed January 5, 2005).

Kagarlitsky, Boris. 2003. "The Fray Near the Borovitsky Gates: Some Want to Convert Money into Power; Others Want the Opposite," *Rodnaya Gazeta*, July 18–24. English translation by Kirill Frolov in JRL 7258, July 21, 2003.

Kang, David C. 2002a. *Crony Capitalism: Corruption and Development in South Korea and the Philippines*, Cambridge and New York: Cambridge University Press.

2002b. "Bad Loans to Good Friends: Money Politics and the Developmental State in Korea," *International Organization* 56: 177–207.

Karklins, Rasma. 2002. "Typology of Post-Communist Corruption," *Problems of Post-Communism*, 49: 22–32.

Karmel, Solomon M. 1996. "Securities Markets and China's International Economic Integration," *Journal of International Affairs* 49: 525–556.

Karush, Sarah. 2002. "Selling Off the Power Company: A Test of Russia's Ability to Reform Economy," San *Francisco Chronicle*, December 21. Reprinted in JRL 6612, December 22, 2002.

Katz, Richard. 2003. *Japanese Pheonix: The Long Road to Economic Revival*, Armonk, NY: M. E. Sharpe.

Katz, Richard S., and Peter Mair. 1995. "Changing Models of Party Organization and Party Democracy: The Emergence of the Cartel Party," *Party Politics* 1: 5–28.

Kaufmann, Daniel. 2004. "Corruption, Governance and Security: Challenges for the Rich Countries and the World," in *Global Competitiveness Report 2004–2005*, Geneva: World Economic Forum 2: 83–102.

Kaufmann, Daniel, and Aleksander Kaliberda. 1996. "Integrating the Unofficial Economy into the Dynamics of Post-Socialist Economies: A Framework of Analysis and Evidence," in B. Kaminski, ed., *Economic Transition in Russia and the New States of Eurasia*, Armonk, NY: M. E. Sharpe.

Kaufmann, D., A. Kraay and P. Zoido-Lobatón. 1999. "Governance Matters," World Bank Policy Research Working Paper 2196, Washington, DC: World Bank. Online at http://www.worldbank.org/wbi/governance/working_papers.htm (viewed July 15, 2001).

Kaufmann, Daniel, Joel S. Hellman, Geraint Jones, and Mark A. Schankerman. 2000. "Measuring Governance, Corruption, and State Capture: How

Firms and Bureaucrats Shape the Business Environment in Transition Economies," World Bank Policy Research Working Paper 2312, online at http://papers.ssrn.com/sol3/papers.cfm?abstract_id=236214 (viewed July 21, 2004).

Keefer, Philip. 1996. "Protection Against a Capricious State: French Investment and Spanish Railroads, 1845–1875," *Journal of Economic History* 56: 170–92.

Keim, Gerald, and Asghar Zardkoohi. 1988. "Looking for Leverage in PAC Markets: Corporate and Labor Contributions Considered," *Public Choice* 58: 21–34.

Kennedy, William. 1983. *O Albany!*, New York: Penguin.

Khan, Mushtaq H. 2002. "Patron–Client Networks and the Economic Effects of Corruption in Asia," in Arnold J. Heidenheimer and Michael Johnston, eds., *Political Corruption: Concepts and Contexts*, 3rd edn, New Brunswick, NJ: Transaction Publishers, pp. 467–488.

Khan, Mushtaq H., and J. K. Sundaram, eds. 2000. *Rents, Rent-Seeking and Economic Development*, Cambridge: Cambridge University Press.

Kilby, Christopher. 1995. *Risk Management: An Econometric Investigation of Project Level Factors*, Washington, DC: World Bank, Operations Evaluation Department.

Kim Joongi. 2002. "Clientelism and Corruption in South Korea," in Stephen Kotkin and András Sajó, eds., *Political Corruption in Transition: A Skeptic's Handbook*, Budapest and New York: Central European University Press, pp. 167–185.

Kim Yong Jong. 1994. *Bureaucratic Corruption: The Case of Korea*, 4th edn, Seoul: Chomyung Press.

1997. *Korean Public Administration and Corruption Studies*, 2nd edn, Seoul: Hak Mun Publishing.

King, Dwight Y. 2000. "Corruption in Indonesia: A Curable Cancer?" *Journal of International Affairs* 53: 603–624.

Kipnis, Andrew B. 1997. *Producing Guanxi: Sentiment, Self, and Subculture in a North China Village*, Durham, NC: Duke University Press.

Kiser, Edgar, and Tong Xiaoxi. 1992. "Determinants of the Amount and Type of Corruption in State Fiscal Bureaucracies: An Analysis of Late Imperial China," *Comparative Political Studies* 25: 300–331.

Kitschelt, Herbert. 1986. "Political Opportunity Structures and Political Protest," *British Journal of Political Science* 16: 57–85.

Klitgaard, Robert. 1988. *Controlling Corruption*, Berkeley: University of California Press.

Klitgaard, Robert, Ronald MacLean-Abaroa, and H. Lindsey Parris. 2000. *Corrupt Cities: A Practical Guide to Cure and Prevention*, Oakland, CA: ICS Press; Washington, DC: World Bank Institute.

Klopp, Jacqueline M. 2000. "Pilfering the Public: The Problem of Land Grabbing in Contemporary Kenya," *Africa Today* 47: 7–26.

2002. "Can Moral Ethnicity Trump Political Tribalism? The Struggle for Land and Nation in Kenya," *African Studies* 61: 269–294.

Klussmann, Uwe. 2004. "A Perfidious Double-Edged Strategy," *Der Spiegel*, June 7. Reprinted, *New York Times*, June 7 (translated by Christopher Sultan).

Knack, S., and Philip Keefer. 1995. "Institutions and Economic Performance: Cross-Country Tests Using Alternative Institutional Measures," *Economics and Politics* 7: 207–227.

Knight, Alan. 1996. "Corruption in Twentieth Century Mexico," in Walter Little and Eduardo Posada-Carbó, eds., *Political Corruption in Europe and Latin America*, Basingstoke: Macmillan, pp. 219–236.

Koo, Hagen, ed., 1993. *State and Society in Contemporary Korea*, Ithaca: Cornell University Press.

Koo, Hagen. 2002. "Civil Society and Democracy in South Korea," *The Good Society* 11: 40–45.

Kostikov, Vyacheslav. 2003. "Dizzy with Success: Russia – Stability under Threat," *Argumenty I Fakty*, July 16. Reprinted in JRL 7253, July 17.

Kramer, John M. 1977. "Political Corruption in the USSR," *Western Political Quarterly* 30: 213–224.

1998. "The Politics of Corruption," *Current History* 97: 329–335.

Ku, Hok Bun. 2003. *Moral Politics in a South Chinese Village: Responsibility, Reciprocity, and Resistance*, Lanham, MD: Rowman & Littlefield.

Kung, Hsiao-Hsia, and Maris Gillette. 1993. *Corruption and Abuses of Power During the Reform Era*, Armonk, NY: M. E. Sharpe.

Kwong, Julia. 1997. *The Political Economy of Corruption in China*, Armonk, NY: M. E. Sharpe.

Lacey, Marc. 2003a. "Kenya's Brand New Day," *New York Times Upfront* 135: 18–21.

2003b. "A Crackdown on Corruption in Kenya Snares Judges," *New York Times*, October 26.

Lambsdorff, Johann Graf. 1999. "The Transparency International Corruption Perceptions Index 1999: Framework Document," Berlin: Transparency International. Online at http://www.transparency.org/cpi/1999/cpi_framework.html (viewed January 5, 2005).

2003a. "How Corruption Affects Productivity," *Kyklos* 56: 457–474.

2003b. "How Corruption Affects Persistent Capital Flows," *Economics of Governance* 4: 229–243.

La Porta, Rafael, Florencio Lopez-de-Silanes, Adrei Shleifer, and Robert Vishny. 1999. "The Quality of Government," *Journal of Law, Economics, and Organization* 15: 222–279.

Larraín B., Felipe, and José Tavares. 2004. "Does Foreign Direct Investment Decrease Corruption?" *Cuadernos de Economica* 41: 217–230.

Lauth, Hans-Joachim. 2000. "Informal Institutions and Democracy," *Democratization* 7: 21–50.

Lavelle, Peter. 2003. "Opinion: The New and Improved Corruption Equilibrium," *The Russia Journal*, reprinted in JRL 7509, February 12.

Lavrentieva, Victoria. 2002. "Whatever Happened to Those Vouchers?" *Moscow Times*, August 15. Reprinted in JRL 6405, August 15.

Ledeneva, Alena V. 1998. *Russia's Economy of Favours: Blat, Networking, and Informal Exchange*, Cambridge and New York: Cambridge University Press.

Lee, Peter N. S. 1990. "Bureaucratic Corruption during the Deng Xiaoping Era," *Corruption and Reform* 5: 29–47.

Leff, Nathaniel. 1964. "Economic Development through Bureaucratic Corruption," *American Behavioral Scientist*, 7: 8–14.

Leite, Carlos, and Jens Weidmann. 1999. "Does Mother Nature Corrupt? Natural Resources, Corruption, and Economic Growth," working paper of the International Monetary Fund.

Leitzel, Jim. 2002. "Corruption and Organized Crime in the Russian Transition," in Michael P. Cuddy and Ruvin Gekker, eds., *Institutional Change in Transition Economies*, Aldershot: Ashgate, pp. 35–54.

Levine, Bertram J. 2004. "Unrecorded Legislative Activities: A Study of How Members of the U. S. House of Representatives Work 'Behind-the-Scenes' to Accomplish Policy and Career Objectives," Ph.D. thesis, Department of Political Science, Rutgers University.

Levy, Brian, and Sahr Kpundeh. 2004. *Building State Capacity in Africa: New Approaches, Emerging Lessons*, Washington, DC: World Bank.

Levy, Daniel C., and Kathleen Bruhn. 2001. *Mexico: The Struggle for Democratic Development*, Berkeley: University of California Press.

Leys, Colin. 1965. "What is the Problem about Corruption?" *Journal of Modern African Studies* 3: 215–3230.

Li, Ke, Russell Smyth, and Yao Shuntian. 2002. "Institutionalized Corruption and Privilege in China's Socialist Market Economy: A General Equilibrium Analysis," Clayton, Victoria: Monash University, Department of Economics discussion papers, October.

Li Lianjiang. 2001. "Support for Anti-corruption Campaigns in Rural China," *Journal of Contemporary China* 10: 573–586.

Liddle, R. William. 1985. "Soeharto's Indonesia: Personal Rule and Political Institutions," *Pacific Affairs* 58: 68–90.

1996. "Indonesia's Democratic Past and Future," *Comparative Politics* 24: 443–462.

Lipset, Seymore Martin, and Gabriel Salman Lenz. 2000. "Corruption, Culture, and Markets," in Lawrence J. Harrison and Samuel P. Huntington, eds., *Culture Matters: How Values Shape Human Progress*, New York: Basic Books, pp. 80–124.

Liu, Alan P. L. 1983. "The Politics of Corruption in the People's Republic of China," *American Political Science Review* 77: 602–623.

Liu, Ch'uang-ch'u, and Rance Pui-leung Lee. 1978. *Bureaucratic Corruption in Nineteenth-Century China*, Hong Kong: Chinese University of Hong Kong, Social Research Centre.

Lo, T. Wing (Tit Wing). 1993. *Corruption and Politics in Hong Kong and China*, Buckingham and Philadelphia: Open University Press, 1993.

Lü Xiaobo. 1999. "From Rank-Seeking to Rent-Seeking: Changing Administrative Ethos and Corruption in Reform China," *Crime, Law, and Social Change* 32: 347–370.

(Lü, Hsiao-Po). 2000. *Cadres and Corruption: The Organizational Involution of the Chinese Communist Party*, Stanford, CA: Stanford University Press.

Lui, Adam Y. C. 1979. *Corruption in China During the Early Ch'ing Period 1644–1660*, Centre of Asian Studies Occasional Papers and Monographs 39.

Lukas, J. Anthony. 1976. *Nightmare: The Underside of the Nixon Years*, New York: Viking Press.

MacIntyre, Andrew. 2003. "Institutions and the Political Economy of Corruption in Developing Countries," discussion paper, Workshop on Corruption, Stanford University, January 31–February 1.

Makarim, Nono Anwar. 2001. "A Path through the Rainforest: Anti-Corruption in Indonesia," in Wilson International Center for Scholars, "Old Game or New? Corruption in Today's Indonesia," Asia Program Special Report 100, pp. 4–8.

Malley, Michael S. 2003. "Indonesia in 2002: The Rising Cost of Inaction," *Asian Survey* 43: 135–146.

Manion, Melanie. 2004. *Corruption by Design: Building Clean Government in Mainland China and Hong Kong*, Cambridge, MA: Harvard University Press.

Mann, Thomas, and Takeshi Sasaki, eds. 2002. *Governance for a New Century: Japanese Challenges, American Experience*, Tokyo and New York: Japan Center for International Exchange

Mauro, Paolo. 1998. "Corruption: Causes, Consequences, and Agenda for Further Research," *Finance and Development* 35: 11–14.

　　2002. "The Effects of Corruption on Growth and Public Expenditure," in Arnold J. Heidenheimer and Michael Johnston, eds., *Political Corruption: Concepts and Contexts*, 3rd edn, New Brunswick, NJ: Transaction Publishers, pp. 339–352.

McCoy, Alfred W. 1989a. *Closer Than Brothers: Manhood at the Philippine Military Academy*, New Haven: Yale University Press.

　　1989b. "Quezon's Commonwealth: The Emergence of Philippine Authoritarianism," in Ruby R. Paredes, ed., *Philippine Colonial Democracy*, New Haven: Yale University Southeast Asia Studies Monograph 32.

　　1993. "Rent-Seeking Families and the Philippine State: A History of the Lopez Family," in Alfred W. McCoy, ed., *An Anarchy of Families: State and Family in the Philippines*, Madison, WI: University of Wisconsin, Center for Southeast Asian Studies, in cooperation with Ateneo de Manila University Press, pp. 429–536.

McCullagh, Declan. 1998. "Banking with Big Brother," *Wired News*, December 10, online at http://www.wired.com/news/politics/0,1283,16749,00.html (viewed October 1, 2004).

McFaul, Michael. 1995. "State Power, Institutional Change, and the Politics of Privatization in Russia," *World Politics* 47: 210–243.

　　2001. *Russia's Unfinished Revolution*, Ithaca, NY: Cornell University Press.

McFaul, Michael, Nikolai Petrov, and Andrei Ryabov. 2004. *Between Dictatorship and Democracy: Russian Post-Communist Political Reform*, Washington, DC: Carnegie Endowment for International Peace.

McKinley, James C. Jr. 2004. "Police Arrest 33 After Lynchings in Mexico City," *New York Times*, November 26.

Mendras, Marie. 1997. "Rule by Bureaucracy in Russia," in Donatella Della Porta and Yves Mény, eds., *Democracy and Corruption in Europe*, London: Pinter, pp. 118–131.

Mishima Ko. 1998. "The Changing Relationship between Japan's LDP and the Bureaucracy: Hashimoto's Administrative Reform Effort and its Politics," *Asian Survey* 38: 968–985.

Mitchell, Richard H. 1996. *Political Bribery in Japan*, Honolulu: University of Hawaii Press.

Montesano, Michael J. 2004. "The Philippines in 2003," *Asian Survey* 44: 93–101.

Montinola, Gabriella. 1993. "The Foundations of Political Corruption: Insights from the Philippine Case," *Asian Journal of Political Science* 2: 86–113.

1999. "Politicians, Parties, and the Persistence of Weak States: Lessons from the Philippines," *Development and Change* 30: 739–774.

Moodie, G. C. 1980. "On Political Scandals and Corruption," *Government and Opposition* 15: 208–222.

Moon Chung-In and Kim Song-Min. 2000. "Democracy and Economic Performance in South Korea," in Larry Diamond and Byung-Kook Kim, eds., *Consolidating Democracy in South Korea*, Boulder, CO: Lynne Rienner, pp. 139–172.

Moran, Jonathan. 1998. "Corruption and NIC Development: A Case Study of South Korea," *Crime, Law and Social Change* 29: 161–177.

Moran, Jon. 1999. "Patterns of Corruption and Development in East Asia," *Third World Quarterly* 20: 569–587.

Moreno, Alejandro. 2002. "Corruption and Democracy: A Cultural Assessment," *Comparative Sociology* 1: 495–507.

Moroff, Holger. 2002. "American and German Fund-Raising Fiascos and Their Aftermaths," in Arnold J. Heidenheimer and Michael Johnston, eds., *Political Corruption: Concepts and Contexts*, 3rd edn, New Brunswick, NJ: Transaction Publishers, pp. 687–710.

Morris, Dwight L. 1996. "Take and Switch (Money Talks)," Washington *Post*, April 15, online at http://www.washingtonpost.com/wp-srv/politics/campaigns/money/archive/money041596.htm (viewed April 7, 2004).

Morris, Stephen D. 1991. *Corruption and Politics in Contemporary Mexico*, Tuscaloosa, AL: University of Alabama Press.

1995. *Political Reformism in Mexico: An Overview of Contemporary Mexican Politics*, Boulder: Lynne Rienner Publishers.

1999. "Corruption and the Mexican Political System: Continuity and Change," *Third World Quarterly* 20: 623–643.

Mortishead, Carl. 2003. "Power Struggle Follows Shift in Influence towards Oligarchs," *The Times* (London), September 18. Reprinted in JRL 7329, September 18.

Moss, David. 1995. "Patronage Revisited: The Dynamics of Information and Reputation," *Journal of Modern Italian Studies* 1: 1.

Murphy, Kevin M., Andrei Schleifer, and Robert W. Vishny. 1993. "Why is Rent Seeking So Costly to Growth?" *American Economic Review* 83: 409–414.

Myers, Steven Lee. 2002a. "A Russian Crime Drama Deepens with Arrests," *New York Times*, November 21.

2002b. "Russia Glances to the West for Its New Legal Code," *New York Times*, July 1.

Myrdal, Gunnar. 2002. "Corruption as a Hindrance to Development in South Asia," in Arnold J. Heidenheimer and Michael Johnston, eds., *Political Corruption: Concepts and Contexts*, 3rd edn, New Brunswick, NJ: Transaction Publishers, pp. 265–279.

Neher, Clark D. 1994. "Asian Style Democracy," *Asian Survey* 34: 949–961.

Nelken, David. 1996. "The Judges and Political Corruption in Italy," *Journal of Law and Society* 23: 95–112.

New York Times. 2004. "Berlusconi Acquitted of Corruption Charges," December 10.

Nye, J. S. 1967. "Corruption and Political Development: A Cost-Benefit Analysis," *American Political Science Review* 61: 417–427.

Nyong'o, P. Anyang'. 1989. "State and Society in Kenya: The Disintegration of the Nationalist Coalitions and the Rise of Presidential Authoritarianism 1963–78," *African Affairs* 88: 229–251.

O'Donnell, Guillermo. 2001. "Illusions about Consolidation," in Larry Diamond and Marc F. Plattner, eds., *The Global Divergence of Democracies*, Baltimore: Johns Hopkins University Press, pp. 113–130.

OECD (Organization for Economic Cooperation and Development). 1998. *Corruption and Integrity Improvement Initiatives in Developing Countries*, New York: United Nations Development Program, and Paris: OECD Development Centre.

2003. "Anti-Bribery Convention: Entry into Force," online at http://www.oecd.org/document/12/0,2340,en_2649_37447_2057484_1_1_1_37447,00.html (viewed January 9, 2005).

Oi, Jean C. 1991. "Partial Reform and Corruption in Rural China," in Richard Baum, ed., *China's Post-Mao Reforms: A Comparative Assessment*, New York: Routledge, pp. 143–161.

O'Leary, Cornelius. 1962. *The Elimination of Corrupt Practices in British Elections, 1968–1911*, Oxford: Clarendon Press.

Opensecrets.org. 2001. "Bankruptcy," March 15, online at http://www.opensecrets.org/news/bankruptcy/index.htm (viewed April 6, 2004).

2004a. "Benefiting from the Benefit?" March 26, online at http://www.capitaleye.org/inside.asp?ID=124. (viewed April 6, 2004).

2004b. "Tracking the Payback," online at http://www.opensecrets.org/payback/index.asp (viewed April 6, 2004).

Ornstein, Norman J., Thomas E. Mann, and Michael J. Malbin. 2002. *Vital Statistics on Congress 2001–2002*, Washington, DC: American Enterprise Institute, online at http://www.cfinst.org/studies/vital/3–3.htm (viewed February 6, 2003).

Papyrakis, Elissaios, and Reyer Gerlagh. 2004. "The Resource Curse Hypothesis and its Transmission Channels," working paper: Institute for Environmental Studies, Vrije Universiteit Amsterdam, online at http://130.37.129.100/ivm/organisation/staff/papers/Papyrakis_and_Gerlagh.pdf (viewed November 30, 2004).

Park Byeog-Seog. 1995. "Political Corruption in South Korea: Concentrating on the Dynamics of Party Politics," *Asian Perspective* 19: 163–193.

Pascha, Werner. 1999. "Corruption in Japan: An Economist's Perspective," based on discussant comments for panel on "Shadow Politics: Political Corruption in Japan," Annual Meeting of the Association for Asian Studies, Boston, online at http://www.uni-duisburg.de/Institute/OAWISS/download/doc/paper23.pdf (viewed January 5, 2005).

Pasquino, G., and P. McCarthy, eds. 1993. *The End of Post-War Politics in Italy: The Landmark 1992 Elections*, Boulder, CO: Westview Press.

Pastor, Robert. A. 2000. "Exiting the Labyrinth," *Journal of Democracy* 11: 20–24.

PCIJ (Philippine Center for Investigative Journalism). 2000. "Can Estrada Explain His Wealth? The State of the President's Finances," Philippine Center for Investigative Journalism, online at http://www.pcij.org/stories/2000/erapwealth.html (viewed January 5, 2005).

Pei Minxin. 1999. "Will China Become Another Indonesia?" *Foreign Policy* 116: 94–108.

——— 2002. "China's Governance Crisis," *Foreign Affairs* 81: 96–109.

Pempel, T. J. 1998. *Regime Shift: Comparative Dynamics of the Japanese Political Economy*, Ithaca: Cornell University Press.

Peng, David R. Yusheng. 2004. "Kinship Networks and Entrepreneurs in China's Transitional Economy," *American Journal of Sociology* 109: 1045–74.

People's Daily Online. 2001a. "Corruption Crackdown Gathers Pace," March 18, online at http://fpeng.peopledaily.com.cn/200103/18/eng20010318_65274.html (viewed October 9, 2003).

——— 2001b. "Details of Xiamen Smuggling Case Exposed," July 26, online at http://english.peopledaily.com.cn/200107/25/eng20010725_75780.html (viewed October 9, 2003).

——— 2002a. "Customs Pinpoint Smuggling-Infested Areas in China," January 24, online at http://english.peopledaily.com.cn/200201/24/eng20020124_89275.shtml (viewed May 13, 2005).

——— 2002b. "Anti-Corruption Struggle Fruitful: Top Judge, Procurator," March 11, online at http://english.peopledaily.com.cn/200203/11/eng/20020311_91882.shtml (viewed October 9, 2003).

Percival, Lindsay. 1997. "Albania: Pyramid Schemes Common across Eastern Europe," *RFE/RL Features*, January 16, online at http://www.rferl.org/nca/features/1997/01/F.RU.970116172653.html (viewed May 17, 2003).

Perry, Elizabeth J. 1999. "Crime, Corruption, and Contention," in Merle Goldman and Roderick MacFarquhar, eds., *The Paradox of China's Post-Mao Reforms*, Cambridge, MA: Harvard University Press, pp. 308–329.

Peters, J. G., and Welch, S. 1978. "Political Corruption in America: A Search for Definitions and a Theory," *American Political Science Review* 72: 974–984.

Pharr, Susan J. 2000. "Officials' Misconduct and Public Distrust: Japan and the Trilateral Democracies," in Pharr and Putnam, eds., *Disaffected Democracies*, pp. 173–201.

2005. "Contributions, Covenants, and Corruption: Politicians and Society in Japan," in Michael Johnston, ed., *Civil Society and Corruption: Mobilizing for Reform*, Lanham, MD: University Press of America, pp. 23–32.

Pharr, Susan J., and Robert D. Putnam, eds. 2000. *Disaffected Democracies: What's Troubling the Trilateral Countries?* Princeton, NJ: Princeton University Press.

Philp, Mark. 1987. "Defining Corruption: An Analysis of the Republican Tradition," International Political Science Association research roundtable on political finance and political corruption, Bellagio, Italy.

1997. "Defining Political Corruption," in Paul Heywood, ed., *Political Corruption*, Oxford: Blackwell, pp. 20–46.

2002. "Conceptualizing Political Corruption," in Arnold J. Heidenheimer and Michael Johnston, eds., *Political Corruption: Concepts and Contexts*, 3rd edn, New Brunswick, NJ: Transaction Publishers, pp. 41–57.

Pizzorno, A. 1993. *Le radici della politica assoluta*, Milano, Feltrinelli.

Political Graveyard. 2004. "Politicians in Disgrace," Biographical Entries, online at http://politicalgraveyard.com/special/trouble-disgrace.html (viewed April 7, 2004).

Pollingreport.com. 2004. "Government and Politics," online at http://www.pollingreport.com/politics.htm. (viewed December 13, 2004).

Popov, Vladimir. 2002. "Strong Institutions are More Important than the Speed of Reform," in Michael P. Cuddy and Ruvin Gekker, eds., *Institutional Change in Transition Economies*, Aldershot: Ashgate, pp. 55–71.

Poteete, Amy R. 2003. "When Professionalism Clashes with Local Particularities: Ecology, Elections and Procedural Arrangements in Botswana," *Journal of Southern African Studies*, 29: 461–485.

Preston, Julia, and Sam Dillon. 2004. *Opening Mexico: The Making of a Democracy*, New York: Farrar, Straus, and Giroux.

Pribylovsky, Vladimir. 2003. "Oligarchs of the Putin Era: A Brief Guide to the Russian Oligarchic System," *Smysl*, May 1–15. Translation reprinted in JRL 7167, May 5, 2003.

Przeworski, Adam. 1995. *Sustainable Democracy*, Cambridge: Cambridge University Press.

Przeworski, Adam, and Fernando Limongi. 1993. "Political Regimes and Economic Growth," *Journal of Economic Literature* 7: 51–69.

Pujas, Véronique, and Martin Rhodes. 2002. "Party Finance and Political Scandal: Comparing Italy, Spain, and France," in Arnold J. Heidenheimer and Michael Johnston, eds., *Political Corruption: Concepts and Contexts*, New Brunswick, NJ: Transaction Publishers, pp. 739–760.

Putnam, Robert D. 2000. *Bowling Alone: The Collapse and Revival of American Community*, New York: Simon and Schuster.

Pye, Lucian W. 1997. "Money Politics and Transitions to Democracy in East Asia," *Asian Survey* 37: 213–228.

Quah, Jon S. T. 2003. *Curbing Corruption in Asia: A Comparative Study of Six Countries*, Singapore: Eastern Universities Press.

Rahman, Aminur, Gregory Kisunko, and Kapil Kapoor. 2000. "Estimating the Effects of Corruption," Policy Research Working Paper 2479, Washington, DC: World Bank.

Rauch, James. 1995. "Bureaucracy, Infrastructure, and Economic Growth: Evidence from U.S. Cities during the Progressive Era," *American Economic Review* 85: 968–979.

Reddaway, Peter, and Dmitri Glinski. 2001. *The Tragedy of Russia's Reforms: Market Bolshevism against Democracy*. Washington: United States Institute of Peace Press.

Reed, Bradley Ward. 2000. *Talons and Teeth: County Clerks and Runners in the Qing Dynasty*, Stanford: Stanford University Press.

Reinikka, Ritva, and Jakob Svensson. 2002. "Measuring and Understanding Corruption at the Micro Level," in Donatella Della Porta and Susan Rose-Ackerman, eds., *Corrupt Exchanges: Empirical Themes in the Politics and Political Economy of Corruption*, Frankfurt: Nomos Verlag.

Reut, Andrei, and Oleg Rubnikovich. 2003. "Prosecutor General's Office Versus a Member of 'Yeltsin's Family,'" *Gazeta*, July 15. Translation reprinted in JRL 7249, July 15, 2003.

Rhodes, Martin. 1997. "Financing Party Politics in Italy: A Case of Systemic Corruption," in Martin J. Bull and Martin Rhodes, *Crisis and Transition in Italian Politics*, London: Frank Cass.

RIA RosBusiness Consulting. 2003. "Russian Capital Flies Back Home," JRL 7471, December 16.

Riedinger, Jeffrey. 1995. "The Philippines in 1994: Renewed Growth and Contested Reforms," *Asian Survey* 35: 209–216.

Ringuet, Daniel Joseph, and Elsa Estrada. 2003. "Understanding the Philippines' Economy and Politics since the Return of Democracy in 1986," *Contemporary Southeast Asia* 25: 233–240.

Roberts, Clayton. 1966. *The Growth of Responsible Government in Stuart England*, Cambridge: Cambridge University Press.

Robertson-Snape, Fiona. 1999. "Corruption, Collusion, and Nepotism in Indonesia," *Third World Quarterly* 20: 589–602.

Rodrik, Dani, ed. 2003. *In Search of Prosperity: Analytic Narratives on Economic Growth*, Princeton, NJ: Princeton University Press.

Root, Hilton L. 1996. *Small Countries, Big Lessons: Governance and the Rise of East Asia*, New York: Asian Development Bank and Oxford University Press.

Rosbalt. 2003. "Russian Businessmen Spend up to USD 33 Billion a Year on Bribes," JRL 7353, October 5.

Rose-Ackerman, Susan. 1978. *Corruption: A Study in Political Economy*, New York: Academic Press.

1999. *Corruption and Government*, New York: Cambridge University Press.

2002. "When is Corruption Harmful?" in Arnold J. Heidenheimer and Michael Johnston, eds., *Political Corruption: Concepts and Contexts*, 3rd edn, New Brunswick, NJ: Transaction Publishers, pp. 353–371.

Rose-Ackerman, Susan, and Andrew Stone. 1996. *The Costs of Corruption for Private Business: Evidence from World Bank Surveys*, Washington, DC: World Bank Development.

Ross, Stanley D. 1992. "The Rule of Law and Lawyers in Kenya," *Journal of Modern African Studies* 30: 421–442.

Rotberg, Robert I. 2004. "Strengthening African Leadership: There is Another Way," *Foreign Affairs*, 83: 14–18.

Round, John. 2002. "The Business of Politics in Magadan," *RFE/RL Newsline*, October 22. Reprinted in JRL 6506, October 22.

Rubinstein, W. D. 1983. "The End of 'Old Corruption' in Britain 1780–1860," *Past and Present* 101: 55–86.

Rustow, Dankwart A. 1970. "Transitions to Democracy: Toward a Dynamic Model," *Comparative Politics* 2: 337–363.

Ruzindana, Augustine. 1997. "The Importance of Leadership in Fighting Corruption in Uganda," in Kimberly Ann Elliott, ed., *Corruption and the Global Economy*, Washington, DC: Institute for International Economics, pp. 133–145.

Ryabov, Andrei. 2003. "The Decline of the Family: Competition and Rivalry among Elites in Russia Should Continue," Vremya *MN*, August 8. Translated in JRL 7281, August 8.

Ryklin, Alexander. 2003. "Politics and Business: The Kremlin Has Failed to Cleanse Russian Politics of Big Business," *Yezhenedelny Zhurnal*, January 2. Translation by A. Ignatkin reprinted in JRL 7030, January 23.

Sachs, J., and A. M. Warner. 2001. "The Curse of Natural Resources," *European Economic Review* 45: 827–838.

Samatar, Abdi Ismail, and Sophie Oldfield. 1995. "Class and Effective State Institutions: The Botswana Meat Commission," *Journal of Modern African Studies* 33: 651–668.

Samuels, Richard J. 2001. "Kishi and Corruption: An Anatomy of the 1955 System," Cardiff, CA: Japan Policy Research Institute, working paper 83, online at http://www.jpri.org/WPapers/wp83.html (viewed January 5, 2005).

Sandholtz, Wayne, and William Koetzle. 2000. "Accounting for Corruption: Economic Structure, Democracy, and Trade Source," *International Studies Quarterly* 44: 31–50.

Satter, David. 2003. *Darkness at Dawn: The Rise of the Russian Criminal State*, New Haven: Yale University Press.

Schlesinger, Thomas J., and Kenneth J. Meier. 2002. "Variations in Corruption among the American States," in Arnold J. Heidenheimer and Michael Johnston, eds., *Political Corruption: Concepts and Contexts*, 3rd edn, New Brunswick, NJ: Transaction Publishers, pp. 627–644.

Schneider, Ben Ross. 1998. "Elusive Synergy: Business–Government Relations and Development," *Comparative Politics* 31: 101–122.

Schopf, James C. 2001. "An Explanation for the End of Political Bank Robbery in the Republic of Korea," *Asian Survey* 41: 693–715.

Schoppa, Leonard. 2001. "Japan, the Reluctant Reformer," *Foreign Affairs* 76–90.

Schwartz, Charles A. 1979. "Corruption and Political Development in the U.S.S.R.," *Comparative Politics* 11: 425–443.

Scott, James C. 1972. *Comparative Political Corruption*, Englewood Cliffs, NJ: Prentice-Hall.

Seabrook, Jeremy. 1998. "Corruption, Collusion, Nepotism," *New Statesman*, October 9: 20–21.

Seagrave, Sterling. 1988. *The Marcos Dynasty*, New York: Harper & Row.

Seibel, Wolfgang. 1997. "Corruption in the Federal Republic of Germany Before and in the Wake of Reunification," in Donatella Della Porta and Yves Mény, eds., *Democracy and Corruption in Europe*, London: Pinter, pp. 85–102.

Seligmann, Albert L. 1997. "Japan's New Electoral System," *Asian Survey* 37: 409–428.

Seligson, Mitchell A. 2002. "The Impact of Corruption on Regime Legitimacy: A Comparative Study of Four Latin American Countries," *Journal of Politics* 64: 408–433.

Seyf, Ahmad. 2001. "Corruption and Development: A Study of Conflict," *Development in Practice* 11: 597–605.

SHCP (Secretaría de Hacienda y Crédito Público). 2000. "Algunas Puntualizaciones" (press release on elimination of secret presidential funds), October 22.

Shefter, Martin. 1976. "The Emergence of the Political Machine: An Alternative View," in Willis D. Hawley, ed., *Theoretical Perspectives on Urban Politics*, Englewood Cliffs, NJ: Prentice-Hall.

Shelinov, Roman. 2003. "Who Has Stolen What in Russia: Review of the Annual Report of the Prosecutor General's Office," translation reprinted in JRL 7096, March 9.

Shelley, Louise. 2001. "Crime and Corruption," in Stephen White, Alex Pravda, and Zvi Gitelman, eds., *Developments in Russian Politics*, Durham, NC: Duke University Press, pp. 239–253.

2005. "Civil Society Mobilized against Corruption: Russia and Ukraine," in Michael Johnston, ed., *Civil Society and Corruption: Mobilizing for Reform*, Lanham, MD: University Press of America, pp. 3–21.

Shleifer, Andrei, and Daniel Treisman. 2004. "A Normal Country," *Foreign Affairs* 83: 20–38. Also available as NBER working paper 10057, October 2003, online at http://papers.nber.org/papers/w10057 (viewed June 14, 2004).

Shleifer, Andrei, and Robert W. Vishny. 1993. "Corruption," *Quarterly Journal of Economics* 108: 599–617.

Sidel, John T. 1997. "Philippine Politics in Town, District, and Province: Bossism in Cavite and Cebu," *Journal of Asian Studies* 56: 947–966.

2000. *Capital, Coercion, and Crime: Bossism in the Philippines*, Stanford, CA: Stanford University Press.

Simis, Konstantin. 1982. *USSR – The Corrupt Society: The Secret World of Soviet Capitalism*, New York: Simon and Schuster.

Sinclair, Barbara. 2000. *Unorthodox Lawmaking: New Legislative Processes in the U.S. Congress*, 2nd edn, Washington, DC: CQ Press.

Sindzingre, Alice. 2005. "Social Networks, States, and Rents: Contrasting Corruption in Africa and Asia," in Michael Johnston, ed., *Civil Society and Corruption: Mobilizing for Reform*, Lanham, MD: University Press of America, pp. 33–60.

Singleton, Solveig. 1999. "Know Your Customer: Know Your Comrade," Cato Institute: Publications, February 4, online at http://www.cato.org/dailys/ 02–04–99.html (viewed October 1, 2004).

Snyder, James. 1992. "Long-term Investing in Politicians; Or, Give Early, Give Often," *Journal of Law and Economics* 35: 15–43.

Stanley, Peter W. 1974. *A Nation in the Making: The Philippines and the United States, 1899–1921*, Cambridge: Harvard University Press.

Steinberg, David I. 2000. "Continuing Democratic Reform: The Unfinished Symphony," in Larry Diamond and Byung-Kook Kim, eds., *Consolidating Democracy in South Korea*, Boulder, CO: Lynne Rienner, pp. 203–238.

Stiglitz, Joseph E. 2002. *Globalization and its Discontents*, New York: W. W. Norton.

Su Ya and Jia Lusheng. 1993. *White Cat and Black Cat*, Guangzhou: Huacheng Press.

Sun, Yan. 1999. "Reform, State, and Corruption: Is Corruption Less Destructive in China than in Russia?" *Comparative Politics* 32: 1–20.

———. 2001. "The Politics of Conceptualizing Corruption in Reform China," *Crime, Law and Social Change* 35: 245–270.

———. 2004. *Corruption and Market in Contemporary China*, Ithaca, NY: Cornell University Press.

Sun-Star (Manila). 2003. "Imelda Marcos Expected to Be in Jail Next Year: Gov't," September 22, online at http://www.sunstar.com.ph/static/net/ 2003/09/22/ (viewed January 5, 2005).

Szilágyi, Ákos. 2002. "Kompromat and Corruption in Russia," in Stephen Kotkin and Andras Sajo, eds., *Political Corruption in Transition: A Sceptic's Handbook*, Budapest and New York: Central European University Press, pp. 207–231.

Tachino, Junji. 1999. "Political Corruption and Governmental Credibility in Japan," University of California-San Diego, Research Program on the Pacific Rim, working paper, online at http://orpheus.ucsd.edu/las/studies/ pdfs/tachino.pdf (viewed January 5, 2005).

Tanzi, Vito, and Hamid Davoodi. 2002a. "Corruption, Growth, and Public Finance," in George T. Abed and Sanjeev Gupta, eds., *Governance, Corruption, and Economic Performance*, Washington, DC: International Monetary Fund, pp. 197–222.

———. 2002b. "Corruption, Public Investment, and Growth," in George T. Abed and Sanjeev Gupta, eds., *Governance, Corruption, and Economic Performance*, Washington, DC: International Monetary Fund, pp. 280–299.

Tat Yan Kong. 1996. "Corruption and its Institutional Foundations: The Experience of South Korea," *IDS Bulletin* 27: 2.

Tavernise, Sabrina. 2002a. "Handful of Corporate Raiders Transform Russia's Economy," *New York Times*, August 13.

———. 2002b. "Police for Hire in Russia's Business Jungle," *New York Times*, July 28.

———. 2003a. "A Russian Tilts at Graft (It Could Be a Quixotic Task)," *New York Times*, February 10.

———. 2003b. "A Crackdown on an Oil Tycoon Shakes Up Russian Politics," *New York Times*, July 22.

Thayer, George. 1973. *Who Shakes the Money Tree? American Campaign Financing Practices from 1789 to the Present*, New York: Simon and Schuster.

Theobald, Robin. 1990. *Corruption, Development and Underdevelopment*, Durham, NC: Duke University Press.

Thompson, Dennis F. 1993. "Mediated Corruption: The Case of the Keating Five," *American Political Science Review* 87: 369–381.

1995. *Ethics in Congress: From Individual to Institutional Corruption*, Washington, DC: Brookings Institution.

Torgler, Benno. 2003. "Tax Morale in Central and Eastern European Countries," presented at a conference on Tax Evasion, Trust, and State Capacity, University of St. Gallen, Switzerland, October 17–19.

Tornell, Aaron. 2002. "Economic Crises and Reform in Mexico," in Stephen Haber, ed., *Crony Capitalism and Economic Growth in Latin America*, Stanford, CA: Hoover Institution Press 5: 127–150.

Toro, María Celia. 1998. "The Political Repercussions of Drug Trafficking in Mexico," in Elizabeth Joyce and Carlos Malamud, eds., *Latin America and the Multinational Drug Trade*, Basingstoke: Macmillan, pp. 133–145.

Transparency International. 2000. *Confronting Corruption: The Elements of a National Integrity System, TI Source Book 2000*. Berlin: Transparency International.

Treisman, Daniel. 2000. "The Causes of Corruption: A Cross-National Study," *Journal of Public Economics* 76: 399–457.

Trent, Logan. 1981. *The Credit Mobilier*, New York: Arno Press.

Troy, Gil. 1997. "Money and Politics: The Oldest Connection," *The Wilson Quarterly* 21: 14–32.

Tsie, Balefi. 1996. "The Political Context of Botswana's Development Performance," *Journal of Southern African Studies* 22: 599–616.

Tulchin, Joseph S., and Andrew D. Selee, eds. 2003. *Mexico's Politics and Society in Transition*. Boulder, CO: Lynne Rienner.

UNDP (United Nations Development Program). 1997. "Corruption and Good Governance," New York: UNDP Bureau for Policy and Programme Support.

United States, Department of Justice. 1995. "Former Congressman Donald E. Lukens Indicted for Bribery" (February 23: Criminal Release #103), online at http://www.usdoj.gov/opa/pr/Pre_96/February95/103.txt.html (viewed April 7, 2004).

United States, Federal Election Commission. 1995. *Twenty Year Report*, online at http://www.fec.gov/pages/20year1.htm (viewed January 5, 2005).

1996. "National Voter Turnout in Federal Elections: 1960–1996," online at http://www.fec.gov/pages/htmlto5.htm (viewed December 13, 2004).

2000. "Voter Registration and Turnout 2000," online at http://www.fec.gov/pages/2000turnout/reg&to00.htm (viewed February 6, 2003).

2001a. "FEC Reports on Congressional Financial Activity for 2000," online at http://www.fec.gov/press/press2001/051501congfinact/051501congfinact.html (viewed April 6, 2004).

2001b. "PAC Activity Increases in 2000 Election Cycle," online at http://www.fec.gov/press/press2001/053101pacfund/053101pacfund.html (viewed April 6, 2004).

2004a. "The FEC and the Federal Campaign Finance Law," online at http://www.fec.gov/pages/brochures/fecfeca.shtml (viewed December 13, 2004).

2004b. "Campaign Finance Reports and Data," online at http://herndon1.sdrdc.com/ (viewed December 13, 2004).

United States, President. 1901. *Immorality and Political Grafting of Roman Catholic Priests in the Philippine Islands: Extracts from [the] Message of the President of the United States*, Girard, KS: B. Rogers.

United States, Senate. 2004. "Senator Ousted," Art & History, Historical Minutes 1878–1920, online at http://www.senate.gov/artandhistory/history/minute/Senator_Ousted.htm (viewed April 5, 2004).

USAID (United States Agency for International Development). 1998. *USAID Handbook for Fighting Corruption*, Washington, DC: USAID Center for Democracy and Governance.

Uslaner, Eric M. 2003. "Tax Evasion, Trust, and the Strong Arm of the Law," presented at a conference on Tax Evasion, Trust, and State Capacity, University of St. Gallen, Switzerland, October 17–19.

Vaksberg, Arkady. 1992. *The Soviet Mafia*, New York: St. Martin's Press.

Van Inwegen, Patrick. 2000. "The Domestic Determinants of Mexico's Constrained Foreign Policy," paper presented at the 26th Annual Third World Conference, Chicago, March 15–18.

Varese, Federico. 1997. "The Transition to the Market and Corruption in Post-Socialist Russia," *Political Studies* 45: 579–596.

2001. *The Russian Mafia: Private Protection in a New Market Economy*, Oxford: Oxford University Press.

Voice of America. 2000. "China Corruption," online at http://www.fas.org/news/china/2000/000308-prc1.htm (viewed October 9, 2003).

Volkov, Vadim. 2002. *Violent Entrepreneurs: The Use of Force in the Making of Russian Capitalism*, Ithaca: Cornell University Press.

Wagle, Swarnim, and Parmesh Shah. 2003. "Bangalore, India: Participatory Approaches to Budgeting and Public Expenditure Management," Social Development Notes 70, Washington, DC: World Bank.

Waquet, Jean-Claude. 1996. "Some Considerations on Corruption, Politics and Society in Sixteenth and Seventeenth Century Italy," in Walter Little and Eduardo Posada Carbó, eds., *Political Corruption in Europe and Latin America*, Basingstoke: Macmillan, pp. 21–40.

Warren, James Francis. 1985. *The Sulu Zone, 1768–1898*, Quezon City: New Day Publishers.

Waters, Sarah. 1994. "'Tangentopoli' and the Emergence of a New Political Order in Italy," *West European Politics*, January 17.

Wawro, Gregory. 2001. "A Panel Probit Analysis of Campaign Contributions and Roll-Call Votes," *American Journal of Political Science* 45: 563–579.

Weber, Max. 1958. *The Protestant Ethic and the Spirit of Capitalism*. Translated by Talcott Parsons, New York: Scribner.

Webman, Jerry A. 1973. "Political Institutions and Political Leadership: Black Politics in Philadelphia and Detroit," New Haven, CT: Yale University, Department of Political Science, unpublished manuscript.

References 255

Wedel, Janine R. 2001. "Corruption and Organized Crime in Post-Communist States: New Ways of Manifesting Old Patterns," *Trends in Organized Crime* 7: 3–61.

Wedeman, Andrew. 1997a. "Looters, Rent-Scrapers, and Dividend-Collectors: Corruption and Growth in Zaire, South Korea, and the Philippines," *The Journal of Developing Areas* 31: 457–478.

1997b. "Stealing from the Farmers: Institutional Corruption and the 1992 IOU Crisis," *China Quarterly* 152: 805–831.

2004. "Great Disorder under Heaven: Endemic Corruption and Rapid Growth in Contemporary China," *The China Review* 4: 1–32.

Wei, Shang-Jin. 1997. "Why is Corruption So Much More Taxing than Tax? Arbitrariness Kills," *NBER Working Paper* 6030.

1999. *Corruption in Economic Development: Beneficial Grease, Minor Annoyance, or Major Obstacle?* Washington, DC: World Bank, Development Research Group, Public Economics. Policy research working paper 2048. http:// www.worldbank.org/html/dec/Publications/Workpapers/WPS2000/series/ wps2048/wps2048.pdf (viewed July 2, 2001).

2000. "How Taxing is Corruption on International Investors?" *Review of Economics and Statistics* 82: 1–11.

Weingast, Barry. 1993. "Constitutions as Governance Structures: The Political Foundations of Secure Markets," *Journal of Institutional and Theoretical Economics* 149: 286–311.

Weir, Fred. 2002. "In Post-Soviet Russia, Politics Proves Perilous Profession," *Christian Science Monitor*, December 27.

2003. "Open Season on Russia's Tycoons," *Christian Science Monitor*, July 17.

Williams, James W., and Margaret E. Beare. 1999. "The Business of Bribery: Globalization, Economic Liberalization, and the 'Problem' of Corruption," *Crime, Law and Social Change* 32: 115–146.

Williams, Robert J. 2000. *Political Scandals in the USA*, Chicago: Fitzroy Dearborn.

Wilson, James Q. 1960. *Negro Politics: The Search for Leadership*, Glencoe, IL: Free Press.

Wines, Michael. 2002. "Muckraking Governor Slain by Sniper on Moscow Street," *New York Times*, October 19.

Wong, Linda. 2004. "Market Reforms, Globalization and Social Justice in China," *Journal of Contemporary China* 13: 151–171.

Woo, Jung Eun (Meredith Woo-Cumings). 1991. *Race to the Swift: State and Finance in Korean Industrialization*, New York: Columbia University Press.

Woo-Cumings, Meredith., ed., 1999a. *The Developmental State*, Ithaca, NY: Cornell University Press.

1999b. "The State, Democracy, and the Reform of the Corporate Sector in Korea," in T. J. Pempel, ed., *The Politics of the Asian Economic Crisis*, Ithaca, NY: Cornell University Press.

Woodall, Brian. 1996. *Japan under Construction: Corruption, Politics, and Public Works*, Berkeley: University of California Press.

World Bank. 1997. "Helping Countries Combat Corruption," Washington, DC: World Bank, Poverty Reduction and Economic Management Program.

References 255

Wedel, Janine R. 2001. "Corruption and Organized Crime in Post-Communist States: New Ways of Manifesting Old Patterns," *Trends in Organized Crime* 7: 3–61.

Wedeman, Andrew. 1997a. "Looters, Rent-Scrapers, and Dividend-Collectors: Corruption and Growth in Zaire, South Korea, and the Philippines," *The Journal of Developing Areas* 31: 457–478.

World Factbook Online, 2004a. "Indonesia," online at http://www.cia.gov/cia/ publications/factbook/geos/id.html (viewed July 25, 2004).

    2004b. "Kenya," online at http://www.cia.gov/cia/publications/factbook/geos/ ke.html (viewed July 22, 2004).

Wright, John R. 1996. *Interest Groups and Congress*, Boston: Allyn and Bacon.

Yablokova, Oksana. 2002. "State Duma Deputy Victim of Ambush," *St. Petersburg Times*, August 23, http://www.sptimesrussia.com/archive/times/ 797/top/t_7212.htm (viewed June 4, 2004).

Yao Shuntian. 2002. "Privilege and Corruption: The Problems of China's Socialist Market Economy," *American Journal of Economics and Sociology* 61: 279–299.

Your Congress. 2004. "Daily Traficant," online at http://www.yourcongress. com/section.asp?section=Daily_Traficant (viewed April 5, 2004).

Index

US
Russia
China

Participation

hi

Econ
Devel   market

Pol Lib t.

Econ
Devel